TYPICAL SURREY

A COMMENTATOR'S SEASON WITH
THE COUNTY CHAMPIONS

Mark Church

To Dad,
Thanks for listening.
Miss you every day.

FOREWORD

2018 was a triumphant year for Surrey County Cricket Club as the club won the County Championship for the first time since 2002, winning 10 games (a feat that included nine in a row). This is the title that the players covet the most, it's the ultimate challenge for a professional cricketer to win a tournament that has spanned three centuries. There is no hiding place or respite as your skills and psychological make-up are laid bare in the most testing of conditions set across 14 four-day games, concluding with five games played back-to-back, with the winner taking all...

This is an up-close and personal account from the boundary, the inside story by Mark Church, BBC London's cricket correspondent (he's been in the role since the dawn of time). Churchie witnessed and called every ball, run, wicket, triumph, frustration and very, very occasional disaster of the 2018 campaign from the confines of the commentary box in a journey that started in sprightly spring conditions on 20 April and finished on a sun-drenched day at the Kia Oval on 28 September.

Alongside the trials and tribulations on the field, the book features a bunch of cricket (and barking!) mad enthusiasts who bring the game to life week-in, week-out through the season for the BBC's domestic coverage, which proudly delivers every ball for every game and gives a "warts-and-all" insight into what it'd like to cover our beautiful game and how the commentary makes it on to the airwaves... which consists chiefly of many hours flogging up and down motorways, a myriad hotels, hostels, campsites and campervans, the moral dilemma of whether or not "to do" tea (cakes and scones) and the daily challenge of making the "competitive" per diems stretch to three courses plus wine...

It's safe to say that the timing of the decision to do a season diary (a decision made alongside Surrey's "visionary" Head of Communications Jon Surtees) was a good one and all that needed was a decent stab at the Championship title and the gentle coaxing of Matt Thacker at *Wisden Cricket Monthly* into helping publish the book. Thank you, Matt!

Of course all the while we were covering Surrey's charge to the title, Churchie was training to run 1,000 miles across 50 days (the small matter of 38 marathons). As I write, the great man is a third of the way through this extraordinary challenge, done to raise funds for Pancreatic Research in memory of his dear father Tony.

Anyway, that's enough scene-setting. Enjoy the book and remember it's only a few more short(ish) months until we do it all over again......

Johnny Barran

INTRODUCTION

When I was little, I used to spend hours in my garage at home playing Test matches.

Bat, ball, brick wall. Day after day I would throw the ball against the wall and hit it back. In my own little world, scoring hundreds against Australia as England's greatest batsman.

And I always commentated. An only child, talking to myself for hours on end whilst hitting a ball in a garage. A psychologist would have had a field day!

But even though all those hours didn't help my cricket, I have ended up talking to myself, and a few others, watching the sport I love for a living. I am a lucky man.

I had always thought about writing a diary of a season following Surrey for the BBC one day. The major problem, as you will find out over the coming pages, is that I'm not very good at writing. I can talk for England but I've always found it quite difficult getting those thoughts down on page.

Before the season started, Surrey's Head of Communications, Jon Surtees came up with the answer. I would write down all my jumbled thoughts, send them to him, and he would turn them into something readable. I'm so glad he persuaded me, because what a summer it has been.

Hopefully this diary gives you an idea of what it is like to cover county cricket in this country. Our domestic game is unique, and the County Championship is a precious commodity that must be treasured and protected.

For Surrey it has been a special summer and I have felt very lucky to be following them during the season. This has been my sixteenth year of covering Surrey for BBC London and I chose a good one to do the diary. I could thank so many people for their help but that would need a separate book in itself.

So,

thanks to Pete Stevens and BBC London for employing me;

thanks to all my BBC colleagues for making a season of cricket so much fun;

thanks to Johnny Barran for putting up with me in the commentary box;

thanks to Surrey CCC;

thanks to all the players across the game in this country. Without all of you, I wouldn't have a job or anything to talk about;

and thanks to the Surrey boys for putting up with me and leaving a big smile on my face.

I hope you enjoy reading this book as much as I did writing it. And I hope you agree with me by the end of the book (if you get that far)… cricket is a bloody wonderful game.

Mark Church, November 2018

DRAMATIS PERSONAE

Mum: My Mum, who I stay with for home games at The Oval. A lovely lady who keeps me fed and watered during the summer. Always been my number one (and only) fan.

Mrs Church: My lovely wife who puts up with me and deserves a medal. Extremely patient with a husband who spends his summer talking to himself.

Isabelle: My daughter and the most important person in my world. She is a big Jason Roy fan and has Guinea Pigs called 'Rikki' and 'Clarke'.

Tysoe: My car is named after the Surrey physio, Alex Tysoe. Just like its namesake, Tysoe is solid and reliable, with a little bit of flair when you need it.

Johnny Barran: The man I see more than my wife during the summer. The Graham to my Gooch in the commentary box and a man who has sung on stage with Frank Bruno and Roy Castle.

Kevin Howells: The leader of the BBC county cricket commentary team. Travels up and down the country and is at the forefront of county cricket coverage on the BBC.

Jon Surtees: Surrey's Head of Communications who is also the head of the community. In fact, he is head of everything. The man who makes this diary make sense.

Joel Pope: Surrey's video and media guru. One of Weybridge's finest and according to England selector James Taylor, the man with the best hands he's ever seen.

Jack Wilson-Mumford: Surrey's social media genius. Manchester City fan extraordinaire and one of the nicest people you will ever meet.

Kevin Hand: The voice of Middlesex cricket on the BBC. I spent three weeks with him in Antigua in 2008 in an all–inclusive hotel with the Middlesex squad. I'm still recovering.

Daniel Norcross: Wearer of silly shirts and *Test Match Special*'s very own. A wonderful broadcaster who has the most complicated drinks order at the bar.

Steve Howes: Without Steve I would never get to where I need to or have anywhere to sleep at away games. My go-to for putting the world to rights.

APRIL

"County Championship cricket is a
brilliant and beautiful thing"

WEDNESDAY 18 APRIL

The cricket season – my eighteenth of ball-by-ball coverage of Surrey CCC – is due to start in two days' time, and England is bathed by a heatwave. Those unfortunate enough to have seen pictures of me will be aware that I am a tan fan, so it's lovely to lie outside in Mum's garden all morning recovering from an early run and going through some stats ahead of the game on Friday.

The afternoon sees me back at the Kia Oval for the first time in six months. Gear successfully installed, ISDN kit* tested and I'm briefed on some swanky new technology. Surrey will be live streaming every game, syncing it up with our commentary. For 2018, they are adding replays, which I am in charge of generating via an iPad. A big responsibility, but it's great that people who can't get to the game are able to watch at home or on their phones.

The evening involves an encounter with new Surrey skipper Rory Burns, when I host a Q&A session for the Surrey Cricket Foundation in Guildford. Mr Burns (as he is not known) seems in confident form answering my questions about leadership. Having commentated on nearly every game of his career, it will be quite the experience watching him lead out Surrey for the first time later this week.

It might sound a strange thing to say but I am very proud of him. He has come a long way from a primary school Q&A I did with him a few years ago, when one of the kids asked him: "Have you ever been married? And if not, why not, because you are a very handsome man."

An ISDN kit is what we broadcast off. Really, it's a glorified phone with lots of buttons and flashing lights. Portable and, normally, very reliable. Have had some moments over the years with them. Generally, they work perfectly until you are just about to go on air and then, for no particular reason, they turn themselves off.

Once you've plugged your microphones and headphones into the ISDN kit, you must remember to put a mic out of a hole in the commentary box otherwise it sounds like you're broadcasting from the toilet. Having said that, at a couple of outgrounds and Rugby League grounds, I have actually broadcast from the toilet! It's very convenient if caught short but the aroma's somewhat off-putting, although that doesn't matter on the radio.

I once had one that burst into flames during an FA Cup game at Southend. Happily, I was able to put it out and borrow another one for the second half.

✳

THURSDAY 19 APRIL

Another perfect day weather-wise, allowing me to engage in some of my favourite pursuits – running and sunning.

The latter part of the morning is taken up giving Tysoe a vigorous clean. My faithful Honda CRV is named after Surrey's Head Physio Alex Tysoe, who also needs to get through a great many miles over the course of the summer. The car is much like Alex; solid, reliable and one of the best in the business.

So vigorous was the clean that I drop off while I am recovering on the sun lounger in the garden. When I wake up, the ECB seem to have announced that they've devised a new format of the game, 'The 100', which will be played by new teams in 2020.

For a while I can't work out if I've dreamt this, have sunstroke or it's really happened. A quick check of the BBC Sport website confirms that it is reality. Once I have picked my jaw up off the floor, I take a quick look at Twitter and the immediate reaction can be best be described as "amused" and "surprised". With so many of the journalists already tucking into the ECB, I wonder if they're aware of the beast they've unleashed here? It will be a topic of conversation up and down the country all summer long.

My initial reaction is, 'what a load of balls', which seems to be the point. I would have loved to be at the meeting.

"Make the game more simple!"

"100 balls?"

"But six doesn't go into 100?"

"I know! 15 x 6 and 1 x 10!"

"What a great idea, that's definitely less complicated!"

End the day, in the grip of a bit of sunstroke, watching *Major League*. A truly classic sports film, there are many parallels with The 100 and I look forward to seeing Chris 'The Wild Thing' Woakes walking out to bowl his climactic ten ball over to some appropriate walk-on music.

✳

FRIDAY 20 APRIL

The first day of the cricket season! Hallelujah! Tysoe and I leave the house (or in Tysoe's case, car park) at 5.15am and arrive at the Kia Oval before 7am. A quick double–check of the broadcasting gear before I head out for coffee and a pre-match run around Westminster. Although The 100 is still going round and round my head, and not in a good way, my thoughts are primarily excitement about the return of the County Championship. Thank God normality has returned.

County Championship cricket is a brilliant and beautiful thing. It has many detractors but most of those haven't been to a cricket ground in a very long time. It's the highest quality domestic cricket tournament in the world, has a wonderful history, many hundreds of thousands of passionate fans and should be protected and promoted at all times. It is very precious.

Joined in the commentary box today by Kevan James* from BBC Solent and Lord Johnny Barran of Broadcastshire**, resplendent in some fresh white chinos. And utterly overexcited. Going back on air at 10.55am feels like coming home to a house full of friends after a winter away and it's wonderful to see regular correspondents welcoming us back on Twitter.

As well as commentating, there is a lot of social planning done on air today. It seems that after we've had our traditional weekend net, Barran is taking Kevan and me to a rooftop pool party tomorrow night. You can't write emojis into diaries, but if you could I'd probably insert the little man with his eyebrow raised at this point. It's only the first day of the season!

Replay button pressing goes well on Day 1. The highlight is when I take the iPad with me for a toilet break and accidentally trigger a replay whilst washing my hands. We are visited in the commentary box by the gentleman who invented the replay button. I feel real pressure with him looking over my shoulder and taking photographs. It's like having Mr Dyson watching you hoover.

The cricket itself is compelling and exciting. Hampshire, through some good signings, look a very competitive outfit and Fidel Edwards is still a terrific bowler. Surrey struggle a little at the beginning due to some quality bowling from the West Indian, but warm to their task as the day goes on before the losses of Burns and Dean Elgar put them on the back foot. Ben Foakes appears every inch the international batsman and Ollie Pope looks class but Surrey don't get enough runs as they lose six wickets for 24 runs after tea.

Three late Hampshire wickets round off a smashing first day and indicate that Hampshire will not have things all their own way over the weekend. There is definitely enough to keep the Surrey quicks interested.

Drive home to see Mum, who I am staying with in Kent during home games this summer after family Church's big move from Sussex to Cardiff last spring. Whilst I do miss Mrs Church and Isabelle, it's important to look after Mum as much as I can after we lost Dad last summer to pancreatic cancer. She's coping well without him, and I'm very proud of her, but it is odd to be launching off on my first season without him to go to for advice, a joke or just a good old chinwag. It's strange to know he wasn't listening to the opening day of the season. I'm currently planning a tribute to him that I will undertake later in the year, trying to raise some money for medical research into the disease.

Kevan James – former Middlesex and Hampshire all-rounder who actually has first-class runs and wickets.

**Lord Barran – Mark Butcher introduced us 11 years ago – an entertainment guru who counts Bobby Davro and Billy Ocean as close friends. A wonderful man, a friend and someone without whom I couldn't do my job. During the summer, Barran and I are like a married couple. He definitely doesn't have any first-class runs or wickets, but does have a fabulous wardrobe and hair.*

✳

SATURDAY 21 APRIL

What a day. I am writing this entry in one of the many spare rooms at Mother Barran's house in the heart of Chelsea. It is gone 3.30am and I need to be up to get to the ground in approximately three hours' time.

Not really sure where to start with today so let's go with the cricket. Surrey have had an excellent day, turning the match around and securing a very strong position. Rikki Clarke and Sam Curran were both excellent with the ball and Scott Borthwick then cemented Surrey's position with a crucial knock in the afternoon session.

Today also gave us the first sighting of *Test Match Special*'s Daniel Norcross this summer. He is hosting a Q&A session with Alec Stewart tonight at Malden Wanderers CC and has popped in for a 'commentary net' as he warms up for a summer on *TMS*. Lovely to see him, even though his choice of shirts has not improved one iota. In fact, today's pick is hideous. He looks like a psychedelic tour guide. Having said that, he is one of the most talented broadcasters I know – and an ardent Surrey fan.

During the lunch break I accompany newly appointed *Evening Standard* Cricket Correspondent Will Macpherson, who looks like he should still be wearing short trousers and sitting on his father's lap – to road test the newly astro-turfed Corinthian Roof Terrace at the Kia Oval. Macpherson had brought along a putter and some golf balls and we enjoyed a short putting competition, using a cup of tea as a hole, which was a great deal of fun. If someone had told the 19-year-old Mark Church that he would be having casual putting competitions in a hospitality area of The Oval...

The highlight of the afternoon session is an extraordinary ten minutes from Johnny Barran, where he seems to be applying for work on a rival station, live on the BBC. With Norcross sat at the back of the box we come up with a childish, but extremely funny plan. I change the labelling of Norcross' number on my phone to 'Adam Mountford', the BBC's Head of Cricket. Norky then rings me and I show the phone to Barran as he is blathering on. He sees my phone with the call apparently coming from the boss and the colour very quickly drains from his face. It is some time before we let him in on the gag and Norcross finds it all so amusing he almost has to be surgically revived afterwards.

After play I enjoy the first net of the summer with Barran, who produces a brand new box of shiny red Dukes for the occasion. He is a truly indefatigable cricketer – and great fun to practise with.

Following that we meet back up with Kevan James, who declined to join us in the nets despite his first-class experience, and climb in a cab to Shoreditch. It is the London Marathon tomorrow and, given the circuitous route that is taken to get to our destination, I think we saw the majority of the course being prepared.

Dinner is a great success – many of the finest cultural touch points of the 1980s ("What was it like playing with Mike Gatting?") are discussed in great detail and my trousers stay on at all times, despite yesterday's promise of a pool party, which is certainly taking place around us but I'm not sure my ugly mug would fit in with all the beautiful people!

What is already a very late night for me then takes an interesting turn when we arrive back at Mother Barran's, where I am due to stay the night. As we approach the front door, Barran mentions that his sister's birthday party is currently ongoing inside and we should put in an appearance before going to bed.

After an hour and a half chatting with some lovely friends of the Barrans, I start the tricky job of ascending the stairs to the attic rooms where we are staying. It's relatively dark and I'm surprised to hear Barran say 'do mind Grandfather' as we near the top. I am pleasantly surprised to hear that his Grandfather is still with us and make an effort to further quieten my footsteps. It turns out it's a historic portrait of Barran Snr, a very handsome man with great hair, much like his grandson.

✷

SUNDAY 22 APRIL

Awake in Chelsea and walk to The Oval on a perfect London summer's day. Those running in the marathon today have got a hot one, that's for sure. Good luck to them all, including Mrs Barran, who is in the elite group. I left her husband sleeping soundly, with his eye goggles in.

Enjoy an early morning cup of coffee with Surrey great Steve Howes before running into Head Coach Michael Di Venuto, Assistant Head Coach Vikram Solanki and Director of Cricket Alec Stewart. They are all in good spirits after yesterday's performance and hopeful of further success today. I am lucky to know all of these blokes and very privileged to call them mates.

Surrey put themselves in an unassailable position on the third day. Ollie Pope hits a brilliant 145 to underline his status as not just one of the finest talents in Surrey but the whole country and he forms a fine partnership with Ben Foakes, who has got be in the mind of my old school alumnus Ed Smith when he shortly selects the squad for the first Test of the summer. You could just pick him as a batsman, he is that good, despite his talent with the keeper's gloves.

When Surrey bowl later in the day, another talented teenager, Amar Virdi takes two wickets in an over. Not just any wickets mind you, he dismisses Hashim Amla and James Vince. Such is his excitement, he runs three quarters of the way to Vauxhall celebrating and needs to hop on the 185 to get back to the ground and finish his over. It's fantastic to see.

A quieter day in the commentary box as Barran is off parenting because Mrs Barran is running the marathon and young John Barran Jnr. has a training session for Hampshire U9s.

The day ends on a more restful note than yesterday as I interview Ollie Pope and then drive back to Kent for dinner with Mum.

MONDAY 23 APRIL

Another early start for Tysoe and I but we again successfully defeat the London traffic and get to the ground in plenty of time.

After getting to the commentary box I head out into London for a walk and go through one of the favourite parts of my day. As I exit the ground through the Alec Stewart Gate, I stop to chat with the effervescent Surrey security guard Dave Gangadeen. He asks if I'm getting a coffee, I reply in the affirmative and ask if he would like a cappuccino fetching. He replies that he is sweet enough already, laughs loudly and I carry on up the road with a spring in my step. A lovely man indeed.

Planning for my tribute to Dad continues with a pre-play meeting with Barry Kitcherside, a wonderful man who is helping to get it organised, before I sit down to read the newspapers and try to understand what Andrew Strauss was talking about yesterday. It seems that he said our game needs to be made far less complicated so mums and their kids are capable of understanding it. I have a huge amount of time for Andrew, having been at Durham University with him, but I'm not sure he's quite got his point across in the right way here and also don't think he believes what he's saying. This new competition is certainly having a troubled launch. Actually, it is less of a launch and more a boat collapsing before it has got out of the boatyard.

An interesting day's cricket, in which Surrey record a maiden victory, is enlivened by Sky Sports News reporter James Cole positioning himself directly next to our effects microphone. This isn't a huge problem but does sometimes cause a ghostly haunt of his broadcasts to appear in the background of our commentary. The nadir comes at the tea break when his cameraman uses some relatively non-BBC Anglo–Saxon to describe his need for a coffee but we all need a coffee and at least it wasn't a private phone conversation, which has happened before.

After losing three wickets in the first session of the day, Hampshire spend the afternoon battling for a draw, with Sam Northeast very much at the heart of things as he scores a century. However, Surrey take wickets at key moments and secure the win late in the day with a fine catch by Ben Foakes off the bowling of Matthew Dunn. It's great to see Dunny back with ball in hand. He's a brilliant bowler and has had some pretty rotten luck with injuries over the past two seasons.

Another couple of maiden sightings today; firstly the great man, cricket journalist Vithushan Ehantharajah (fortunately known widely as Vish for on-air purposes), who comes into the commentary box at lunchtime and then top comedian, Surrey fan and *News Quiz* host Miles Jupp, who pops up during the afternoon. I once visited Miles on the set of *Rev*, an experience that will always be a highlight of my life.

It's always a pleasure to interview the players, especially after a win, so I end the working day having enjoyable chats with Messrs Burns and Virdi before climbing into Tysoe and hitting the road back to Mum's. Barran calls on the way to say that he is coming to Manchester this weekend, which is excellent news. The red carpet is already at the dry cleaners.

TUESDAY 24 APRIL

Sleep in until 8am before breakfasting with Mum on fresh box of granola. Sometimes it's truly the little things in life.

Go for a long run around the lanes before taking the train back up to The Oval to conduct another Q&A for the Surrey Cricket Foundation, this time with Gareth Batty and umpire Neil Bainton alongside Rory Burns.

Come up with a good gag on the way up about Burns having a 100 per cent record as captain only to see it stolen by Foundation boss Paul Taylor in his intro. Despite that, the session goes well with some fascinating insights into captaincy and umpiring.

Slightly shocked on the train ride home to be presented with a large picture of Will Macpherson on the back page of the *Evening Standard* but enjoy reading his new column nonetheless. I call him 'Grisham' because writes lots of stories and they are always based on one theme.

Check the football scores when I get home and am delighted to see that my official lookalike Jurgen Klopp has enjoyed a good night.

WEDNESDAY 25 APRIL

A domestic morning with Mum followed by a trip for Tysoe and I back to Wales. Go for a lovely walk with Mrs Church and pick the little one up from school.

A great family evening ensues with the only intrusion from work a quick call from Barran to arrange a podcast recording session tomorrow.

❋

THURSDAY 26 APRIL

Head to the local gym for a workout and bump into the great Welsh rugby player Ieuan Evans. Always good to see a legend and it's much better than when I once made a fool of myself opening the door of the toilet cubicle for Sir Gareth Edwards, but that is another story.

Podcast recording goes very well. Barran calls in from his country club and we enjoy going over the first week of the season.

Pack my bag and bid the latest set of farewells to Mrs Church and the little one and climb back into Tysoe for the trip to Manchester. Mercifully, I discover that the hotel is actually within the ground so I can't possibly get lost! There is a magnificent picture of Beefy Botham as I emerge from the lift. Next to it is a picture of Beyoncé – what a combination.

Before heading for dinner I notice, online as I'm in the north, that Grisham has a big story about new development plans for The Oval in the *Evening Standard*. They look great. Indulge in the first 'Hilton Burger' of the summer. There will be many more to come.

❋

FRIDAY 27 APRIL

Up early for a pre–commentary run and I take great delight in jogging around the other Old Trafford. Grab a quick breakfast before undertaking the long commute to the commentary box, where I accompany two young ladies setting up a conference for Hiscox. I talk drivel the entire way around the ground and then realise they are based in the room opposite me all day. Never mind.

After a maiden encounter with Old Trafford Dave (a legend), I'm greeted in the commentary box by Kevin Howells (a joy!) and Scott Read (also a joy!).

Shortly after setting up, it starts raining, so I end up on Five Live Sports Extra discussing curly fries, Alex Davies and Ollie Pope – filling desperately until the inevitable is announced, the day is called off and we can all return to our quarters.

Enjoy dinner with the real Tysoe, Di Venuto and Surrey's Strength and Conditioning Coach Darren Veness. We walk a mile to an Italian restaurant that has an abandoned sofa outside and one speaker playing 'Italian' music. Despite this, a great night is had – it is brave from the Head Coach to choose the Prawn Cocktail, but he seems very happy with his choice – experience!

Upon returning to the hotel I'm accosted by a very drunk but very nice gentleman who has made a break from the Builders' Awards being hosted next door. A long discussion ensues about the various merits of brickwork, paving and cement. To bed with hope for better weather tomorrow.

SATURDAY 28 APRIL

Starting the day with another run, keeping the floodlights of Old Trafford as a reference point, I go past the Italian restaurant from last night (the sofa is still there). I take a right, then another right and realise I'm lost. I keep going before admitting failure and asking for directions back to the hotel.

Go to pick up a coffee and bump into Kevin Howells in the coffee shop before walking to the ground and finally getting to commentate on some cricket.

Surrey start well, with Lancashire reduced to 23/3 thanks to some outstanding bowling from Jade Dernbach. Then Shiv Chanderpaul does what Shiv Chanderpaul does and Lancs get back into it.

Some outrageously good fielding keeps Surrey in it but Lancs pull it back in the final session. I interview the Head Coach after play; he is disappointed with the day but pleased that the prawn cocktail hasn't been seen again. All in all an, excellent day on the wireless.

Head back to the hotel, very tired, and fall asleep fully dressed with the Chennai Super Kings and Mumbai Indians on the hotel TV. Wake up at 2am and pick up the game where I'd fallen asleep, on repeat. Such is modern life.

SUNDAY 29 APRIL

Up early for breakfast with lots of Manchester United fans who have travelled from London and are staying at the hotel in order to attend their game with Arsenal today. No Arsenal fans. The highlight, by far, is watching Alec Stewart grappling with the waffle maker. One of England's greatest players, yes. But hopeless at making waffles.

Lancashire continue their dominance with Bailey and Mennie adding a record ninth wicket partnership. Surrey lose Mark Stoneman early on. He has started the season out of form but I have no doubt he will score stacks of runs this summer. It's always tough with the 'England' question following you around.

Barran arrives mid-morning and is delighted to find out we've been promoted to Five Live Sports Extra again. He runs off to put his suit and tie on.

Borthwick and Burns play nicely on a flattening pitch but for the second time this season, Surrey collapse after tea, undone by some patient bowling from Lancashire.

An undoubted highlight of the season so far is Ben Foakes unfurling a delightful cover drive at the same time as Manchester United score around the corner. The roar of delight from 85,000 is perfectly appropriate for the quality of the shot.

Post match is another interview with the Head Coach before I take the tram to Sale with Scott Read and Kevin Howells. Have a Facetime chat with Isabelle during the ride where she shows me the gap where her tooth used to be. This is big news and that'll be another £2 from the tooth fairy. Inflation is a bugger.

Shortly after hanging up I see an amazing sign on the metro platform that says "Do not ride your horse – dismount". Can't imagine there are many horses on the Metrolink but something must have happened to require the sign.

Another lovely Italian meal, this time in a restaurant without a sofa outside. I choose a magnificent meat platter thanks to the toss of a coin. I call correctly, otherwise it would have been its fish alternative.

We are joined for a pint afterwards by Lancashire media–man and former Surrey staffer James Price before I take a cab back to Old Trafford and head to bed.

❇

MONDAY 30 APRIL

Surrey battle through a tough day to secure a draw that they will be very pleased with after a below-par performance over the four days.

Stoneman and Burns start the day with great discipline before Ollie Pope and Ben Foakes get together for most of the afternoon. I think the Pope/Foakes partnership could be one that all Surrey, and maybe England, fans come to enjoy over many seasons.

It is left to teenagers Sam Curran and Ryan Patel to see out the game, which they do well and Surrey emerge with their heads held high. It's been another brilliant advertisement for county cricket.

On the drive back to Cardiff I reflect on another great trip to Old Trafford as I listen to Tottenham v Watford on the wireless. It's such a lovely ground and we're always treated so well there. From Dave on the door all the way through the club, it's a grand old place to go and work.

With the efforts of Read, Howells, Barran and the BBC's Matt Parkinson we had an excellent commentary box for the week and, from my perspective, my season with the microphone has started very well.

I have my £5.70 ready for the Severn Bridge and get home at 11pm, in time for a bowl of granola before bed.

❇

Top: morning breaks on the first day of the season, seen from the commentary box; bottom: Johnny Barran models Daniel Norcross' hat on 21 April.

Clockwise from top left: a pre-season Q&A with the Surrey captain; up at Old Trafford with Gary Neville, sort of ; 'Grisham" MacPherson's cricket column; with Brian Lara this time; Barran arrives, beaming; an early-season net with a manic Barran.

SURREY V HAMPSHIRE

Venue: The Kia Oval, Kennington
Date: 20th, 21st, 22nd, 23rd April 2018
Toss: Surrey
Result: Surrey won by 139 runs

Points: Surrey 20; Hampshire 3
Umpires: RK Illingworth, DJ Millns
Scorers: PJ Makepeace, KR Baker, JH Savill

SURREY	1ST INNINGS	R	b	2ND INNINGS	R	b
*RJ Burns	c Northeast b Edwards	46	118	c McManus b Abbott	10	17
MD Stoneman	lbw b Edwards	4	6	b Abbott	24	28
SG Borthwick	lbw b Edwards	5	7	lbw b Abbott	74	133
D Elgar	c McManus b Wood	44	114	lbw b Wood	20	43
+BT Foakes	lbw b Dawson	46	73	b Edwards	81	161
OJD Pope	lbw b Abbott	34	85	c Rossouw b Dawson	145	191
SM Curran	c Wood b Dawson	5	9	lbw b Dawson	13	25
R Clarke	c Wood b Dawson	5	16	c Dawson b Edwards	7	27
JW Dernbach	b Edwards	0	7	c McManus b Edwards	8	5
MP Dunn	c Rossouw b Dawson	0	5	not out	9	28
GS Virdi	not out	0	1	did not bat		
Extras	(4 b, 5 lb, 4 nb, 9 w)	22		(9 b, 3 lb, 2 nb, 2 w)	16	
Total	(all out, 73.1 overs)	211		(9 wickets, dec, 109.3 overs)	407	

Fall of wickets: 1-8 (Stoneman, 1.6 ov), 2-23 (Borthwick, 5.1 ov), 3-110 (Burns, 38.6 ov), 4-114 (Elgar, 41.4 ov), 5-187 (Pope, 64.1 ov), 6-202 (Curran, 67.3 ov), 7-203 (Foakes, 69.4 ov), 8-210 (Clarke, 71.3 ov), 9-211 (Dernbach, 72.5 ov), 10-211 (Dunn, 73.1 ov)
Fall of wickets: 1-20 (Burns, 4.2 ov), 2-41 (Stoneman, 8.5 ov), 3-86 (Elgar, 22.3 ov), 4-173 (Borthwick, 50.1 ov), 5-304 (Foakes, 81.1 ov), 6-332 (Curran, 87.2 ov), 7-363 (Clarke, 98.2 ov), 8-379 (Dernbach, 100.1 ov), 9-407 (Pope, 109.3 ov)

HAMPSHIRE	O	M	R	W	Wd	Nb		O	M	R	W	Wd	Nb
Abbott	18	1	61	1	4	-	Abbott	19	2	72	3	1	1
Edwards	15	3	38	4	-	1	Edwards	23	1	130	3	-	-
Wheal	15	3	54	0	-	1	Dawson	37.3	7	85	2	-	-
Wood	14	7	19	1	-	-	Wood	16	2	56	1	1	-
Dawson	11.1	2	30	4	-	-	Wheal	14	0	52	0	-	-

HAMPSHIRE	1ST INNINGS	R	b	2ND INNINGS	R	b
JHK Adams	c Foakes b Clarke	17	48	c Stoneman b Clarke	21	53
+LD McManus	lbw b Clarke	22	33	b Dunn	4	45
CP Wood	lbw b Curran	2	22	(9) lbw b Curran	26	66
*JM Vince	lbw b Clarke	6	19	(3) lbw b Virdi	33	47
HM Amla	lbw b Clarke	55	83	(4) lbw b Virdi	21	39
SA Northeast	c Foakes b Curran	6	21	(5) c Foakes b Dunn	129	254
RR Rossouw	lbw b Dunn	4	14	(6) lbw b Virdi	29	68
LA Dawson	c Foakes b Dernbach	6	22	(7) b Dernbach	3	13
KJ Abbott	b Curran	23	35	(8) c Burns b Virdi	29	36
BTJ Wheal	lbw b Curran	0	4	lbw b Dernbach	10	49
FH Edwards	not out	0	0	not out	5	25
Extras	(2 b, 4 lb)	6		(12 b, 6 lb, 4 nb)	22	
Total	(all out, 50.2 overs)	147		(all out, 115.3 overs)	332	

Fall of wickets: 1-37 (McManus, 12.3 ov), 2-42 (Adams, 14.1 ov), 3-52 (Wood, 19.6 ov), 4-52 (Vince, 20.2 ov), 5-63 (Northeast, 27.1 ov), 6-79 (Rossouw, 31.4 ov), 7-116 (Dawson, 40.2 ov), 8-147 (Abbott, 49.2 ov), 9-147 (Wheal, 49.6 ov), 10-147 (Amla, 50.2 ov)
Fall of wickets: 1-29 (Adams, 15.4 ov), 2-29 (McManus, 16.4 ov), 3-83 (Amla, 30.1 ov), 4-84 (Vince, 30.5 ov), 5-150 (Rossouw, 56.2 ov), 6-163 (Dawson, 61.4 ov), 7-206 (Abbott, 70.2 ov), 8-245 (Wood, 85.2 ov), 9-313 (Wheal, 105.5 ov), 10-332 (Northeast, 115.3 ov)

SURREY	O	M	R	W	Wd	Nb		O	M	R	W	Wd	Nb
Dernbach	10	3	21	1	-	-	Dernbach	27	6	86	2	-	1
Curran	16	6	39	4	-	-	Curran	16	5	44	1	-	-
Clarke	15.2	6	39	4	-	-	Virdi	33	7	79	4	-	-
Dunn	9	0	42	1	-	-	Clarke	21	7	46	1	-	-
							Dunn	11.3	3	41	2	-	-
							Borthwick	7	1	18	0	-	1

LANCASHIRE V SURREY

Venue: Emirates Old Trafford, Manchester
Date: 27th, 28th, 29th, 30th April 2018
Toss: No toss made
Result: Match drawn

Points: Lancashire 12; Surrey 8
Umpires: PJ Hartley, RA Kettleborough
Scorers: C Rimmer, PJ Makepeace, AJ McCarrick

LANCASHIRE	1ST INNINGS	R	b	2ND INNINGS	R	b
KK Jennings	lbw b Curran	15	26			
H Hameed	c Elgar b Dernbach	4	24			
+AL Davies	c Dunn b Dernbach	4	6			
*LS Livingstone	lbw b Dernbach	48	88			
S Chanderpaul	c Borthwick b Virdi	65	149			
DJ Vilas	c Borthwick b Curran	13	19			
SJ Croft	c Foakes b Virdi	62	112			
J Clark	c Pope b Virdi	78	101			
JM Mennie	not out	68	107			
TE Bailey	c Dunn b Virdi	66	84			
G Onions	did not bat					
Extras	(1 b, 9 lb, 6 nb)	16				
Total	(9 wickets, dec, 118.5 overs)	439				

Fall of wickets: 1-15 (Hameed, 6.6 ov), 2-23 (Davies, 8.6 ov), 3-23 (Jennings, 9.2 ov), 4-111 (Livingstone, 38.1 ov), 5-128 (Vilas, 43.3 ov), 6-206 (Chanderpaul, 64.5 ov), 7-252 (Croft, 76.3 ov), 8-321 (Clark, 96.2 ov), 9-439 (Bailey, 118.5 ov)

SURREY	O	M	R	W	Wd	Nb		O	M	R	W	Wd	Nb
Dernbach	29	6	93	3	-	-							
Curran	26	0	106	2	-	-							
Dunn	24	7	88	0	-	-							
Patel	16	0	62	0	-	2							
Virdi	23.5	2	80	4	-	1							

SURREY	1ST INNINGS	R	b	2ND INNINGS (F/O)	R	b
*RJ Burns	c Davies b Bailey	28	108	c Jennings b Livingstone	33	117
MD Stoneman	b Onions	0	4	c Vilas b Bailey	29	90
SG Borthwick	c Davies b Onions	79	137	b Bailey	0	8
D Elgar	c +Vilas b Bailey	34	85	c Vilas b Clark	14	61
+BT Foakes	lbw b Clark	34	62	c Vilas b Bailey	57	119
OJD Pope	b Bailey	17	60	c Livingstone b Bailey	41	98
SM Curran	lbw b Livingstone	9	16	not out	9	23
RS Patel	not out	4	36	not out	9	27
JW Dernbach	c Jennings b Bailey	7	11	did not bat		
MP Dunn	lbw b Onions	1	11	did not bat		
GS Virdi	c +Vilas b Onions	4	10	did not bat		
Extras	(8 b, 6 lb, 4 nb)	18		(7 lb)	7	
Total	(all out, 89.4 overs)	235		(6 wickets, 90.3 overs)	199	

Fall of wickets: 1-2 (Stoneman, 1.4 ov), 2-100 (Burns, 34.5 ov), 3-131 (Borthwick, 48.6 ov), 4-171 (Elgar, 61.4 ov), 5-202 (Foakes, 71.5 ov), 6-217 (Curran, 76.6 ov), 7-218 (Pope, 80.1 ov), 8-228 (Dernbach, 82.4 ov), 9-231 (Dunn, 85.6 ov), 10-235 (Virdi, 89.4 ov)
Fall of wickets: 1-53 (Stoneman, 26.5 ov), 2-53 (Borthwick, 30.1 ov), 3-68 (Burns, 42.3 ov), 4-90 (Elgar, 49.3 ov), 5-176 (Foakes, 80.6 ov), 6-177 (Pope, 82.5 ov)

LANCASHIRE	O	M	R	W	Wd	Nb		O	M	R	W	Wd	Nb
Bailey	22	5	54	4	-	2	Bailey	19	12	13	4	-	-
Onions	19.4	6	49	4	-	-	Onions	19	6	41	0	-	-
Livingstone	18	4	36	1	-	-	Clark	12	3	29	1	-	-
Mennie	16	2	47	0	-	-	Mennie	15	5	44	0	-	-
Clark	12	4	32	1	-	-	Livingstone	22.3	5	59	1	-	-
Croft	2	0	3	0	-	-	Croft	3	1	6	0	-	-

"How the England selectors
continue not to mention him is one
of life's great mysteries"

TUESDAY 1 MAY

Wake up to a rude shock – it appears that it's May already. Not quite sure how that happened and Isabelle is unable to give me any insight as I take her into school.

A morning of Ps – paperwork and podcasts. The second is considerably more enjoyable than the first. On this occasion, rather than the regular effort with Barran, we are recording a pilot episode of a new BBC London cricket podcast, so am joined down the line by Kevin Hand, who has spent the season so far coming in off an extremely long run about The 100.

It all seems to go very well but it will now be up to the internal vagaries of the BBC to see if our babbling ever hits the podcasting airwaves in the wider world. I do hope so because Barran seems to have somehow got our current effort banned by Apple, before it even got posted, which is not hugely helpful in driving more people to listen to it.

At lunchtime I head out for a five mile run as part of continued preparations for the tribute I am doing for Dad later in the year. After a few different ideas were thrown into the pot, it has been decided that I will be running 20 miles a day for 50 days during October, November and December. Writing this down does not make it any less intimidating!

Helpfully, it's almost exactly five miles from my commentary box at The Oval to Lord's, so that will be my route – four times a day, ground to ground for 50 days. 1,000 miles in total. I think I might go mad by the end of it.

I pick up Isabelle from school and am greeted by the news she has come first in the 400m today. A very proud moment and we celebrate by making a vegetable bookmark for her homework.

Still waiting for the return of the heatwave...

✻

WEDNESDAY 2 MAY

Another quiet day in Wales, enlivened by an encounter with a digger while out running. They are seemingly building several million new homes nearby, which is an interesting process to watch happen – but does bring occasional challenges for the amateur runner and would-be house seller.

Into Cardiff in the afternoon where I walk past the newly named Sophia Gardens, Cardiff. I'm sure I recognise the name from somewhere before but can't quite put my finger on it somehow.

After picking up Isabelle for the second day in the row, I mount my faithful Tysoe and drive to Mum's, accompanied by commentary on official lookalike Jurgen Klopp's Liverpool playing Roma. It doesn't seem entirely straightforward but they eventually come out on top. Good old Jurgen…

*

THURSDAY 3 MAY

A quiet morning catching up with Mum and helping her with some domestics before heading for a lovely lunch at The Swan in West Peckham. The Kentish iteration of Peckham doesn't have a great deal in common with its south London namesake – and on this particular occasion I think I prefer the ambience of the Garden of England.

After my experience in Manchester I again choose the meat platter, and enjoyment levels are lifted further as two teams walk out to play a match on the cricket pitch opposite the pub. Utterly glorious, quintessential England in the sun.

Back at Mum's I'm sat down minding my own business when I feel a small explosion in my pocket. I check out the situation to discover that Surrey have announced the signing of Indian captain Virat Kohli for the month of June, which is quite the coup to say the least. My next move is to turn on the TV, where I see the good old yellow ticker tape on Sky Sports News, confirming my suspicions that it's exciting news.

There have been rumours circulating for a little while, but now it's official – the highest profile signing in county cricket since the likes of Brian Lara and Shane Warne played for Warwickshire and Hampshire. Fairly certain it will increase the reach of the online BBC commentary too. Exciting times ahead…

There is some predictable criticism on Twitter that Surrey are allowing Kohli to find his form in English conditions ahead of the India series later this year but I think that's rubbish. To have players of his quality and celebrity around county cricket can only benefit the game.

A check of Twitter shows a few people who have responded to the news with comments around "typical Surrey". I agree with this – but possibly not for the same reasons. Similar to Kumar Sangakkara three years ago, it's a huge and confident signing that will add huge amounts to the dressing room, a potentially vast number of runs on the pitch and a unique opportunity for some exciting young players to learn from one of the greatest batsmen of the modern age. There is not one county that would have turned down this opportunity and if it is 'typical Surrey' then it is because of the boldness and audaciousness of the move. Bravo Mr Stewart. It also occurs to me that this signing might make it an even better year to be attempting my first 'proper' season diary!

Later in the day, the Surrey website tells me the squad for the Worcestershire game starting tomorrow. Sadly, Matthew Dunn is injured, but it's good to see that Rikki Clarke's sore throat has cleared up and Gareth Batty's back is nearly recovered.

I pop over to see Stuart Barnes, the former Surrey bowling coach who lives near to Mum. Lovely to catch up and hear about his new ventures in the world of property. A very focused man indeed!

Head to bed and dream of successfully persuading Virat Kohli to join Barran and me for a podcast at Reading service station.

FRIDAY 4 MAY

Rudely awoken by the call of a 5am alarm but the sun is shining on the drive to The Oval so all feels well in the world.

Get to the ground so early that the commentary box is still locked on my arrival but a kind lady helps me find the key so I can conduct the necessary checks. Go for a sit in the sun on the TV camera balcony in front of the commentary box and fall asleep.

Awoken by the arrival of Chris Egerton (a fabulous broadcaster who has a voice that could melt butter) and we eagerly discuss the glorious weather forecast for the next four days. We also catch up, having not seen each other for a couple of years. The last time I saw him was in Northampton and I had forgotten my trousers (a long story).

Surrey win the toss and bat and the day is dominated by a classic Rory Burns century. How the England selectors continue not to mention him is one of life's great mysteries – by this stage I'm not even sure if the great John Nettles could get to the bottom of it in an episode of *Midsomer Murders*.

Ben Foakes once again looks class and a young but exciting Worcestershire attack give a very good account of themselves.

There is a lot of Kohli chat, both on and off air and I'm interviewed by *BBC Sport* about his potential impact on Surrey and county cricket. It's fair to say I'm quite excited.

Have coffee with John Norman, the *talkSPORT* cricket producer. He is a lovely man and is currently at the helm at a fascinating time for broadcasting in the sport.

Return to the commentary box to discover Barran researching campervans for our trip to Scarborough at the end of the next month. Not the worst idea he's ever had but I'm slightly concerned when I look at the screen on his laptop and he appears to be looking at Bon Jovi's tour bus.

Away from The Oval it's been a ridiculous day at Chelmsford where Essex are playing Yorkshire. 22 wickets have fallen, including Alastair Cook, Joe Root and Jonny Bairstow, who all fell cheaply as they attempt to get time in the middle ahead of the upcoming Tests with Pakistan.

With Burns still going strong, I enjoy an afternoon chat with Dean Wilson (*Mirror*) and Lawrence Booth (*Mail* and *Wisden Almanack* editor), who have popped in to get a gander at Surrey's early season form.

Burns is not out overnight and his response to a congratulatory text ("Cheers Church") is simple, to-the-point and entirely in character.

A late highlight of the day is a photograph I see online of Jimmy Anderson's astonishing new haircut. It can't be a good sign for the lad that the subsequent discussion centres on trying to work out whether he looks more like Billy Idol, Philip Schofield or Gary Barlow circa 1992. However, both Barran and I have already had episodes of 'peroxide crisis' in our lives and can relate to what he's tried to do – and we haven't taken 700 Test wickets.

Drive back to Mum's in time for a quick ham sandwich before bed.

✳

SATURDAY 5 MAY

Another glorious day, another early arrival and another 'cappuccino encounter' with David Gangadeen on my way out for a wander along the Thames.

Catch up with Steve Howes before play and emerge with a spring in my step after the world has been firmly put to rights.

Burns continues onto 193 and I write a brilliant line about "how he has set his stall out like many will this Bank Holiday weekend" for the BBC Sport website. It doesn't make the website. Gutted.

An interesting discussion about the last time a county opening pair opened the innings for England, as this Stoneman/Burns partnership is very capable of doing just that one day. Thankfully, our educated and interested listeners come up with the answer of Mark Butcher and Alec Stewart.

With Barran on family duties, I'm joined all day by Dick Davies, a stalwart of BBC Essex, and we discover, on air, that we have a mutual love of musical theatre. My favourite is 'Me and My Girl' starring Emma Thompson and Robert Lindsay. Once again listeners help with our recollections and I remember that Frank Thornton, from 'Are You Being Served?', was also in the production when I saw it at the Adelphi.

Worcestershire begin their reply in solid fashion, with Daryl Mitchell looking particularly good as they end the day on 135/1.

A post-match interview with Rory Burns concludes with the phrase "ho-hum" (by him). The man is a class act.

The drive home is lively. Lots of people out and about for the Bank Holiday and I enjoy listening to the commentary of Tony Bellew beating David Haye on the other side of London as another ham sandwich is enjoyed before bed.

❊

SUNDAY 6 MAY

It's getting hotter and hotter and the early morning drive to The Oval is very enjoyable, watching London wake up to a summer Sunday.

Start the working day by indulging in a short moment of heaven as I bake myself on the camera terrace with a coffee before I'm called to the ISDN kit to act as a Chris Egerton's stunt double for a 10.30am update on BBC Hereford and Worcester.

Shortly before play we're joined by Norcross, the floral-shirted colossus, and then Barran, who returns on fine form as ever.

The majority of the day is spent watching Joe Clarke compiling 157 runs. He is a lovely player to watch and definitely one for England in the future. Time. He has lots of time.

Norcross is producing the coverage for BBC Radio Five Live Sports Extra and has a lot of fun with Barran, telling him we're off the wider network every time he comes on air. For some reason, this remains funny all day and never gets old. He falls for it each and every time.

At The Oval, the game is clearly heading for a draw and the pitch seems to be getting better and better but the game at Chelmsford draws to a remarkable conclusion with Yorkshire picking up the win, despite their performance on Friday. Astonishing stuff and who knows how crucial it could be come the end of the season?

The post-match interview today is with Conor McKerr, another of Surrey's crop of hugely promising youngsters. A very impressive young man.

Driving home is as pleasurable as driving in, although some of the sights I see are somewhat less family-friendly as London is now coming to the end of its sunny Bank Holiday Sunday. There will be some sore heads and shoulders tomorrow.

MONDAY 7 MAY

"The hottest early May Bank Holiday ever," proclaims Tysoe's car radio as I pootle up to The Oval for the final day of the match. There is an amazing mix of early risers and late sleepers on the streets of south London this morning.

Apparently, it's hotter than Miami today. I wonder for a while if they are wringing their hands on the radio in Florida, hugely upset that they're colder than London. I'd like to think so.

No Barran for the final day, he's competing in the village run back in Hampshire, but Norcross enlivens proceedings in another silly shirt.

The draw is confirmed but an excellent day's cricket is highlighted by Surrey off-spinner Amar Virdi, who continues his superb start to the season by taking the final four wickets to fall to end up with six in the match. I don't want to get ahead of myself, he is only 19 years old, but he does have a lot about him and gives the ball a genuine rip.

Another classy innings from Scott Borthwick secures the draw and he goes past 8,000 first-class runs in the process. The day ends with Norcross and Egerton gathered around the ISDN kit listening to BBC Tyne and Wear's Martin Emmerson describe Durham's dramatic victory over Leicestershire.

A post-match interview with coach Di Venuto provides the usual sensible take on the game and plenty of excitement about the impending arrival of Virat Kohli.

The highlight of the drive home is giving Norcross a lift from the Vauxhall End to Oval tube station, which takes him probably five times as long as walking, because of the traffic, and the day ends with a cold beer and a ham sandwich in the garden before bed.

TUESDAY 8 MAY

A recovery day for both Surrey players and Surrey ball-by-ball commentators.

Still at Mum's, I go for a run in the morning, followed by a podcast with Barran. He's also having a recovery day, at his exclusive country club, after getting too excited about Virat Kohli last week.

See some reports filing in from the players' afternoon meeting with the ECB about The 100. I think my recent dream about commentating on Christopher Biggins bowling to Brian Lara is now closer to fruition than ever before.

A lovely new feature on the Surrey Facebook page this evening is called '*Game in a Minute*' where they've taken some splendid photography of the game and paired it with key bits of our commentary. It actually makes me sound like I know what I'm talking about.

Go for a second run of the day before settling in to watch Southampton beat Swansea this evening. Going for two runs in a day may seem excessive but when you've committed to running four sets of five miles every day for 50 days in the autumn, it's essential training!

✳

WEDNESDAY 9 MAY

A quiet day is made quieter by paperwork in the morning and another run in the afternoon.

Out for dinner with Mum this evening. She's in good form, which is great to see.

✳

THURSDAY 10 MAY

I made a bold decision earlier this year to get my golf clubs out of the garage and try to play a bit more over the summer and so I meet up with Stuart Barnes and his lovely wife Emily for 18 holes at a nearby course.

I've not played in two years but despite this I'm able to navigate the course using only a four iron, a driver and a pitching wedge, losing only ten balls – largely into various different water-filled obstacles.

For what it's worth, there is also a putter in my bag but I've applied it so badly in the past I actually prefer to put with my wedge. Don't ask.

My driver is a new addition to the set, donated by Surrey physio Alex Tysoe after he heard I was getting back into the game. It has a magnificent pink shaft and, given my success with it, potentially magical properties.

In the evening Mum and I go a memorial service held at the hospice where Dad was cared for last year. It's an amazing place full of amazing people and the service provides a good opportunity to sit and think about Dad.

Thoughts also turn to Dave Callaghan (DC), a great BBC colleague from Yorkshire who we tragically lost just before the start of the season. Surrey play Yorkshire at the Kia Oval tomorrow, and I have to say it will be very strange indeed not to be joined by DC for one of the great matches in county cricket.

Given that the Test match summer has yet to start, Yorkshire are able to play both Joe Root and Jonny Bairstow, so the early promise shown by Surrey's young players will be given its biggest test yet. A fascinating prospect if ever there was one and a proper match up of two good sides.

*

FRIDAY 11 MAY

What a day for Ollie Pope. For him to end the day on 131* is testament to his talent and potential. This lad is really something.

Rikki Clarke's 70, in which he passes the amazing landmark of 10,000 first-class runs, is also crucial to Surrey's position. He is a cricketer I admire hugely, playing the best cricket of his career after his return to Surrey last season.

It's doubly fantastic for Messrs. Pope and Clarke that their exploits are broadcast nationwide on BBC Five Live Sports Extra. It's always good to get the boost of being on the major network and I'm pleased today's cricket has given us lots to talk about.

I'm glad to be joined by Kevin Howells and Isabelle Duncan, who I have not worked with before but turns out to be excellent company, both on air and away from the microphone, especially as it seems initially that Barran might not be in situ today.

Then, just as the first ball of the day is bowled, he bursts through the door at the back of the commentary box, all in a flap because his car was caught behind Micky Stewart at the Alec Stewart Gate and he was delayed. He is noticeably buoyed by the Five Live boost and is on cracking form throughout the day.

With our friends from Yorkshire all tuning in, I source advice on air for the best place to park the campervan in Scarborough and by the end of the morning session feel much more prepared for the road trip than I did at 11am.

Another highlight of the day is, undoubtedly, an interview between Kevin Howells and Surrey Chief Executive Richard Gould during the tea break. Gould is fascinating on a number of potentially explosive topics and the presence of John Etheridge from the *Sun*, Dean Wilson from the *Mirror* and Lizzy Ammon from the *Times* in the commentary box during the interview indicates that Howells may have got himself something of a scoop.

Dean Elgar, who played well for his 61 today, is the post-match interview. It must be quite something for teenagers like Ollie Pope to have such an experienced operator to learn from, especially with no Kumar Sangakkara to tap into this summer.

Tysoe and I have a great listen on the way home as the Cardiff Blues nip Gloucester by a single point in the European Challenge Cup Final. A great comeback by the Blues in the second half, beautifully covered by my BBC colleagues.

Change up from a ham sandwich to a chicken roll – but the end result is the same – bed with indigestion.

✳

SATURDAY 12 MAY

Well batted Ollie Pope, who took his hard work of yesterday and built on it wonderfully to walk off the field unbeaten on 158. It has been a brilliant innings and he has really put a marker down for the rest of his season.

No Barran because he has a big day closer to home as his Churt Wasps U9 outfit play their cup final against rivals Wokingham and Bracknell Pumas. I'm delighted to report they win 2-1 in extra time, with Little John scoring the winner. Barran posts a picture of the celebrations and I enjoy noticing the monikered 'JB' on his tracksuit.

Back at The Oval, Surrey take three wickets to reduce Yorkshire to 40-3 and, sadly, that's that for the day as the rain comes and just doesn't shift.

This does give me the opportunity of a slightly freer rein on my BBC London updates, which need to come much more frequently at the weekend. We end up talking campervans and Scarborough, a discussion which gives rise to a fantastic story from their studio guest, former England footballer Paul Parker, about being in a hotel with Gazza during Italia '90. Amazing.

The weather is slightly better in Malahide, Dublin, where Ireland are able to get their maiden Test match underway after being rained off yesterday. Feel very proud of Gary Wilson and Tim Murtagh, two old boys of Surrey who are playing in the historic game and it's fantastic to see former Surrey Head Coach Graham Ford coaching again in international cricket.

With the rain, I drive home earlier than scheduled and am therefore able to catch the full broadcast of the *Eurovision Song Contest*. I love the heavy metal/

folk number from Denmark and am once again patriotically disappointed to see the GB entry finish 24th out of 26, as well as negotiating a stage invader.

SUNDAY 13 MAY

If Friday was the day for Ollie Pope, then Sunday is all about Sam Curran. He sets out his stall early by trapping England captain Joe Root lbw from the sixth ball of the morning and just doesn't let up all day.

He finishes the first innings with six wickets, receives his full county cap at lunchtime and takes his 100th first-class wicket during the afternoon session. Think about getting over to see him to ask for the lottery numbers for later but can't leave the commentary box.

To borrow a phrase from captain Rory Burns, I'm absolutely chuffed to bits for him. He is a lovely lad with all the talent in the world and people tend forget he is still only 19 years of age.

Despite a powerful effort from Jonny Bairstow this morning, Surrey enforce the follow on and then take another five wickets in the afternoon. The highlight of the second innings so far has been Amar Virdi bowling Joe Root, who has been dismissed twice in a day by Surrey teenagers, with the perfect off-spinner.

The moment is beautifully brought to the wider listening public by Barran, who has taken to describing Virdi as 'the young Surrey twiddler'.

As expected, the post-match interview with Sam is full of happiness and satisfaction for the young man and gives me the boost required for a planned net session with Barran in the indoor school. We are joined by Isabelle (Duncan, not my daughter, who is sadly still back in Wales) and Barran brings his special yellow ball, the one that only seems to swing in to right-handers. Isabelle proceeds to smash him everywhere.

Post-net dinner with Barran at 'Big Easy' in Chelsea. As we arrive the live band stops and almost everyone leaves. An amazing meal though, featuring the largest prawn cocktail I've ever had. We go for a beer afterwards and for one moment I did actually think we were in the seniors' version of *Made in Chelsea*.

Back to Mother Barran's for a sleep after a very enjoyable evening.

MONDAY 14 MAY

Surrey conclude a brilliant win within 45 minutes of the morning session, taking the last five wickets in ruthless fashion. Sam Curran nabs three of them to secure ten in the match.

The post-match interview with a very happy Rory Burns is highlighted by his response to my question about captaining Virat Kohli, which isn't something many people get to do. He says, with a wink, that 'Kohli will be lucky to be captained by me'. A brilliant response and typical of Burns.

Last year I wrote a short piece paying tribute to Gareth Batty for his Testimonial programme. Very occasionally, I am asked to sign this by people and this happens again today. I normally wouldn't record this in the diary but Vish takes a photo of me doing it and then sends it out to his many thousands of Twitter followers with the caption: "Just another big name doing big-name duties at Surrey." Thank you very much.

Say goodbye to Isabelle and Barran, who heads off to continue organising an event with a Daniel Craig lookalike who looks more like Sean Connery. Another superb week in the commentary box.

On the drive back to Mum's, I listen to ECB Chairman Colin Graves, who has conducted an extraordinary interview with *Test Match Special*'s Simon Mann. I'm really not sure what's going on in our wonderful game at the moment – but it's certainly not good.

Back in time to watch some highlights of Kevin O'Brien's century for Ireland (he always picks the big occasion) with a chicken sandwich (changing it up again) before I head to bed after a tremendous four days.

TUESDAY 15 MAY

Drive back to Cardiff listening to Jeremy Vine on Radio 2. All the chat is about the Royal Wedding. My overriding thought is astonishment on how many 'wedding experts' there seem to be in the world.

England announce their squad for the first Test and I'm delighted to see that Mark Stoneman has been retained. He is a quality performer and I really hope he makes a massive hundred next week.

My old mate Charlie Dagnall is doing updates from Malahide where Ireland at one stage have Pakistan 15-3 and an incredible upset is on the cards. In the end Pakistan pull it out of the bag but what an occasion it's been for Ireland Cricket. They've conclusively shown that they deserve to be at the top table of the world game.

There is a lot more chat about Colin Graves – and his statement that kids just aren't interested in cricket. This gets better and better. I'm not quite sure what he means by any these comments but I'm sure all will become clear at some point. Hopefully before 2020.

Back to Wales in time to pick up my Isabelle from school and we head straight to the park for a massive ice cream before going to home to play some Xbox and attempt some very hard maths homework.

Delighted to find out that my DVD of *The Greatest Showman* has arrived. Disappointed to find out I seem to be the only one in the house that wants to watch it and so head out for a run instead!

❊

WEDNESDAY 16 MAY

Take Isabelle to school in time for her yoga class (!). What a start to the day for my little girl!

Today's agenda is a trip to Bristol with Mrs Church. We end up in the River Cottage Café, surrounded by lots of books by Hugh Fearnley-Whittingstall.

Pick Issy up from school to news that she has run the 50m in 9.57 seconds. Buy her a Crunchie to celebrate.

The day ends with me reading *The Midnight Gang* by David Walliams to Isabelle, for what may be the tenth time. Honestly, I think I enjoy it more than she does!

❊

THURSDAY 17 MAY

Say goodbye to Mrs Church and then drop Issy off at school before heading back down the M4 to Mum's, ahead of the first game of the Royal London One Day Cup, which starts at The Oval tomorrow.

The journey east is soundtracked by Nottinghamshire commentator Dave Bracegirdle, who is joined by Messrs. Howells and Read for Notts v Lancashire on Five Live. Delighted to hear Read get the phrase 'danger zone' into the very first over of commentary. We are both big *Top Gun* fans and have a private battle to jam as many references in as we can over the summer.

Surrey name their first 50-over squad of the season, which is without Mark Stoneman because of his England duties. However, he hasn't reported in to join the squad yet and offers to come and do a stint in the commentary box with us, which is terrific news.

With the news that we'll be joined by BBC Bristol's Anthony Gibson for the Somerset game tomorrow, the preparations are finalised for the start of the white ball summer. Bearing in mind they've lost the last three Lord's finals, can Surrey go one step further and win it this year?

When I get to Mum's I head out for a long run and return to the news that we've been invited to watch the Royal Wedding with some of our closest family friends. I've been asked to provide ball-by-ball commentary, so spend a while working out how balls will be involved in the celebrations and what type of bat Meghan will be using.

✳

FRIDAY 18 MAY

Wake early from white ball dreams to drive to The Oval and get everything ready for an 11am start.

On the way back from my coffee collection walk I start to realise there are considerably more children than normal in the area and quickly realise that this is the match that has been selected for Surrey's annual Schools Day. On past form there are likely to be around 5,000 kids in the ground – it's a fantastic occasion and always sounds great on the radio!

Before we start, I spend some time online researching potential campervans for our trip to Scarborough next month. It seems like Barran and I will be joined by Surrey Head of Communications Jon Surtees, which makes the whole thing seem a bit more realistic. We may need a bigger van.

When the XI is announced at the toss it becomes clear that Surrey are giving a debut to Will Jacks, another of their talented teenagers. Very much looking forward to watching him play. The other thing that is revealed at the toss is the presence of England selector Ed Smith, in a lovely pair of white trousers.

Barran arrives and is in cracking form after a hosting a gig at Café de Paris last night. Tonight he will be Michael Buffer at one of his regular White Collar boxing nights. What a man he is! Michael Buffer, not Barran.

Play starts, soundtracked by the excited screams of 5,000 local children. I try to work out what they're screaming at because, as we've all been told by the ECB Chairman, kids don't like cricket. Very confusing.

The game isn't great from a Surrey perspective. They're rattled out for 129, which Somerset chase down with the minimum of fuss. A bad day at the office.

Highlight for me is being joined in the box by Mark. Stoneman. We have a fascinating chat ahead of the first Test of the summer. He's a smashing fella and I hope he scores a tonne of runs against Pakistan – he deserves to.

The early finish allows our attention to turn to the serious business of podcasting and Barran and I record a magical Royal Wedding podcast with Daniel Norcross. Barran's experience – "when I was at school with Henry Windsor", being a particular favourite of mine – and Norcross' rampant Marxist republicanism make a hell of a combination and I think it is likely to raise a few smiles in all the right places.

Drive back to Mum in the glorious sunshine and reward myself with a cold beer before bed. Mum is very excited about the wedding tomorrow. As am I if I'm honest.

❇

SATURDAY 19 MAY

ROYAL WEDDING DAY!

Up early to post the podcast before heading out for a run. Make sure I'm back in plenty of time to put on my finery and head over to our friends Eric and Karen's house to watch the drama unfold.

It's a lovely service and it's great to see Becks and George Clooney in attendance. The ball-by-ball commentary that was requested doesn't really materialise, largely because no balls, apart from 'Golden Balls', were involved in the proceedings. Maybe next time.

The afternoon unfolds in the garden as we watch the FA Cup Final between Chelsea and Man Utd. Alec Stewart will be a happy man tonight.

In the evening Mum and I go out with friends to have a meal to remember Dad. It's been nearly a year since he passed away. It has gone very slowly – but also far too quickly, if that makes any sense. I miss the old man very much and I don't think I'm the only one.

He adored cricket and I will always be very glad that the final broadcast of mine he heard was Kumar Sangakkara scoring a century at Lord's. He would have enjoyed that.

✻

SUNDAY 20 MAY

Take Mum to a memorial service at Riverhill Gardens in Sevenoaks. It's a lovely morning, with the sun shining brightly at one of Dad's favourite places.

Conscious of the trip to Hampshire tomorrow, I spend the afternoon giving Tysoe a proper buff up and end the day with another five mile run.

✻

MONDAY 21 MAY

Up early to pack for the trip to Hampshire and thoughts again turn to Dad, who passed away a year ago today.

Jump into Tysoe and head for Southampton. The radio is still full of people talking about Meghan's dress and other details about the Royal Wedding.

Arrive at the Ageas Bowl and initially struggle to find a parking pace until Surrey Assistant Head Coach Vikram Solanki strolls along and offers me his. Even his reversing is elegance personified.

Climb into one of the Ageas Bowl hotel lifts to head up to the broadcasting area to check the set-up. I wouldn't normally mention this specific detail of the day, but the lifts at this ground have a mind of their own and tend to deposit you where they feel like it, rather than where you have asked for.

Upon arrival I use my key card to access the commentary box. This may sound odd but it's a unique arrangement here, where we broadcast from hotel rooms situated on the TV gantry which are temporarily converted to commentary boxes. I'm greeted by Kevan James and Kevin Howells and immediately realise that today will be a good day.

It feels like an appropriate day to do some more planning for my run, so I phone Maggie Blanks from the Pancreatic Cancer Research Fund. All very exciting and plans are coming together nicely.

For the first time this year we're also joined by our friends at Sky Sports and I say hello to Rob Key as he makes his way to the putting green at the Ageas Bowl golf course for some pre-match practice.

We have a very full commentary box today as myself and the Kevins are joined by Hampshire and England's injured all-rounder Liam Dawson, Barran and Kris Temple, who has brought cake for his birthday. Barran and Temple must surely be the smoothest commentary pair on the circuit.

Barran, as ever, is full of beans. On this occasion it is down to Little John's performance for Hampshire U9s yesterday and he regales us all with a ball-by-ball account of the event.

On the field, Surrey win the toss and bat and Will Jacks gets them off to a good start before the experienced heads of Dean Elgar and Rory Burns capitalise to get them in a strong position. However, a flurry of wickets and some rain put things up in the air before Scott Borthwick and Rikki Clarke play extremely well to post 262/7 off 44 overs.

More rain means Hampshire need 227 off 34 overs and, despite the rain, we still have an interval where I'm delighted to find some hot cottage pie has my name on it.

Rilee Rossouw gets Hampshire off to a belting start and it seems that Surrey are all but out of the game before Clarke and Gareth Batty bowl brilliantly and the game swings once again. It all gets very tense but fair play to Joe Weatherley and Lewis McManus, who get Hampshire over the line with seven balls to spare.

It's back-to-back losses for Surrey in the One Day Cup but they started this competition poorly last year and still made the final.

Great news arrives from Jon Surtees during the evening session. He has secured us a campervan for Scarborough! Not only that, it's being lent to us by a firm called Spaceships UK, who have agreed to the deal in return for a little promotion. I have visions of a photoshoot with Barran draped over the bonnet in various shades of cashmere but quickly put them to one side.

Eventually leave the ground at 11pm after a long day and get back to Mum's at 1am. What to do? Watch highlights of the game with a bowl of granola. Rock 'n' roll.

✳

TUESDAY 22 MAY

Wake up far too early for someone who'd only got back in the house at 1am the previous night and head out for a six-miler. With all this sun and all this running, the tan really is coming on very nicely.

Help Mum with some paperwork before heading to Nizels Golf Club for another 18 holes with Stuart Barnes. As ever I arrive far too early and promptly fall asleep in the sun before waking up to see Barnes arriving with his legs out!

I play like Rory McIlroy for the first three holes, whilst Barnes is all over the shop, twice not getting his drive past the ladies' tee. However, bearing in mind he already has his legs out, I agree that nothing else needs to follow and we continue.

Alex Tysoe's (human version) pink driver is going like a dream but I still can't putt and my game falls apart after hitting a duck (which was stunned but OK) and Barnes wins on the last hole.

Back at Mum's it's lovely to see my Auntie Sue and to find out that Surrey have Jason Roy back from the IPL for tomorrow's match against Gloucestershire.

Mum and Sue are off to the Chelsea Flower Show tomorrow but then, bizarrely, Mum says: "After Chelsea I really fancy some Royal London One Day Cup cricket" (or something like that), so it is decided that her and Sue will come to The Oval tomorrow afternoon.

Pack my bags to head back to Cardiff after the game tomorrow – there is a swimming gala for Isabelle on Thursday morning that I don't want to miss.

✳

WEDNESDAY 23 MAY

Up at 5am and straight into Tysoe. Arrive at The Oval and the commentary box is all set up by 7am.

Await the arrival of Bob Hunt from BBC Gloucestershire, who is one of the legends of the cricket commentary scene, despite his habit of shouting: "Come on the shire!" during a commentary.

Barran arrives just as the coin goes up. The toss is won by Rory Burns, who decides to bowl first – a change of tactic for Surrey.

Surrey bowl well and have their visitors in trouble for periods but they recover and post a very solid 282.

Stay on air during the start of the interval to allow me to interview Surrey's Accessibility Officer, Theresa Peters. She has been at the club for a long time and really is doing some fantastic work in her new role to help make it easy and welcoming for people with accessibility issues come to The Oval.

Dash down to leave tickets for Mum on the gate and get back just in time for the start of the Surrey innings. Jason Roy goes in the first over but after that, Will Jacks dominates with the bat. He is only 19 years old and plays the best innings I've ever seen for a lad in his third game. He has every shot in the book and dominates the scoring, bringing up his maiden hundred with a six. Just brilliant.

Mum and Auntie Sue arrive and I bring them up to the commentary box. I'm really proud to have them there and they are charmed by Bob, who brings them slices of Victoria sponge and scones.

Jacks eventually goes for 121. What an effort. Surrey get nailed for apparently spending tonnes of money but here is another 19-year-old coming through the system and immediately making an impact. He receives a richly deserved standing ovation on the way off. Ben Foakes makes 50 and Surrey move to a thoroughly professional first win in this year's competition.

Say goodbye to Mum and Auntie Sue and head off to interview Jacks. Quite rightly, he is very excited by how he has played and it's lovely to meet him for the first time.

Send the interview back to the BBC, a very easy process these days. When I first started, you had to wait for a producer back in the studio to find enough time to 'capture' your interview back in the studio whilst you sent it down the ISDN line. These days you just slap it into your laptop and e-mail it. Technology!

Bid an emotional farewell to Bob Hunt, who revealed today that he had been Bruce Forsyth's paperboy *and* an extra in *Casualty*! What a man.

As I'm packing up Tysoe to drive back to Cardiff, I hear a rumour that Kohli might not be fit for next month. Choose to ignore it. We've booked the bloody campervan and everything!

Arrive back in Cardiff at 11pm. It's been a long old day but spirits are lifted when I find a brand new box of granola in the cupboard. A Will Jacks hundred and fresh granola – days don't get much better than that.

❋

THURSDAY 24 MAY

A huge morning.

Take Isabelle to school and then head straight to the Cardiff International Swimming Pool for her swimming gala.

It's like the Olympics as I secure a seat in the front row to make sure I have prime position for the Year 3 breaststroke final. Sitting there waiting I realise what Michael Phelps' family must have been through all those times.

Shortly before the start of the race I hear that Virat Kohli is definitely not coming to play for Surrey because of a neck injury he picked up in the IPL. As important as this is, I file it to one side for now. Priorities and all that.

When the moment comes, Issy takes a sitting start whilst everyone else dives in. Always the individual, my girl. However, she powers along brilliantly and for a moment looks set to take the win before being pipped at the line into silver medal position.

I'm so proud of her and give her a standing ovation as she receives her medal. I've already sorted the rights to the exclusive interview and will be conducting it later on.

Head home in time to hear the start of the *TMS* summer. England win the toss and bat and are immediately in a bit of trouble at Lord's. Go for a long run and by the time I'm back, they're in a lot of trouble.

Pick Issy up from school and fulfil my part of the 'exclusive interview' deal by bringing along a large bar of chocolate. Conduct the interview and then watch the Channel 5 highlights of a poor day for England's batsmen at the Test match. I think some people may have underestimated Pakistan.

And yes, sadly, Kohli is not coming due to injury. A decision needs to be made on the campervan.

FRIDAY 25 MAY

Spend the day with Mrs Church and Issy. A great time includes shopping (dull), eating (nice) and watching *The Greatest Showman* for the fifth time (Jackman is special).

Pakistan are still on top in the Test as I mount the running machine at the gym and start watching. I bang out 10km and then head home for peanut butter on toast and bed.

❈

SATURDAY 26 MAY

Climb back into faithful Tysoe for the drive to Kent. It's raining in Cardiff as I leave but as I get further along the M4 the sun comes out and with *TMS* soundtracking the journey, it flies by.

By the time I get to Mum's, England are five down but I'm able to spend an enjoyable afternoon in the garden with *TMS* as Buttler and Bess stage a recovery.

Do a turn for BBC Essex looking ahead to tomorrow's game in Chelmsford before heading inside to watch Fulham win the Championship play-off final. Delighted for Rory Burns, who will be a happy man tonight.

The Champions League final this evening sees Twitter have a complete meltdown over poor Karius. These days, if you make a mistake everyone's got an opinion, including Johnny Barran, Liverpool's biggest fan. He bleeds red and one day I will take him to Anfield so he actually gets to watch them!

❈

SUNDAY 27 MAY

Today's game necessitates an early start, as I need to make it through the Dartford Tunnel. Of course, I manage this and arrive at the ground far too early.

Wander into Chelmsford for a coffee and hear lots of a talk of thunderstorms today. Let's hope it remains at the 'talk' stage, eh?

Get set up in the commentary box with my BBC Essex colleagues and catch up with former England batsman James Taylor, who is at the game today as a scout for England. He's an inspirational and lovely bloke – and was a bloody good player. He tells me his autobiography is out soon, and with all he has been through I have no doubt it will be a massive success. I will make sure I pick up a copy.

Felstead School Steel Band are playing ahead of the game – they are amazing and play the *Dr. Who* theme perfectly before the toss.

Surrey win it and bowl, a brilliant effort in the field on a really good batting track keeping Essex to 294.

A group of lads on a stag do turn up and add to the atmosphere as they attempt to start a Mexican wave. Looking at the state of them, I'm surprised they can count to five, let alone co-ordinate a mass participation event.

The Surrey chase is lovely to watch. Jason Roy looks in prime form with 88 and Dean Elgar plays a smashing innings in the last game of his current spell with Surrey. Ben Foakes is the icing on the cake with a gorgeous unbeaten knock to take Surrey home by six wickets with five overs to spare. A neat, tidy and very professional performance.

Interview Elgar afterwards. He is exactly what you want from an overseas player. A quality performer and a quality bloke in the dressing room.

Drive back to Mum's afterwards listening to the fall-out from England's nine–wicket loss. The main thing that strikes me is the arrogance of everyone talking about how bad England were. There should be a lot more focus on how good a very young Pakistan team is.

Get home in time for a ham sandwich and part two of the superb *A Very English Scandal* on the BBC, with Hugh Grant playing Jeremy Thorpe. He really is a tremendous actor.

Spent the day experiencing slight laptop issues, which is never much fun. I've decided to go for the old 'switch on, switch off' technique and head to bed hoping it works again in the morning.

✳

MONDAY 28 MAY

Awake and immediately feel stressed about the laptop's recovery process so the first thing I do is check how it went – it works! Huge relief.

Head off for a beautiful Bank Holiday run, the sun is shining and there is barely a cloud in the sky. Return home to the news that Mark Stoneman has been dropped for the Headingley Test – I do feel for him but he is too good a player not to come back even stronger.

A quiet afternoon with Mum sees the announcement of the Surrey squad to play Sussex tomorrow. It's frankly ridiculous – Morkel, Stoneman and Tom Curran have all come back into the squad. By my calculations, 77 per cent are home-grown talent but I still see 'Typical Surrey' out there on Twitter.

I receive a text from Daniel Norcross saying he will be with us tomorrow and the game is on the network. Poor old Barran is missing a network game – away for half term with the family, which will include many hours of Little John bowling to him on the beach.

✳

TUESDAY 29 MAY

Aboard Tysoe by 5.15am and head to The Oval to rebuild the commentary box and grab a coffee. It's a cloudy morning but the forecast says we should be OK, with no rain.

On the way back to the ground I bump into Jason Roy, and it's lovely to catch up with the great man, who is in cracking form. He's another one whose first game I'm very proud to have commentated on and it has been great to see his career grow and grow.

I also see Sam Curran, who is bowling really well this season and is one of the nicest lads on the circuit. This Surrey dressing room is packed with good people.

Adrian Harms from BBC Sussex arrives; it's always lovely to broadcast with Adrian and great to see him. Norcross arrives in a surprisingly sober shirt and everything gets set up for the Five Live broadcast.

The coin goes up half an hour before play – and then it starts to rain. And it keeps raining. Really frustrating because, on paper, this is a cracking game.

We spend time constructively debating the England Test team with Norcross, Harms and 'Legside' Lizzy Ammon from the *Times*. My "Joe Root needs to play youngsters and think ahead" idea is met with a muted response. I do feel he needs to put his stamp on the team and the first step in that is giving young players a go.

Lunch – lamb and mashed potato – goes down very well with those press that are here.

Then Armageddon strikes south London. Torrential rain floods the outfield and puts paid to any chance of cricket. Lee Fortis and his groundstaff, the hardest working team in show business, have a long evening ahead of them.

I say my goodbyes and head for the car, bumping into Chris Jordan on the way. I've a real soft spot for CJ – he's an incredible talent who, for some bizarre reason, was never used properly when he was at Surrey. I'm so pleased to see his career blossom at Sussex and he's still one of the coolest blokes I know.

Leave London and head back to Cardiff. I get a bit of a shock when I'm halfway up the M4 and hear Five Live say in their sports bulletin: "and we have full commentary on Surrey v Sussex from The Oval on Sports Extra at the moment". There might be commentary on some fishing, but not much else!

Get home at 9pm and enjoy a nice evening with Mrs Church watching the latest *Planet of the Apes* film.

WEDNESDAY 30 MAY

Head to the gym for an early session and then sit in the café watching *Homes Under the Hammer* with Dion Dublin. There is no better start to the day.

Pick up Isabelle from her friend's house, where she has had a sleepover. It's half term week so we head off for a swim. Spend three hours in the pool playing tag and 'How Long Can You Hold Your Breath For?' [HLCYHYBF]. I'm still swimming in my Surrey shorts circa 2009 – must buy some trunks.

Spend some time in the afternoon setting up my JustGiving page for the run in memory of Dad. It's all getting very real now and I'm going public with it on Friday.

On 8 October I will leave The Oval and run to Lord's, a five-mile route I will repeat four times a day for 50 days. It will be 200 runs and 1,000 miles in total, all to raise money for Pancreatic Cancer Research Fund.

Later in the day I hear the brilliant news that Sam Curran has been called into the England Test squad for the Headingley Test. He will take it all in his stride and I really hope he plays. He will certainly do some damage and it's a hell of an opportunity for him.

I head to bed and am soon joined by Isabelle, who wants to have a chat about the day. The one thing I really miss during the cricket season is my family – but I am still very lucky and have the best job in the world.

❊

THURSDAY 31 MAY

I'm in charge today, so with half term still in full swing Isabelle and I head into Cardiff to spend the £10 note Granny sent up with me from Kent.

I spend two hours stood outside 'Smiggle' whilst Isabelle decides which pens and pencil case she wants to take back to school next week. As I begin to lose the will to live, Isabelle decides on a nice pencil case with pineapples on the front.

Back to the swimming pool for another swim and HLCYHYBF? (see 30 May) session. Manage a minute to smash my PB and emerge from the water like one of those whales you see on *Blue Planet*.

Head home for the hard part of the day, saying goodbye to the girls again. After ten years of saying goodbye to the family I find I'm much better at it, but I still really miss them.

Head back down the M4 to Mum's to prepare for the game at Beckenham tomorrow, getting there around 9.30pm. After a quick cup of tea I head for bed. I realise it's June tomorrow – where did that come from?!

❊

Clockwise from top: The trusty Tysoe; making an effort for the Royal
Wedding; Kevin Howells and Johnny Barran in 'action'; chilling with Issy.

Clockwise from top left: Izzy Duncan and Barran shooting the breeze; and then netting together; Daniel Norcross sporting the 'Victorian Bath Mosaic', one of his less flamboyant shirts; 5,000 schoolkids enjoy Schools Day at the Kia Oval; with Steve Waugh this time; May the Fourth be with you.

SURREY V WORCESTERSHIRE

Venue: The Kia Oval, Kennington
Date: 4th, 5th, 6th, 7th May 2018
Toss: Surrey
Result: Match drawn

Points: Surrey 9; Worcestershire 11
Umpires: JH Evans, AG Wharf
Scorers: PJ Makepeace, PM Mellish

SURREY	1ST INNINGS	R	b	2ND INNINGS	R	b
*RJ Burns	c Mitchell b Morris	193	408	c Barnard b Twohig	30	72
MD Stoneman	run out (Barnard)	28	61	lbw b Morris	20	34
SG Borthwick	c Cox b Leach	10	29	not out	82	154
RS Patel	c Cox b Leach	10	19	c Head b Morris	25	59
+BT Foakes	c Cox b Barnard	72	105	not out	11	42
OJD Pope	c Mitchell b Leach	32	102	did not bat		
SM Curran	b Leach	0	8	did not bat		
R Clarke	lbw b Morris	38	62	did not bat		
SC Meaker	b Twohig	13	31	did not bat		
C McKerr	not out	10	24	did not bat		
GS Virdi	c Mitchell b Tongue	11	20	did not bat		
Extras	(8 b, 3 lb, 6 nb)	17		(3 b, 2 nb)	5	
Total	(all out, 144.2 overs)	434		(3 wickets, dec, 60 overs)	173	

Fall of wickets: 1-50 (Stoneman, 19.4 ov), 2-87 (Borthwick, 31.4 ov), 3-99 (Patel, 37.4 ov), 4-224 (Foakes, 72.6 ov), 5-293 (Pope, 103.5 ov), 6-295 (Curran, 105.4 ov), 7-384 (Clarke, 128.5 ov), 8-403 (Burns, 134.4 ov), 9-415 (Meaker, 137.6 ov), 10-434 (Virdi, 144.2 ov)
Fall of wickets: 1-38 (Stoneman, 13.4 ov), 2-74 (Burns, 22.3 ov), 3-136 (Patel, 43.4 ov)

WORCESTERSHIRE	O	M	R	W	Wd	Nb		O	M	R	W	Wd	Nb
Leach	36	4	96	4	-	3	Leach	4	2	11	0	-	-
Barnard	25	4	73	1	-	-	Tongue	8	2	28	0	-	1
Tongue	25.2	3	88	1	-	-	Twohig	22	3	62	1	-	-
Morris	29	5	85	2	-	-	Head	16	5	36	0	-	-
Twohig	20	2	60	1	-	-	Morris	6	1	21	2	-	-
Head	8	0	21	0	-	-	D'Oliveira	3	0	12	0	-	-
Mitchell	1	1	0	0	-	-	Mitchell	1	1	0	0	-	-

WORCESTERSHIRE	1ST INNINGS	R	b	2ND INNINGS	R	b
DKH Mitchell	lbw b Clarke	81	139			
BL D'Oliveira	lbw b Clarke	23	51			
TC Fell	c Meaker b Curran	88	220			
JM Clarke	lbw b McKerr	157	280			
TM Head	b Virdi	50	56			
+OB Cox	lbw b Virdi	0	1			
EG Barnard	c and b Virdi	66	135			
BJ Twohig	c Patel b Virdi	9	30			
*J Leach	c Borthwick b Virdi	18	20			
JC Tongue	c and b Virdi	9	21			
CAJ Morris	not out	0	6			
Extras	(8 lb, 14 nb, 3 w)	25				
Total	(all out, 158.4 overs)	526				

Fall of wickets: 1-48 (D'Oliveira, 17.1 ov), 2-139 (Mitchell, 47.1 ov), 3-256 (Fell, 86.2 ov), 4-336 (Head, 106.5 ov), 5-336 (Cox, 106.6 ov), 6-460 (Clarke, 135.3 ov), 7-475 (Twohig, 142.2 ov), 8-505 (Leach, 148.3 ov), 9-523 (Tongue, 154.4 ov), 10-526 (Barnard, 158.4 ov)

SURREY	O	M	R	W	Wd	Nb		O	M	R	W	Wd	Nb
Curran	21	4	62	1	-	-							
Clarke	33	10	90	2	-	-							
Virdi	41.4	7	105	6	-	1							
McKerr	16	1	76	1	1	3							
Patel	17	3	57	0	-	1							
Meaker	22	1	93	0	1	1							
Borthwick	8	0	35	0	1	1							

SURREY V YORKSHIRE

Venue: The Kia Oval, Kennington
Date: 11th, 12th, 13th, 14th May 2018
Toss: No toss made
Result: Surrey won by an innings and 17 runs

Points: Surrey 24; Yorkshire 4
Umpires: DJ Millns, MJ Saggers
Scorers: PJ Makepeace, JT Potter

SURREY	1ST INNINGS	R	b	2ND INNINGS	R	b
*RJ Burns	c Pujara b Brooks	9	18			
MD Stoneman	lbw b Bresnan	10	23			
SG Borthwick	c Lyth b Shaw	5	20			
D Elgar	b Root	61	101			
+BT Foakes	c Bairstow b Patterson	18	35			
OJD Pope	not out	158	224			
SM Curran	c Bairstow b Patterson	19	34			
R Clarke	c Lyth b Brooks	71	91			
C McKerr	c Pujara b Bresnan	29	49			
JW Dernbach	c Root b Patterson	14	7			
GS Virdi	c Leaning b Bresnan	1	7			
Extras	(4 b, 10 lb, 4 nb, 1 w)	19				
Total	(all out, 101.1 overs)	414				

Fall of wickets: 1-15 (Stoneman, 6.3 ov), 2-19 (Burns, 7.2 ov), 3-40 (Borthwick, 13.2 ov), 4-69 (Foakes, 22.5 ov), 5-137 (Elgar, 43.6 ov), 6-162 (Curran, 52.6 ov), 7-291 (Clarke, 81.2 ov), 8-373 (McKerr, 95.1 ov), 9-404 (Dernbach, 98.4 ov), 10-414 (Virdi, 101.1 ov)

	O	M	R	W	Wd	Nb		O	M	R	W	Wd	Nb
Bresnan	26.1	5	98	3	-	1							
Brooks	18	0	91	2	-	1							
Shaw	17	2	76	1	-	-							
Patterson	27	2	107	3	1	-							
Root	11	1	27	1	-	-							
Brook	2	1	1	0	-	-							

YORKSHIRE	1ST INNINGS	R	b	2ND INNINGS (F/O)	R	b
A Lyth	lbw b Curran	6	17	c Clarke b Virdi	58	130
AZ Lees	c Elgar b Dernbach	0	1	c Borthwick b Dernbach	4	12
CA Pujara	c Borthwick b Curran	17	29	b Curran	0	3
*JE Root	lbw b Curran	14	26	b Virdi	23	62
HC Brook	c Foakes b Curran	17	26	lbw b Virdi	8	33
+JM Bairstow	c Clarke b Dernbach	95	94	c Foakes b Clarke	29	64
JA Leaning	lbw b Clarke	20	49	lbw b Clarke	28	87
TT Bresnan	c Borthwick b Curran	1	6	c Foakes b Curran	1	4
SA Patterson	c Pope b Clarke	5	37	b Curran	0	1
J Shaw	c Elgar b Curran	29	44	b Curran	0	4
JA Brooks	not out	5	18	not out	4	1
Extras	(6 b, 7 lb, 6 nb, 1 w)	20		(1 b, 3 lb, 8 nb, 1 w)	13	
Total	(all out, 57.2 overs)	229		(all out, 66.1 overs)	168	

Fall of wickets: 1-1 (Lees, 0.2 ov), 2-7 (Lyth, 3.6 ov), 3-34 (Pujara, 11.1 ov), 4-41 (Root, 13.6 ov), 5-88 (Brook, 19.3 ov), 6-155 (Leaning, 35.4 ov), 7-158 (Bresnan, 36.5 ov), 8-183 (Patterson, 45.5 ov), 9-203 (Bairstow, 50.2 ov), 10-229 (Shaw, 57.2 ov)
Fall of wickets: 1-9 (Lees, 4.6 ov), 2-10 (Pujara, 5.5 ov), 3-66 (Root, 28.4 ov), 4-99 (Lyth, 38.2 ov), 5-102 (Brook, 40.5 ov), 6-151 (Bairstow, 60.5 ov), 7-164 (Bresnan, 63.6 ov), 8-164 (Patterson, 65.1 ov), 9-164 (Shaw, 65.5 ov), 10-168 (Leaning, 66.1 ov)

SURREY	O	M	R	W	Wd	Nb		O	M	R	W	Wd	Nb
Dernbach	18	2	81	2	-	-	Dernbach	13	4	24	1	1	-
Curran	16.2	2	54	6	-	-	Curran	17	6	47	4	-	-
Clarke	16	2	47	2	-	2	Clarke	17.1	3	41	2	-	-
McKerr	3	0	16	0	1	-	Virdi	19	1	52	3	-	4
Virdi	4	1	18	0	-	1							

JUNE

"Rory Burns says his team 'will not flirt with form'. It's brilliant, but I've no idea what it means"

FRIDAY 1 JUNE

Wake to the news that my instinct was correct last night and it is, in fact, June. Leave the house in Tysoe at 5.30am because I'm not sure how long it will take to get to Beckenham and want to make sure I beat the traffic.

Arrive at Beckenham at 6am – it wasn't as far I thought and there was no traffic. That's early, even for me. Park up and fall asleep in the car and have an amazing dream in which Sam Allardyce is appointed Read Madrid manager after Zidane steps down.

Wake up and am not sure where I am, but am convinced that the Madrid fans will be getting used to the long ball game at the Bernabeu next season.

At 7am I announce details of my run to the world and tweet my fundraising page for the first time. Amazed by all the lovely messages of support that come in – it's all very real now and that tends to focus the mind a bit. 1,000 miles – that's quite a long way!

I take a wander to find out where we're broadcasting from. I do love an outground because you can end up working from some amazing locations. During one broadcast, made from a farmer's field in Wales, I missed a couple of overs of commentary whilst he had to let his cows out. On another occasion, I commentated on a whole game whilst only able to see half the ground because we were behind the sightscreen.

Today there are no such problems and I'm delighted to discover that BBC Kent Sports Editor Matt Cole came down yesterday and ran an ISDN lead 100m from the pavilion kitchen to a specially constructed gazebo. When I discover that he built the gazebo himself, I'm even more impressed.

The written press have their own marquee. This was meant to be Kohli's first game, so a big tent was ordered. There is now considerably less press and I wonder if Johnny Barran might have space to host a garden party this afternoon.

Eventually some other people arrive, including Surrey and England bowler Tom Curran. It's good to chat to him and also get a close up look at the new blonde streak in his hair that has recently appeared.

Joined by Matt Cole and by Adam Williams from BBC Sport Onli
us today, when I bump into a photographer from the *Sunday T*
to take a picture of Morne Morkel. He asks me if the great Sou'
recognisable; I reply that he's 6ft 5" and he agrees that that sh

Surrey win the toss and bowl, but as we go on air from the gazebo there is still no sign of Barran. Shortly into the game, my phone buzzes with a text from him saying that he's stuck in his car in the car park, and may be a little late. I have visions of him having to clamber out of the sun roof because he's parked too close to a wall or another car but it turns out that he's actually gone to the wrong ground, parked up, walked to the pavilion and then realised it was a bit quiet for a game of professional cricket. Eventually he finds the gazebo and is very excited with our set-up. With the marquee next door, he's in his natural habitat.

The pitch is an absolute belter and Kent bat first and rack up 384 – TC is the pick of the Surrey bowlers with three wickets.

At half time, Barran and I record a new podcast outside the gazebo. All is going well until we start to notice lots of ants on the table we are broadcasting off. It transpires Matt Cole has constructed the gazebo on top of an ants' nest. There is a small army of ants going up my trouser leg but fortunately we are rescued by Anna from Kent CCC, who hears about our wildlife danger on the radio and quickly makes her way over with some ant repellent!

Given the quality of the pitch, I think Surrey have a real chance of chasing this total down. However, they never get any partnerships going and despite 68 from Jason Roy, they are all out at 5.30pm and Kent win by 221 runs.

That man Darren Stevens takes 6-25. He is an extraordinary cricketer and I reckon he will still be scoring runs and taking wickets when he's 80.

It's a busy old day in Beckenham but away from the game the biggest news of the day is Sam Curran making his England Test debut at Headingley. He's presented with his cap by Graham Thorpe and takes a wicket – and there is a lovely moment here as Scott Borthwick (twelfth man) takes his phone out to TC at third man so he can watch his brother's first over in Test cricket.

Conduct an honest interview with coach Di Venuto at the end and Surrey now really need a miracle to make the knock-out stages of this competition.

It's been a lovely day at Beckenham and the early finish means the drive back to Mum's can be soundtracked by the end of the first day on *TMS*.

Ham sandwich, Day 1 Test highlights, bed.

❊

SATURDAY 2 JUNE

Up early for a ten-mile run. All goes well and I get a lovely surprise when I get back and look at the JustGiving page. People are already generously donating, including the likes of Rikki Clarke, RJ Burns and former Surrey batsman Michael Brown. Very, very touched.

Spend the afternoon in the garden with *TMS*. Dom Bess is batting really well again as nightwatchman, although he hasn't really had a bowl. It is a much better performance from England, who within a week have gone from a disaster to a quality side – such is the fickle nature of our sport.

Take Mum to the village hall to drop off some cup and saucers (all rock 'n' roll) and then head to the Papermakers pub for a lovely meal.

As I tuck into my Chicken Supreme, I keep an eye on Sam, who finishes 16*, and the England football team, who beat Nigeria 2-1 in a World Cup warm-up. Very much looking forward to soon being able to get my 'Harry Kane sausages' for the BBQ.

Head home from an early night to find the South Africa v Wales rugby match being televised on Channel Four. A very pleasant surprise and it's made better by being able to watch a good win for my adopted homeland. It still doesn't get me a discount on the Severn Bridge though.

SUNDAY 3 JUNE

Step into Tysoe at 6am and drive to The Oval where I leave the car and walk to Lord's – it's a good chance to get a look at the route I'll be taking during my charity run in October, November and December – 200 times!

The sun is shining and I stop in St. John's Wood High Street to have a cup of coffee and watch the world go by. It's a very glamorous part of London and I always feel like a scruff when I'm here. A little tip: charity shops in St. John's Wood always have amazing clothes at very reasonable prices.

Make my way into Lord's – it's always a special day coming to the 'Home of Cricket' – it has a unique feel to it and I feel very privileged every time I broadcast from the ground.

Head up to the Media Centre – the big spaceship – and am greeted by the wonderful sight of a freshly brewed pot of coffee – it's going to be a great day.

We use the *TMS* box for games at Lord's because it's the only box with a window for the effects mic to be dangled out of – without the effects mic it would sound like we're broadcasting from the toilet.

The next event is the arrival of Kevin Hand – one of my oldest broadcasting friends, he has been covering Middlesex for many years and is a tremendous man of the radio. Back in 2008 we went to Antigua together to cover the ill-fated Stanford Series – it was an amazing couple of weeks and we spent a lot of time at the all-you-can-eat buffet. In fact, we spent much of that fortnight with our mouths open.

One sadness of this season is that we will not get our eight days together in the Championship. This is down to Middlesex getting relegated last season – and it had nothing to do with a crossbow.

Middlesex win the toss, bat and Kev and I settle into the day. There is no Barran today, he is recovering from his dinner with Rudimental last night. As you do.

As well as the game in front of us, we keep an eye on the Test match and see Sam get out for 20. He looked very good and it could well be a three-day Test.

Surrey bowl very well to restrict Middlesex to 234. Paul Stirling plays nicely for Middlesex but he never really gets going and Tom Curran is outstanding with 4-33.

During the interval Kevin and I record a podcast which largely seems to focus on his eating habits and Han Solo, two of the greatest loves in his life.

Surrey's chase does not start well but Burns and Foakes put together an intelligent and skilful partnership. These two love batting together in one--day cricket. Burns goes for 40 but Foakes completes his third 50 of the competition this year. He does look international class and England must find a way of getting him into the Test side.

Talking of which, Sam takes a wicket as England wrap up an innings victory at Headingley. It looked like a good performance from England but I find it all a bit dull that most of the chat is about how England responded to criticism from a former England captain. I think it's probably more likely that they responded to how crap they were in the first Test.

The series is well poised at 1-1 – I can't wait for the decider! Oh, hang on, that's it for Test match cricket until August. No wonder the most beautiful form of the game is struggling.

Back on the field at Lord's, Ollie Pope joins Foakes and together they move Surrey towards the winning line. Foakes is out just before the end for 86 but Pope (52*) sees Surrey home in very mature fashion. A six-wicket win and, somehow, Surrey are still in with a shout of making the play-offs.

At the end of the game I have the huge privilege of walking across the Lord's outfield to go and get interviews. Whenever I do this I always stop for a second and just have a look around dreaming that I am playing in a Test match (and scoring a hundred of course).

Interview Rikki Clarke who's very happy with the performance and full of praise for Foakes. Email the interview to the BBC, pack my bag, say an emotional goodbye to Kevin and make my way to St. John's Wood tube station.

Travel back to The Oval, pick up Tysoe and drive back to Mum's in time to sit with a beer and a sandwich watching the final part of *A Very English Scandal* with Hugh Grant. Like all great batsmen, he has matured very nicely.

Before I turn in, I take one final look at the JustGiving page and am overwhelmed by the amount of support I'm already getting.

Head to bed reflecting on a very neat and tidy day.

❋

MONDAY 4 JUNE

A rest day begins with a brief spot of podcast editing before a morning of paperwork is lifted by a trip to Kelly Holmes' coffee shop in Tonbridge to meet Stuart Barnes. It's lovely to catch up on his news – the property empire seems to be building nicely.

Head back to Mum's and take her into town where I have a much-needed haircut. I only have a couple of 'chops' a year and that is because I am very lazy.

I can never go to a proper hairdresser after a devastating incident in my 20s. I went to a very fashionable salon where they offered to wash my hair first. A very attractive lady took me over to the basin and I proceeded to kneel on the chair and put my head in the basin. Cue lots of laughter, as all you could see was my chino-clad bottom pointing across the room. It still makes me shiver to think of it.

Anyway, fortunately this haircut was more successful and I give it a first outing with a ten-mile run. The run goes well and I'm beginning to feel a bit more like I know what I'm up to with training, which is good news.

A lovely fish pie for supper – a much-neglected dish the fish pie – before I help Mum get ready for her trip to Cardiff tomorrow for the WI Conference.

I have a new-found respect for the WI, who kindly helped out at Dad's funeral last year. They were like the Special Forces and did everything with military precision.

Mum is staying in a hotel for a couple of nights and is on the WI coach in the morning. She reveals that Huw Edwards, the BBC newsreader, is the guest speaker. I ask her to quiz him about how his hair always looks so good at 10pm.

Head to bed after chatting to Mrs Church back in Cardiff. It's slightly annoying that we've moved to Cardiff and the whole family, including Mum, will be there for the next couple of days whilst I am in Kent and Glamorgan are the visitors to The Oval on Wednesday. Such is the life of a cricket commentator.

✻

TUESDAY 5 JUNE

Early start as I take Mum to meet the coach at Tesco. After waving the coach off I head for a very long run. Check the JustGiving page when I get back and am astonished to see a donation from Sam Billings; yes, he of Kent, England and IPL fame. His donation gives me renewed motivation.

A quiet afternoon leads into quite the most wonderful evening of TV I have enjoyed in some time. It appears the History Channel are showing all the official Fifa films of the tournament from different World Cups.

I settle in to France '98, narrated by Sean Bean, and enjoy Michael Owen's goal against Argentina, all the mystery of the final with Ronaldo and Petit's pony tail – magic.

After that, Sky Sports Golf is showing the documentary on the 'Miracle at Medinah', the 2012 Ryder Cup. I am a sucker for sport with inspirational music and find myself in tears as José Maria Olazábal describes the third day singles and Justin Rose points to the picture of Seve Ballesteros on his sleeve and then up to the sky.

What an evening – all watched with a bowl of granola.

Mum lets me know she has got to Cardiff and has slipped out of the hotel, undercover, to go and see Isabelle – what a rebel. Head to bed with visions of Mum in camouflage, diving into bushes on the M4.

WEDNESDAY 6 JUNE

Up early for the drive to The Oval. Rebuild the commentary box and then work out what Surrey need to do to qualify for the play-offs. It turns out they need to beat Glamorgan and then hope Kent beat Essex and Hampshire beat Somerset.

I meet Surrey Fielding Coach Chris Taylor for some breakfast. He was part of that amazing Gloucestershire one-day side that were seriously ahead of the curve in terms of fielding and has turned that experience into becoming one of the best fielding coaches in the business. He tells me about a brilliant new app he's invented called Pro Fielder, which monitors players during the game and comes up with unique fielding stats. Fielding is the new rock 'n' roll and I think Taylor has got something very special on his hands.

Tonight's game is a day/nighter and my early arrival has caused panic in Tooting where Daniel Norcross briefly thinks he needs to be at Chelmsford for 11am before realising his game is also a day/nighter.

BBC Radio Wales' Nick Webb arrives to join today's commentary. He is a wonderful broadcaster, also the voice of Welsh rugby, and I have spent many happy hours listening to him during the Six Nations.

We're also joined by former Glamorgan captain and keeper Mark Wallace. He was a tremendous cricketer who played something ridiculous like 230 consecutive first-class games. He is now working for the PCA, which must be interesting at the moment!

Surrey win the toss and bowl, with Sam Curran back in the side, fresh from his England cap at Headingley.

Morne Morkel bowls beautifully and Glamorgan find themselves 0-2. Surrey continue to bowl well after that and restrict their visitors to 266, in front of another really good crowd.

Barran is in very good form, enjoying discussing catching with Mark Wallace. The Glamorgan captain and East Bergholt stalwart together at last.

During the interval I catch up with Will 'Grisham' Macpherson from the *Evening Standard* who says he will run a leg with me this winter – I will hold him to that. Maybe he will turn it into his latest novel?

Surrey's chase is as good as their bowling, led by Will Jacks with 80 and a captain's 68 from Rory Burns. The problem is Essex have beaten Kent which makes it all rather academic as Surrey cannot qualify.

Wallace comes out with the line of the season on commentary when he describes an old Glamorgan player by saying: "His career was ended by a dodgy chicken bhuna in Maidstone." It has happened to many.

Surrey win with ten overs to spare – a really professional performance – but the overriding feeling in an interview with Rory Burns is 'what might have been'. It will be strange not going to the one-day final this year, having been at the last three.

Pack up broadcasting equipment, say farewell to my Welsh friends and jump into Tysoe, arriving home at midnight, in time for peanut butter on toast, Sky Sports News and then bed.

❄

THURSDAY 7 JUNE

The alarm goes off at 6.45am and I wobble out of bed. Just one of those mornings where you feel a bit groggy. Sadly I didn't even have a beer last night – must be my age.

Jump into Tysoe and make a mad dash for the train to London to cover the match between two Surrey XIs and the touring Australian Aboriginal XIs. It's 150 years since the first Aboriginal side came to these shores and Cricket Australia have arranged another tour to celebrate the anniversary. On the original tour, the first and last games were played at The Oval, so it's great that space has been found in the busy schedule for this game.

It's a hugely emotional occasion and amazing to hear the history and sense of pride from the touring sides.

A number of journalists are here to cover the occasion and it's lovely to bump into Mel Farrell from Cricinfo; she did a run earlier in the year – 501 miles in honour of Brian Lara's 501 – which gave me the inspiration for my efforts this winter.

It's also great to see Ebony Rainford-Brent, Surrey's Director of Women's Cricket as well as a commentator for *Test Match Special* and Sky Sports – her Surrey Women's team are playing in the first game and acquit themselves very well, coming away with a close win.

In the second game, the Surrey XI is made up of players from the Surrey Championship so it's great to be able to catch up with old friends like Chris Murtagh and Tom Lancefield, former Surrey players who are now ploughing a different furrow whilst still playing club cricket at a very high level.

I sit with Lee Fortis and the groundstaff during the game, and try to persuade Fortis to join us in Scarborough. On that front, great news! The campervan is all booked up and sorted. It looks like an articulated lorry but I'm very excited about our trip to the seaside.

Conduct some interviews and send them back to the BBC before packing up the rest of the broadcasting equipment because we're off to Hampshire tomorrow.

I get the train to Mum's. She has returned safe and sound from her WI adventure. I'm very proud of her as it's the first time she's been away on her own since Dad died.

Go for an evening run and then try and watch England v Costa Rica, the last warm-up before the World Cup. I fail miserably and turn over to BBC1 just in time for *DIY SOS* and spend the next hour crying, as I always do, watching Nick Knowles and his team convert a house for someone who really deserves it after a tough time in their lives. I can never get through the bit where Nick shows them around their new home without sobbing.

Head to bed (England won 2-0 by the way – next stop Russia and the World Cup!). Off to Hampshire tomorrow, Championship cricket is back; hooray!

❊

FRIDAY 8 JUNE

Awake to blue skies and the sun shining and spend the morning doing paperwork, drinking coffee and packing my bag for the trip to Hampshire.

Having been on the road for many years I have my Championship away trip packing routine down to a fine art and am happy to reproduce it here as a public service of sorts.

1. Always pack your toothbrush first, because it's so easy to forget.

2. Load in the pants and socks.

3. Next in are a couple of shirts and pairs of trousers

4. Followed by two tank tops and a cardigan

5. Running gear

6. Good book

7. Glasses

8. ISDN kit

9. Headphones

10. Phone charger

11. Press pass

These are all the essentials and they are stashed in Tysoe's boot, along with my golf clubs because there has been some talk about a round of golf this evening.

Say goodbye to Mum and head for Southampton. I always enjoy a Friday afternoon drive because Simon Mayo and Mark Kermode are on Five Live with their film review show.

I arrive at the Ageas Bowl just as Kermode starts his review of *Jurassic World – The Lost Kingdom*. It's amazing how long those dinosaurs have been about.

We are staying at the lovely hotel in the ground – a four-minute commute from my room to the commentary box.

Join Chris Taylor, the real Alex Tysoe and Surrey's media guru Joel Pope (a former Leicestershire wicket-keeper – described as having 'unbelievable hands' by no less than James Taylor) for a round of golf – Pope and Church v Tysoe and Taylor.

We halve the first but then Pope and Church proceed to put four balls in a lake on the second. My phone immediately starts buzzing and I see words of encouragement from Sam Curran and Ollie Pope, who are watching on from the hotel. Sam's says 'shot' with a water emoji whilst Ollie goes even simpler with four emojis of a rowing boat.

Taylor and Tysoe are both very good golfers but Church and Pope somehow hang in there, despite no one being able to find the 11th. We even use the GPS system on Taylor's phone, still to no avail.

Joel Pope plays a couple of extraordinary shots but the battle ends on the 17th when I four putt needing to have two-putted to take it down the 18th.

Handshakes all round, followed by a club sandwich and a beer on the hotel terrace. This is followed by a proper catch-up with Michael Di Venuto, who has had enough of the golf stories after five minutes.

Go to bed and fall asleep dreaming of holing a 12-footer to win the Ryder Cup.

SATURDAY 9 JUNE

7am wake-up and head down to breakfast, which actually takes longer than it will do for me to go to work. Granola followed by peanut butter on toast – always the same.

It's difficult to know when to leave for work but old habits die hard and I leave the room at 8.30am. Arrive at work at 8.34am and find Kevan James already in situ and enjoy a lovely catch-up on all sorts of topics. We dissect the Barran-inspired evening in Shoreditch House from earlier in the summer and make the decision to have a net on Monday evening.

The weather looks good and Surrey win the toss and bat. Morne Morkel is making his Championship debut and the Hampshire new-ball attack of Dale

Steyn, Fidel Edwards and Kyle Abbott definitely has an international feel about it.

Incredibly, Surrey are 1-2 at the end of the first over, after losing Mark Stoneman to a good one from Fidel Edwards and then Scott Borthwick, who is run out looking for a quick single to get off the mark.

Rory Burns and Ryan Patel rebuild brilliantly though, putting on 82 until Patel goes just before lunch.

There is a delayed start to the second session due to a 'precipitation situation' as it tells us on the big screen – at the Ageas Bowl that means rain is coming.

The rest of the day belongs to Burns and Ben Foakes. Burns bats beautifully and his driving through the covers is exquisite. He moves to his century, against an international attack, with the minimum of fuss. How this lad has not had the England call is still one of the mysteries of the modern world. He is day-in, day-out the most consistent opening batsman I have seen.

Foakes yet again looks class and Surrey close on 216-3, Burns 108*, Foakes 68* – pretty good after being 1-2. The day ends with a gentleman doing a lap of the ground in nothing but his pants, which are round his ankles. As streaks go, it's not the most committed and it's slightly bizarre walking past him to get an end-of-day interview. Only at county cricket.

Head back to the room, change and go for a run. Decide to go around the golf course and this time find the 11th hole. Discover Alex Tysoe practising on the putting green before heading to the bar for a sandwich and a pint.

Discuss the campervan we are taking to Scarborough with Alec Stewart. He seems suitably unimpressed.

Then a man who turns out to be a wandering magician joins us. He proceeds to perform some amazing tricks, including making a pea disappear from under a glass. Members of the Surrey squad are as impressed with this as Stewie was unimpressed by our campervan.

Join George Dobell, chief cricket writer at Cricinfo, for a catch-up. George is one of the best and hardest-working journalists in the game and a lovely man. Much of our chat is about Rory Burns and England. As George puts it: "he is becoming hard to ignore for all the right reasons".

I say goodnight and head for bed, where I watch highlights of South Africa beating England at Ellis Park in an extraordinary game of rugby.

After that I watch Tyson Fury make his long-awaited comeback against a man who looks about 4ft 2" and 12 stone. Fury wins (as expected) and I head to sleep, dreaming about a Rory Burns drive being turned into a rabbit by a magician who then streaks onto the outfield.

✳

SUNDAY 10 JUNE

Wake up and realise it's going to be a big day when there's a major incident at breakfast.

I am joined by Alec Stewart and am delighted to be in such unflappable company when it becomes clear that the peanut butter has run out. Stewart's experience is invaluable, reinforcements are called for and the situation is calmed.

It is always a privilege to breakfast with Stewie and – whilst I don't want to give away any state secrets – he does like a bowl of porridge in the morning.

I make my way at a leisurely pace to the commentary gantry and watch Surrey warm up, accompanied by Whitney Houston's *I Want to Dance with Somebody* coming out of the players' iPod. A lovely mix of 80s classics follows and all is right in the Surrey world.

This spirit is taken throughout the second day as Surrey enjoy a tremendous three sessions. Rory Burns and Ben Foakes extend their partnership to 199; Burns scores a quite brilliant 151 and Foakes, who deserved a 100, falls 10 runs short. Surrey are all out for 368 and we are then privileged to watch one of the best all-round bowling displays I've seen in many years.

Surrey are relentless. If Jade Dernbach and Sam Curran don't get you, Morne Morkel and Rikki Clarke will. These four would have knocked over most sides and Hampshire are all out for 135 with Clarke taking a fivefer.

It is yet another outstanding performance from a remarkable cricketer. He has kept himself very fit, is hugely experienced and is now playing some of his best stuff back at his home county. I've known him ever since I started this silly job of mine and not only is he an outstanding cricketer, he's also a smashing bloke.

Surrey enforce the follow on but we never get back out there due to bad light.

After play I wander round to interview Clarke. Naturally, he is delighted but not as delighted as George Dobell, who is a huge Clarke fan and can hardly attach his camera to his tripod his hands are shaking so much!

George later tells me that Dale Steyn has said some very complimentary things about Rory Burns. England should listen because Steyn knows what he's talking about.

I head out for a run and have to sidestep a flurry of guests arriving for a wedding in all their finery, before watching Soccer Aid, which looks a wonderful occasion at Old Trafford. Kevin Pietersen is playing at the heart of defence for the Rest of the World XI and Usain Bolt is up front.

On KP, I know he has divided opinion but I take as I find and in his time at Surrey he was always very good to me and I have a huge amount of time for the bloke. And he was a bloody good batsman – better than he was at the heart of defence for the Rest of the World XI…

Over dinner I see the great Rahul Dravid chatting with the Surrey coaches and the old journalistic antennae prick up before I realise that India A are training at the Ageas Bowl and he hasn't signed for Surrey.

Head to bed to watch highlights of Scotland's amazing win against England at The Grange. It is a fully deserved victory and it looked a fantastic atmosphere. A kick up the backside for England.

Drop off to sleep and dream that Mel Gibson, dressed as William Wallace, is hooking David Willey for six. Freedom!

MONDAY 11 JUNE

Early breakfast and a lovely start to the day as Isabelle rings me before school to read to me. It is going to be a good day! Sit on the golf club terrace in the sun doing some paperwork (correspondence, as I like to call it).

Barran is coming today and I notice a red carpet has been rolled out in reception. I'm not sure if this is for Barran or the wedding that was taking place last night.

Up to the commentary gantry as Barran arrives, with Kevan James already in situ. We are having a net after play tonight, thanks to Will Atkins, the Hampshire press officer. We are all overexcited. Well, Barran and I are.

Play gets underway and once again the Surrey bowlers are outstanding. The balance to the attack is lovely and Amar Virdi gets amongst the wickets with his off-breaks. Ben Foakes' stumping of James Vince is quite brilliant and Surrey look a very professional and ruthless outfit.

During the afternoon we discover that Johnny Barran has become BBC London's Scotland cricket correspondent, after their famous win yesterday. He knows everything about Scottish cricket, apart from who plays for them, where they play and who their next fixture is against.

Surrey wrap up an emphatic innings victory on the stroke of tea. They have looked very good in this game and Rory Burns is suitably "chuffed" at the end, adding that his side "will not flirt with form". It's brilliant but I've no idea what it means.

"Ruthless" is the word being used by the journalists to describe this performance.

The sun is shining as I pack up all the broadcasting equipment and change before heading to the nets, where I discover Barran fast asleep, using one of his pads for a pillow. I wake him up and he takes ten minutes to put on all his 'bits and pieces' for a bat.

Kevan James arrives and shows that you never lose it. It takes him a little longer to loosen up but he then gets the taste for it and Barran needs to be at his very best to see off the man who took 13 fivefers in first-class cricket.

Will Atkins arrives and produces leg-breaks of the highest quality that slightly ruin Barran's good work against Kevan James. It's fair to say that he couldn't pick them.

I then go in for a bat and it's a complete disaster as I fail to locate the ball with the bat on numerous occasions. My humiliation is completed when Barran traps me lbw just before the net comes to an end.

Head back to the hotel, shower, change and pack my bags before heading downstairs to shake a few of the Surrey players by the hand. They can be very satisfied with their work over the last few days.

Drive back to Mum's and am sitting with peanut butter on toast at the kitchen table by 10pm. It has been a lovely four days down in Hampshire and once again I realise how lucky I am to do this job.

TUESDAY 12 JUNE

Thanks to Surrey's three-day victory, I have an extra day to myself and spend the morning helping Mum put stuff in a skip. We are now starting the process of clearing some of Dad's stuff out of the garage. It is a hard job because neither of us want to throw anything away. However, Dad was a keen golfer and I do make the amazing discovery of a cupboard full of golf balls – it is a right result after my appalling performance at the Ageas Bowl.

Can I just say at this point how proud of my Mum I am? Losing your partner of 45 years must be terrible and Mum went through an awful lot when Dad was ill. It was only six months from his diagnosis until the day he died, so there was not much time to get ready for it.

Cricket has always been a huge part of our lives – Mum used to watch Dad and I would score. Then Mum and Dad came to watch me and were there when that inevitable day dawned when I knew I wasn't going to play for England and I thought about a career in radio.

However, at that point I was studying politics at Durham University, which didn't really go hand-in-hand with being the next Des Lynam. But I did some student radio, loved it, did a postgraduate course, started getting work with GLR and BBC Surrey and ended up doing a job I love.

The only reason I mention all of this is that Dad always backed me up, encouraged me and never put me under too much pressure. He was always my biggest critic but also my biggest fan and I was lucky to have him by my side.

I am so proud of Mum because she has lost her best friend as well as her husband but she is getting on with it and although it's really hard for her, she hasn't stopped.

The reason I am doing my charity run in October is that in some small way I want to try and help other people to not have to go through what we did with Dad, because it was bloody horrible.

Great news at lunchtime. I had emailed Adam Mountford, the producer of *Test Match Special*, telling him about my run and asking whether there was any chance of getting a mention on *TMS* this summer. Adam is the busiest man in the world and a brilliant producer of a real institution. He has replied to my email and says the run will get a mention during the ODI between England and Australia at The Oval tomorrow, and would I be available to have a chat with Jonathan Agnew in the interval? It's amazing and I can't thank Adam enough. Dad would have been so proud to get a mention on *TMS*.

Go for a long run in the afternoon after finishing loading the skip. The sun has come out and pounding the lanes of Kent it begins to hit me that this Surrey squad could win the Championship. There is a cracking balance to the side and Morne Morkel is that point of difference.

Surrey are second in the table and their next game is at Guildford against Somerset, who sit top. Should be a hell of an occasion.

Receive a late afternoon email from Maggie, the CEO of the Pancreatic Cancer Research Fund, with a number of designs for the official logo of the run. They are all amazing but I decide on one that looks like a cricket scoreboard. It's all beginning to come together.

A quiet evening. Mum and I are heading to Cardiff tomorrow and thanks to Surrey's three-day win, we have an extra day to get organised.

Watch the highlights from the first Rugby Union Test between South Africa and England in Johannesburg in bed. It's a mad, mad game but England need to start winning.

As I drift off, Burns' mantra, 'don't flirt with form' comes into my head. Decide that it's a good philosophy for life – the problem is I don't flirt and never have any form.

✳

WEDNESDAY 13 JUNE

Up early for the trip back to Cardiff and am greeted with an e-mail from Spaceships UK, who are very kindly providing us with a campervan for the road trip to Scarborough. As you'll have heard, this was Barran's idea, but he is now not coming up with us but is driving himself, meaning I'll be in charge of the campervan – the email contains a picture of our van. It is enormous – more like the Bon Jovi tour bus.

Pack up Tysoe and head back to Cardiff with Mum. Good journey, plus Mum goes to sleep after five minutes, which means I can listen to *TMS* and the ODI from The Oval. Australia are batting first but finding it hard work.

Apparently, 'sandpaper' fours and sixes are being handed out at Vauxhall Tube, after the ball tampering scandal a couple of months ago. Personally, I thought the whole thing got blown out of proportion – what Australia did was stupid, cheating and one of the worst plans of all time. But they didn't murder anybody, they just handled the whole thing terribly, but we all make mistakes.

One thing I do like is a bit of humour and the sandpaper fours and sixes sound brilliant. I don't think everyone sees the funny side but if you dish it out you have to expect it back when you stuff up.

It's nice to get home. Isabelle is at school so get Mum settled in and then make sure I am somewhere quiet for my call from *TMS*. There is a mad panic as our wifi drops out for 20 minutes but thankfully it comes back on again just before they ring.

Spend an amazing couple of minutes chatting to Aggers about the run and I provide Charles Dagnall with a ton of ammunition when I read out my JustGiving page details, including the 'www dot' part. I've known him for many years and he has a field day with this on air. He was a cracking bowler for Leicestershire and Warwickshire and is now a very talented broadcaster. He is also very, very funny.

It was amazing to be on *TMS* and Mum is very pleased when she receives a number of texts from family and friends saying they heard me!

Isabelle gets home from school and it is lovely to see her. There are lots of hugs, tears and running around before she tells me to calm down and I pull myself together.

It's lovely for Issy to see 'Granny Anna' and the day ends with a chapter of *World's Worst Children* by David Walliams.

It's nice to be home, and even better as England have beaten Australia in the ODI.

✳

THURSDAY 14 JUNE

Take Isabelle to school and then head home – for today the World Cup starts in earnest and it means the country will come to a grinding halt whenever England play.

I still remember my tears from Italia '90 when, aged 15, I was sat in a pub in Eastbourne, on a cricket tour as England lost on penalties to Germany. The three pints of lager I'd had didn't help my emotions at that age but I still remember that horrible moment when Chris Waddle blazed it over the crossbar.

Eight years later there were more tears as David Beckham got sent off against Argentina and David Batty missed in the penalty shoot-out. We'd had eight years to get better at penalties, I'm in my mid 20s, and still we can't get it right.

What will happen this time? Well, the good news is, after an open press conference, I know how the squad will be spending their spare time – watching *Love Island* and playing computer games back in the hotel. These are the things that matter.

I head to the gym and get a good run done before going with Mum to pick Isabelle up from school. She has a big day tomorrow, sports day, so we chat about channelling her inner Usain Bolt for the 50m sprint.

During the day I keep an eye on the One Day Cup play-offs – I fancy Kent for the competition, they looked very good against Surrey and have cricket's Gandalf, Darren Stevens, playing for them. The bloke is a magician and still one of the best cricketers in this country.

Kent beat reigning champions Nottinghamshire and Yorkshire beat Essex, so next week's semis will be Hampshire v Yorkshire and Worcestershire v Kent.

The World Cup kicks off and I catch a bit of Russia v Saudi Arabia – Russia win the opener and everything looks spectacular on the TV. The ITV studio looks like they have stolen the set of Blockbusters, leading to many jokes on Twitter about Lee Dixon 'asking for a P please Bob'.

I take Isabelle swimming and manage to break two sets of goggles, which is a tremendous effort from me. One of life's great mysteries is how you adjust the straps in a pair of swimming goggles. You need to be a bloody astrophysicist to work it out and my frustration leads to me snapping the straps. The second incident brings the swimming to a premature end and the only thing that smooths the waters is a hot chocolate and a slice of Victoria sponge.

Have a peanut butter on toast supper and then read another chapter of *World's Worst Children*. Embarrassingly, I fall asleep before Isabelle and she has to wake me up to ask me to stop snoring because she cannot get to sleep.

Wake up and head to bed but check Twitter beforehand to see an amazing video of Barry from Eastenders singing at the opening ceremony of the World Bowls Championships. Robbie Williams at the World Cup v Barry from Eastenders singing *Something Inside So Strong* – I know which I'd rather see. Good old Barry.

FRIDAY 15 JUNE

Up early to take Isabelle to school. It's sports day and there are some nerves knocking about. I get her fired up with *The Greatest Showman* soundtrack in the car, where we also discuss dipping at the line and go over yesterday's chat about channelling your inner Usain Bolt.

I head over to Cardiff Met University. I've been lucky enough to do a few lectures for their Sports Broadcasting course over the winter and I meet the Head of the Course, Joe Towns, who was a very successful journalist for BBC Wales. There are a lot of talented broadcasters on his course – I actually learned lots from them – and Joe seems really pleased with how the first year has gone. I'm hoping to be involved again this year, after the run.

It's amazing how big sports broadcasting is now and, with the advent of social media and iPhones, it has just got bigger. Gone are the days where you just reported a goal, now it has to be accompanied by a clever gif, video and stats – there's a massive market out there but I still believe there is room for old gits like me in the modern world.

I also meet up with Robert Taffurelli, who I did some lecturing for on the specialist journalism course. Cardiff Met is a fantastic university and their sports facilities are really impressive.

The really handy thing for me is Isabelle's sports day is taking place at the Cardiff Met Indoor Athletics centre – so after cups of coffee with Joe and Robert, I wander over and meet Mrs Church and the two grannies. We make our way to the seats and my nerves are going haywire.

Isabelle's first event is the 400m. She has a very steady first lap and then times her break to perfection and wins in Kelly Holmes' style. I quietly pretend I have hay fever so no one thinks I'm crying.

After a very solid standing long jump and 'throwing the howler' comes the 75m. Isabelle has the middle lane and all our chat about inner Usain Bolt hopefully will now come to fruition.

Izzy gets a brilliant start and never looks back as she crosses the line in first place. Again, my pretend hay fever kicks in.

There is a tense 20 minutes waiting for the overall results. I feel as nervous as when Roy, Burns, Stoneman or Foakes get into the 90s.

And then the announcement: "The gold medallist in Year 3, Isabelle Church."

Wow – as Issy gets her gold medal, it is possibly the proudest I have ever been. The only person who will be prouder is her Grandpa Tony, who would have been watching from a nice pub in the sky.

I drive back from sports day with Mum and then nip out for a quick run before heading over to some friends in the evening for a terrific BBQ, being held to honour the World Cup clash between Portugal and Spain.

It's a tremendous game and I spit my burger out as Cristiano Ronaldo equalises for Portugal with a ridiculous free kick. It's genius from Ronaldo and he even remembered to pull his shorts up before he took the kick, so it looked like he was wearing a pair of speedos.

At the BBQ, a friend who is attending tomorrow's ODI in Cardiff asks me who he should keep an eye on. "Jason Roy is due a big score," is my reply – this gentleman thinks I know what I'm talking about, so I hope Jason makes me look good.

Home at 10pm to discover an email from Barran informing me that he has ordered a 'draft lager system' for the campervan in Scarborough. He will also have the responsibility of slopping out and cooking.

Surrey have also announced the signing of Theunis de Bruyn for the Guildford and Scarborough games. Another shrewd signing, to fill the void left by Kohli – I saw him bat against Australia this winter and he looked very organised.

*

SATURDAY 16 JUNE

Wake up feeling slightly hungover, which is a concern after two beers last night. Isabelle heads off to drama club and I head to the gym.

I have always been told by coaches over the years that preparation is vital, so I start my run as New Zealand and France kick off in the second match of the their ongoing rugby Test series.

I finish the run as NZ beat France, and am showered and changed in time to watch the first half of Australia v France in the World Cup. Meanwhile, down the road at Sophia Gardens, Jason Roy is starting to make me look clever as he gets off to a flying state in the second ODI.

I order a coffee and settle in for Australia v Ireland in the second Test of their rugby series, whilst on the other TV, Australia equalise against France and Jason moves to 50 on my phone.

Ireland take control over Australia in the rugby, France go 2-1 up and Jason moves to a sublime century. Ireland beat Australia, Jason makes 120, I finish my third coffee and get home four hours after I left, having had a very constructive morning.

Head back to the gym with Isabelle for two hours in the swimming pool and provide vocal duties to allow my daughter to choreograph some synchronised swimming to *The Greatest Showman*.

Thankfully I can see a gym television from the pool and watch Shaun Marsh stroke a lovely hundred in the ODI as Isabelle perfects her underwater handstands and I pretend to be Hugh Jackman.

Home for supper just as England beat Australia and I watch the highlights as we do Isabelle's homework.

Very proud that I have managed to keep across all the sport today – but in a subtle manner.

I fall asleep as Brazil open their World Cup campaign. What a day! Also delighted that Kent have beaten Worcestershire to reach the Lord's final.

❊

SUNDAY 17 JUNE

Father's Day. Very touched as I am woken up by Isabelle, who has two cards for me and the following presents:

• a pair of swimming trunks

• a notebook

• a keyring with 'World's Best Dad' written on it

Reflect on how she has been brought up to be a shrewd girl as we head back to the swimming pool so I can wear my new trunks and make notes about her synchronised swimming in my new notebook.

I'm so lucky to be with Isabelle today but really miss my Dad as we head into Cardiff for a Father's Day lunch at Zizzis. Lovely pizza with my girls and then a massive treat: Mrs Church takes me to the cinema to see *Solo: A Stars Wars Story*.

Now I'm a massive Stars Wars fan. I was born in 1973, so when Episode 4 came out in 1977, I was in pole position to see it 20 times in the cinema. I've been waiting to find out how Han met Chewbacca for 41 years.

As I sit with my popcorn I love every minute of the film. It's exactly as a Star Wars film should be – fun and full of memorable moments. As a kid I wanted to be Han. Sadly, due to Mum's excellent cooking I was more like Jabba the Hut.

I get home for a coffee and we watch a documentary on being the England football manager. England's first game is against Tunisia tomorrow. I have told Isabelle that the game is on every channel on the telly from 6.15 to 9pm – I'm not sure she believes me.

✻

MONDAY 18 JUNE

Take Isabelle into school and then head to the gym.

I left the house with the washing machine not working and get home after the gym and immediately find myself heading to one of the numerous retail parks in Cardiff and following Mrs Church into a massive Curry's warehouse.

She heads to the washing machine section but my eye is caught by someone playing the most beautiful cover drive on a huge HD TV. It is only James Vince, and I am very grateful that Mrs Church is indecisive on the washing machine selection front because I can watch Vince stroke 171 in the second One Day Cup semi-final against Yorkshire. Mrs Church is not amused that she didn't find a washing machine but I have been blessed to watch James Vince in full HD and surround sound.

Pick Isabelle up from school and, guess what, we go swimming again. I remind Isabelle that the football is the only thing on TV this evening, but nobody in Wales seems bothered that I need to be home by 6.15pm and the traffic moves far too slowly. Do they not realise my country made the World Cup?

When I get home I'm greeted by Messrs. Lineker, Lampard, Shearer and Ferdinand. The normal conversations take place ahead of England's opening game, 'the weight of '66' etc.

The game kicks off – England start brilliantly and go one up thanks to Harry Kane – we are definitely winning the World Cup. Isabelle decides to support Spurs but then Tunisia equalise from the penalty spot – we're not going to make it out of the group.

It's 1-1 at half time and Isabelle heads off to get ready for bed, but then bargains with her Mum, using the tactic, 'If I don't watch, Daddy says it will be very unlucky'.

The second half is horribly dull until, with a minute to go, Kane scores the winner. England are winning the World Cup again. Isabelle claims all the credit for the win and informs her Mum that she will to have to stay up and watch every England game during the World Cup because she is a Spurs fan and "Harry Kane plays for Spurs, and he's the captain Mummy".

I put her to bed and then start packing for the start of a two-week road trip. I leave Cardiff tomorrow and the first stop is Guildford for the game against Somerset.

TUESDAY 19 JUNE

Let the road trip begin.

I start the day by taking Isabelle to school. I still find it very difficult to say goodbye, even after all these years. I get upset but she seems more bothered showing off her new state-of-the-art water bottle to her friends.

Head home, pack car and head out of Cardiff. Down the M4 again, onto the M25 and then come off at Junction 10 because all roads lead to Guildford.

Arrive at Woodbridge Road and am immediately struck, once again, by what a lovely ground it is.

Over the years we have broadcast from a great many locations around the place here. In the early days we used to sling a long network cable out of the pavilion window and sit in the back row of the Members' Stand. With the sun out it was a perfect view. When it rained, bin bags, umbrellas and plastic bags became our best friends as we battled to keep all the broadcasting equipment dry.

We then moved down to the boundary edge for a number of years. This position required more long leads, lots of gaffer tape and the use of the Surrey gazebo, which was a tremendous contraption. It was great for keeping out the rain but had an unfortunate habit of taking off if the wind got up.

Last year, the old pavilion was being pulled down so we ran a long lead from a wheelie bin in the garden of the groundsman's cottage to our temporary home next to the public toilets. Our effects microphone had to be carefully positioned, so we did not have a constant flushing ruining the ambience of our commentary.

This year, Guildford and Surrey have built a brand spanking new pavilion and I am dropping in to test the broadcasting equipment works and see where our temporary home is.

I love outground cricket but it can sometimes lead to a few hours of being like the A-Team to get us on air. On this occasion I needn't have worried because the new pavilion is quite magnificent and we are situated on a rather lovely roof terrace, right next to a plug and our ISDN point.

The view of the ground is fantastic and magically, all the broadcasting equipment works first time. Because this is a top-of-the-table clash, Kevin Howells from Five Live will be joining us once again, which is tremendous news. And Barran will be delighted we are 'al fresco' because it will enable him to work on his suntan.

After a quick coffee with Joel Pope, I wander back to the car where I have left Mum reading her book. I'm really looking forward to getting started tomorrow and can rest easy tonight knowing all the equipment is working.

On the drive back to Mum's I put *TMS* on the wireless and proceed to listen to England launch Australia all over Nottingham.

Arrive back at Mum's just in time to see England post a record score in One Day Internationals. I do find it odd that people are now complaining that England are scoring too many runs and 'it's not a fair contest between bat and ball'. They were not saying that two weeks ago when England lost to Scotland.

Dinner and then an early night, hoping for sun tomorrow.

❋

WEDNESDAY 20 JUNE

It's a 5am kick-off to try and beat the M25 and am delighted to find that Tysoe arrives at Guildford just an hour later, giving time for another sleep in the car.

I awake to see Johnny, the Guildford CC groundsman, opening the gates and he greets me with a "thought it would be you" – my early morning reputation has clearly preceded me.

Make my way to new pavilion and set up all the broadcasting equipment and then head to the Woodbridge Road café for a coffee. It's a cracking place next to the ground that also has an eating challenge advertised as 'The Mega Breakfast'. This comprises a ten-egg omelette, six rashers of bacon, five sausages, and baked beans. If you eat it all in under 30 minutes you get your money back along with a t-shirt. Not sure I'll go for it this morning but maybe one day.

I wander back to the ground and am delighted to find Natalie Greening-Doyle, the Surrey analyst, up on the third floor with us. She is incredibly good at her job, logging every ball of every game and providing vital information to the team. She has set up our gazebo from last year, but it is a breezy morning and there is a slight concern it could take off at any moment.

Kevin Howells arrives in fine form as always, shortly followed by BBC Somerset's Antony Gibson. We decide our new commentary position is somewhat akin to the captain's deck on HMS Guildford.

Surrey will bat first on an overcast morning and Arun Harinath has come into the side in place of Mark Stoneman. Earlier in his career, Arun provided me with one of my most emotional moments on air, when he scored his maiden first-class hundred. He is a very talented batsman who has had to stay patient for his chance. He will have fond memories of Guildford, having scored a hundred in both innings of a game here against Glamorgan a couple of years ago. Will Jacks also makes his County Championship debut.

Barran arrives shortly before the start of play, delighted with the new position and threatening to wear shorts tomorrow. He immediately christens the new pavilion 'the spanking pavilion'. I think he missed the words 'brand' and 'new' in his excitement to debut the phrase. Having been listening to Colin Graves all summer I know that cricket wants to appeal to a new audience – maybe this is the way forward?

Surrey make a good start but Harinath falls before lunch for 48. During the break I wander over to the coffee tent to find a cardboard cut-out of Virat Kohli. Sadly, this is the nearest he has got to Guildford this summer but a plan is hatched to take the cut-out with us in the campervan to Scarborough.

I also receive a lovely email from the people at Worboys Shirts. Barran is an ambassador for them and they have kindly agreed for me to have an ambassadorial role for them as well! They make the most beautiful shirts and are very kindly sending me a rather lovely light blue number to wear. Barran and I are strange looking models but we'll give it a shot!

The afternoon continues to go well for the Surrey batsmen against the Somerset attack. Rory Burns makes 66, Ryan Patel 48 and Scott Borthwick looks in sublime form, making 83. Ollie Pope then guides Surrey to stumps with another high-class 50.

There has been an excellent crowd for the first day and Guildford is the most lovely ground. Surrey have backed up their performance at the Ageas Bowl on the first day and I think they will be quietly satisfied.

It has been a very good day of broadcasting from the roof – at times the wind caused problems and there was a moment when the gazebo did actually take off and may have gone clean off the roof had it not been for the sterling efforts of BBC Surrey and Sussex's Johnny Cantor. Still, it gave us plenty to comment on!

On the drive back home I discover that Gareth Southgate has dislocated his shoulder celebrating a goal at England training. Save it for the Panama game on Sunday, Gareth.

One of the main talking points of the first day was our campervan trip to Scarborough. It now transpires we have nowhere to stay on Saturday night, so after I get back to Mum's I make some peanut butter on toast and spend time googling which service stations we can park at on the M1.

Go to bed eagerly looking forward to tomorrow – not least because Mum is coming to work with me!

✻

THURSDAY 21 JUNE

After yesterday's ludicrously early arrival I decide a bit of a lie-in is in order, so Mum joins me in Tysoe at 5.30am and we make our way to Guildford.

Mum is very excited about a day at the cricket, and our meeting about the run at lunchtime with Barry Kitcherside. However, I think some of the excitement wears off when we arrive at the ground at 6.45am. You can never be too early.

I get set up on the roof and Mum genuinely enjoys watching the groundstaff get the ground ready for the day, saying it's like watching the orchestra get ready for a big performance, a line I steal for use on commentary later in the day.

Mum meets Alec Stewart and tells him of our trip to Barbados in 1994, when Stewie made his two hundreds in the Test. Those hundreds were very, very special. I was just sad to miss the final day – when England won – with sunstroke caused by falling asleep on the beach on a rest day.

Back to Guildford and Surrey are in a good position overnight and that turns into a fantastic position in the morning as Ollie Pope moves to his third Championship century of the summer. He is a very special talent.

There is great amusement on air as Barran has come today looking like a member of a yacht club. He also cannot work out how to put his headphones on over his hat, which leads to much banging and crashing on air.

Surrey are all out for 459, with Pope making 117 and Mum and I walk over to meet Barry at lunchtime. I can't quite believe it when he says that all the money made from the raffle in the hospitality tent is going towards the run – people's generosity is really blowing me away.

Mum is kindly invited to stay in the marquee for lunch and I leave her deep in conversation with Surrey great Martin Bicknell. Fingers crossed her inswinger will be coming out perfectly by this evening.

I then return to the commentary roof and witness an extraordinary afternoon of cricket. Surrey's bowlers are exceptional again, much like they were at the Ageas Bowl. Morkel, Dernbach and Clarke are relentless and four Clarke wickets see Somerset 135-4 at tea.

After tea, Rory Burns throws the ball to Ryan Patel, who has two first-class wickets to his name. He goes on to produce the most remarkable spell of swing bowling, taking five wickets in 11 balls to leave everyone speechless, apart from Barran who is on commentary at the time and utters the immortal line: "never in my 11 years of broadcasting have I ever seen anything like this".

Ryan then takes his sixth wicket as Somerset are suddenly all out for 180. He finishes with figures of 3.2 overs, six wickets and five runs.

Surrey enforce the follow on and Somerset are 17-0 at stumps as statisticians around the world try to find out if Ryan has a world record in terms of number of balls to get to five wickets. I interview him afterwards and I don't think he can quite believe what has happened.

Pack up the broadcasting equipment and find Mum, who was employed to draw the raffle during the tea break. She has had a wonderful day and the phrase 'Typical Surrey' can again be used, for making her feel so welcome and giving her such a lovely time.

Peanut butter on toast rounds off another very satisfactory day.

✳

FRIDAY 22 JUNE

Set off at 5.30am, armed with a cake mix recipe for Surrey analyst Natalie – as promised by Mum yesterday!

On the drive, it occurs to me that the game could be over today. Most importantly, this would give Surrey another Championship win – but it would also give us a whole day tomorrow to start the "Campervan Road Trip" to Scarborough.

Before the start of play I am treated to the most wonderful surprise when the new Chairman of Selectors, Ed Smith, comes up to the roof. I was at school with Ed but haven't seen him for a few years. Personally, I think he is the perfect man for the job and it is lovely to catch up on the last few years with him. It is also very interesting to try and work out who he is here to watch.

The morning starts perfectly for Surrey when Morne Morkel traps Matt Renshaw LBW with his first ball of the morning. Surrey's bowlers are once again relentless and after 40 minutes of play, Somerset are four down.

I don't like to tempt fate, but phone calls are made to the campsite in Scarborough, saying we will be arriving earlier than we thought tomorrow!

After lunch, Surrey continue to pick up Somerset wickets and it is left to Jade Dernbach, a man of Guildford, to put them on the brink with a wonderful spell of swing bowling. Morkel then applies the coup de grâce, taking the final wicket as Surrey complete another emphatic innings victory. It's their first victory at Guildford in 16 years and has been an outstanding effort. Rory Burns is a very satisfied captain in the post-match interview.

The other fantastic piece of news is that we can now take our time picking up the campervan tomorrow and driving to Scarborough.

We have had three of the most wonderful days on the 'Guildford Veranda' – brilliant weather, wonderful company on air and some great cricket to watch. We are all quite sad to pack up the equipment but the good news is the cardboard cut-out of Virat Kohli has made it to the car for the campervan journey.

Head back to Mum's to discover she is going to a party down the road – she has a better social life than me!

Watch highlights of the first two England rugby Tests against South Africa ahead of the third Test tomorrow. I fancy an England win, with Danny Cipriani starting at fly half.

Head to bed for an early night. The road trip starts properly tomorrow.

*

SATURDAY 23 JUNE

I write this entry sat under the stars at midnight in the Scarborough campsite. We made it and it has been a magnificent day.

Early start this morning at Mum's. Run, toast and packing for the road trip. Even at 44 I need looking after and Mum points out it might be a good idea to take a towel on the trip. She also presents me with a bag of essentials (bread, tea bags, coffee, peanut butter, torch and first aid kit). Good old Mum.

Pack Tysoe and drive up to The Oval where I meet Jon Surtees (communications guru at Surrey) and Jack Wilson-Mumford (one of the media team at Surrey and a very talented lad).

I have remembered to pack the cardboard cut-out of Virat Kohli and when I see the amount of equipment we are taking – plus bags, food and Kohli – I am very glad we are taking a taxi to pick up the campervan.

Taxi arrives and we pack everything into it for an hour and a half crawl to Spaceships UK, the rental company in Wraysbury, just outside Heathrow.

As soon as we see the campervan we know it is very special. Emblazoned on the side is the Surrey badge, in bright orange no less! Spacehips have kindly given us the campervan for the week in return for some social media activity.

We take a first look inside the van – it is very spacious with some lovely features including an electric step to get in and out. It feels just like the Millennium Falcon.

Once all the equipment, bags and Kohli have been packed into the van, I do a quick piece for BBC London and we are ready for the off.

It's now 3.30pm and it dawns on me that I am actually going to have to drive the campervan. It is by far the biggest vehicle I have ever driven and with Jack strapped into the dining room and Jon alongside me in the cab, I conduct my final checks before take-off and we are away.

All roads lead to Scarborough and we find the M25 with no problems. All is seemingly going very well, but we then sit in a traffic jam for two hours and our Scarborough ETA is pushed back to 10pm.

Finally we get moving and, once we have an open road, the campervan is a pleasure to drive. I relax enough to listen to the third rugby Test on Five Live.

Cipriani has a cracking game and as we come off the M1, England secure a much-needed win.

I am actually enjoying the van until navigator Surtees takes us off the 'big roads' and onto the country lanes. A terrifying couple of hours ensues, as we negotiate narrow lanes and steep Yorkshire hills. For a while I think we're lost and I certainly do not have the confidence to attempt a three-point turn.

But then – hallelujah – a sign to Scarborough! Now I know how Lawrence of Arabia felt when he finally got out of the desert. Navigator Surtees rings the campsite to let them know we are almost there and, six and a half hours after leaving Wraysbury, we pull into the 'Scarborough Camping and Caravanning Club' site, park the van in the car park and head to reception.

We are told to follow a lovely gentleman on his bike in the van, and he guides us into Pitch 11, our home for the next six nights. Thankfully I do not have to reverse the van into our pitch and I feel a quiet satisfaction when I turn off the engine. We have made it to Scarborough!

Chaos then takes over as we try and plug the van into the electricity supply in the pitch black. We get there in the end and decide we deserve a pint, discovering 'Scalby Manor', where we beat last orders and relax with a well-earned pint of Italian draught lager.

We also discover that Scalby Manor does an all-you-can-eat breakfast, which is a real bonus, as the pub is only a five-minute walk from the campsite and we haven't brought any proper food.

Head back to the campervan to discover we have no bedding or pillows. This is a blow and a hasty series of text messages are dispatched to Barran, instructing him to bring pillows and blankets with him tomorrow.

The first use of the public facilities reminds me of being back at boarding school but, finally, at 1am, I climb the ladder into the driver's bunk, looking forward to a good night's sleep.

Wake up at 3am, needing the toilet, freezing cold. Clamber down the ladder and head across the field to the public facilities. It seems to be warmer outside the van than in it. Put all my clothes on and clamber back into my bunk, thinking a hotel might have been a better idea.

✳

SUNDAY 24 JUNE

Wake up in the bunk and look at watch, which says 8.30am. I have agreed to run with Jack this morning, so clamber down the ladder, put on my running gear and wake him up.

Jack puts on his running gear and looks at his phone.

"Churchie, my phone says it's 4.30", he says.

We head back to bed, realising I have been looking at the time I set my alarm for.

Three hours later, Jack and I do actually get up and head off for a run. It is a glorious morning and the daylight shows the campsite in its full glory. There are some magnificent campervans and caravans on show and all is good in the world.

As we go for our run, Jon heads off to find the cricket ground. Jack and I discover the beach and run along the promenade for an hour. It is the perfect way to introduce ourselves to Scarborough, and we even discover the apartments where the team are staying, which look lovely.

We run to the harbour, turn around and head back to the campsite. A quick shower and then off to Scalby Manor for the all–you–can–eat breakfast. We all feel much better after a couple of trips to the buffet.

Jon gets in touch with his colleagues from Yorkshire to find out what time we are meeting at the ground. Later this afternoon apparently, so, with the sun shining, we set about getting to know the campervan a bit better.

The reason we were so cold last night was the fact that we had the air conditioning on at the lowest temperature and had basically been sleeping in a fridge. Won't be making that mistake again.

We use cardboard Virat Kohli as a makeshift clothesline to dry towels and running gear in the sun. We then meet the neighbours and discuss the match. They are Yorkshire members and are here for the week. I must say the camping community is very friendly.

We then set off to find a pub where we can watch England v Panama. Discover The Ivanhoe and get ourselves a table slap-bang in front of the telly. There is an excited atmosphere in the pub, but the first ten minutes are like watching a wrestling match, as Panama decide their best chance of success is to try and take out as many England players as they can.

England settle down and suddenly they are 5-0 up and everyone in the pub is singing and telling each other: "This is the year!"

At half time I wander back to the campsite with my expert football knowledge telling me that England might win the game. Fall asleep outside the campervan until I sense a presence standing over me. I look up to see Surrey CCC Chief Executive Richard Gould, who is also staying at the campsite, in his Winnebago. I give him the official tour of the campervan and he is suitably impressed, especially with the electric step.

Jon and Jack return as England win 6–1. Eight goals in two games. What is going on?! Normally England have drawn their first two matches and have to win the last game to qualify for the last 16. This time, they have already qualified with a game to spare. Not quite sure how to react.

We collect up all the equipment and then get a cab down to North Marine Road, home of Scarborough CC. We arrive at the ground to be greeted by the Surrey squad training in the sun. Scarborough is a beautiful ground and you can feel the weight of cricketing history surrounding the place.

Find our broadcasting box and, once I have located the keys, let myself in. Everything works first time, which is a relief.

Tomorrow, Surrey will make history, alongside Yorkshire, as they will be streaming the whole game on the internet for people to watch for free, using four cameras. The stream will also be on Sky Digital platforms, enabling fans to watch the whole game live.

It is an exciting development and Jon and Jack spend an hour getting all the appropriate equipment plugged in.

This is the first time I've been back to Yorkshire since we lost our BBC colleague Dave Callaghan earlier this year. Not only was 'Cally' a wonderful man, he was a wonderful broadcaster and this game at Scarborough will not be the same without him. In his honour, the campervan has officially been named Cally.

With everything working, we head back to the campsite and check on Johnny Barran's progress up the M1. He has become a key man because he has pillows and duvets. His ETA is "11pm skipper!", so we wander back to Scarborough and indulge in a very pleasant curry.

Finally, Barran arrives, so we head back to the campsite and take him to the pub for a drink.

Before we set off, Jack, Jon and I had agreed we would refrain from using the en suite toilet inside the campervan, but Barran immediately tells us he is intending on using these facilities in the night, when nature calls. We have to keep the talent happy, and he did bring pillows and duvets.

We lost Jack to the players' five-star apartments this afternoon, so Barran takes his place in the top bunk. He seems to have brought an awful lot of stuff for five days, but we realise that most of this is his 'TV presenter's wardrobe', as he will fronting the stream this week. He has certainly brought enough clothes for the occasion.

Finally clamber into my bunk at 1am and never has a pillow and duvet felt so good.

✻

MONDAY 25 JUNE

6am alarm call and I immediately discover that Barran did use the toilet in the campervan overnight. I hope he knows how to dispose of the materials, because I am going nowhere near it.

Walk to the ground with Jon. The weather is glorious, and it always feels much more civilised to walk to the ground. I have been put in charge of unlocking the commentary box and am very pleased to discover I have remembered the keys.

Kevin Howells – a man with great Scarborough experience – arrives as I'm turning the key and after plugging everything in he takes me down to his favourite café for breakfast. A magnificent poached egg on toast follows and as we return to the ground, more and more spectators are piling in for the day's play.

Back in the commentary box, BBC Leeds' Tim Steere has arrived – also with us this week is Jamie Reid, who is acting as a 'third voice' on the commentary. Lovely to see the pair of them and we all enjoy watching Barran making his way to the middle to conduct the toss for the live stream.

Yorkshire win it and bat under clear blue skies. Mark Stoneman has come back into the side for Arun Harinath in the only Surrey change from Guildford. Jade Dernbach gets off to a flyer with the early wicket of Alex Lees. Even in the opening stages, there is the feel that this could be a special game.

As I complete my first stint of commentary for the BBC, Cheteshwar Pujara is taking 70 minutes to get off the mark, and when I'm done there I head to the bleachers to provide commentary for the live stream. All seems to be going well and it's great to have replays and a vision mixer who can show viewers pictures of the subject you're talking about.

I'm soon joined by the great Jack Brooks. As always, one of Yorkshire's finest bowlers is in great form and I rather enjoy my taste of 'TV' commentary.

Surrey bowl extremely well in the morning session, but one thing I've noticed is there seems to be a very vocal element of the crowd in one corner of the ground. Yorkshire are two down at lunch then Amar Virdi takes two wickets in an over shortly after the break to have the home side in trouble.

Midway through the afternoon I see Rory Burns speaking to the umpires and pointing to the 'vocal' corner of the ground and when Rikki Clarke bowls Gary Ballance, he celebrates vigorously in that direction. Surrey seem really fired up.

Yorkshire are six down but Bresnan and Tattersall come together to put on a hundred partnership for the seventh wicket. Both fall late in the day, but Yorkshire have fought their way back into the game.

As the players make their way off, there seem to be ongoing discussions between some of the Surrey guys and the umpires.

Grab an interview with Ryan Sidebottom, Surrey's bowling consultant, and he seems very pleased with the way Surrey have bowled today.

Jon is very satisfied with the first day of the live streaming and it has been a cracking day, both in the commentary box and the bleachers.

However, on the way back to the campervan we discover that one of the Surrey players has allegedly been the victim of racist comments from the crowd during play. If this is true, it's unforgivable and explains why the players were so fired up.

Back at the campsite we crack open a Peroni and reflect on the day. We have watched some fantastic cricket and I am very pleased for Jon that his live streaming has gone well. Barran seems very happy with his day of 'TV presenting' and spends quite a bit of time watching himself back on his phone. Ever the professional. It is just a huge shame that things have been marred by some idiot in the crowd.

We head into Scarborough and refuel with another curry. Over dinner, we try to persuade Barran not to use the en suite facilities in the campervan, but our requests fall on deaf ears.

Climb into my bunk at midnight. The great news is that we have discovered how the heating works. Getting quite good at this camping lark.

❋

TUESDAY 26 JUNE

6am alarm for a run. As I step out of the campervan (using the brilliant electric step), I get quite a shock.

I cannot see more than 10 feet in front of my face due to a 'heavy mist'. I manage to find my way out of the campsite and down to the beach. The weather is the complete opposite to yesterday. The temperature has dropped and, if it stays like this, I cannot see play starting on time.

An hour later I return to the campsite and, after a shower, leave Barran in bed with his eye mask and products on. Rumour has it he was seen in lycra yesterday, doing a 'high intensity workout' on the campsite. Not sure our neighbours will ever recover from seeing that.

On arrival at the ground, I head to the café with Jon and Kevin. Lots of Surrey supporters are there and some of them are discussing the alleged racist comment directed at a Surrey player yesterday. All very sad.

It is extremely misty at the ground but play gets underway on time. Surrey do not bowl well, and Yorkshire are allowed to add some crucial runs. They are eventually all out for 337 and as Surrey head out for their reply, the mist disappears, and blue sky and sun returns.

Mark Stoneman's run of bad luck continues as he is given out caught behind to a ball he clearly doesn't feel he has hit. I actually think he shows some restraint

– at one point it looked like he might just knock his stumps out of the ground in frustration.

He managed to stop himself but at lunchtime it emerges that Surrey have been penalised five penalty runs for a combination of his response and a comment made in the morning session by Jade Dernbach.

After all that happened yesterday – and the run Mark Stoneman has been going through recently – it seems to me that on this occasion, officialdom have stuck to the letter of the law rather than using common sense.

Cricket is an emotional game and, yes, players should try to keep their emotions in check – but sometimes I think you need to look at the bigger picture.

During the lunch break I am a guest on the live stream discussion panel. It's thoroughly enjoyable and I am very glad that my hair looks rather resplendent on camera. Sadly, it doesn't make up for the rest of my appearance. I look like a slightly younger David Dickinson, having spent far too much time in the sun.

It also emerges during lunch that Ryan Patel was the victim of the alleged racist comment from the crowd yesterday. It is all being dealt with by the relevant people, but it is very sad that some idiot has made this something that needs to be discussed.

During lunch, the mist returns and much of the afternoon is spent in the BBC box discussing sea frets. I have never seen anything like it and batting is extremely tough. Yorkshire use the conditions very well and the umpires do a good job keeping the players out there.

At certain moments during the afternoon the players disappear completely into the mist, only to re-emerge again moments later. All we need is a parrot and a pirate ship to make the atmosphere complete.

Ollie Pope bats out of his skin to get Surrey through to stumps with Morne Morkel but Surrey are behind in this game and face a test of their credentials tomorrow.

Head back to the campervan to discover that our cardboard Virat Kohli is a little soggy, having been left outside all day. Although not as soggy as my clothes that I had left out to dry!

Head into Scarborough and meet some of the Yorkshire communications team for a steak at the Brewers Fayre and the excitement levels go up a notch when it is discovered that the Guardian have written a very favourable piece about the live streaming.

Barran is beside himself when he discovers we have both had a namecheck. He has had an interesting evening. Before we set off for dinner, he decided to 'clear out' the en suite toilet but without watching the instructional video beforehand. I'm not quite sure what happened, but he is a shadow of his former self all evening.

A video of him attempting to 'isolate the toilet' has somehow made its way onto social media and I am hoping he will feel better after a good's night sleep.

✳

WEDNESDAY 27 JUNE

What a day. If a team is serious about winning the title these are the pivotal days. Surrey have turned the game on its head and are now in pole position to make it four consecutive wins.

The day began at 6am with another run, but this time in lovely weather along the beach. The fret has disappeared, and we are back to the weather of the opening day.

Head to the ground with Jon and join Kevin in the café for breakfast. The common consensus is that this could be a key day for Surrey's title aspirations.

Ollie Pope plays brilliantly in the morning, finishing 69* and keeping Surrey just about within touching distance. And then the bowlers take over.

Dernbach, Clarke and Morkel are exceptional and, in favourable batting conditions, they knock Yorkshire over for just 151. It is a brilliant display from Surrey, leaving them needing 228 to win with 30 overs remaining in the third day.

Much of the talk in the commentary box is how ruthless Surrey have been again and Morne Morkel finishes with a much–deserved first five-wicket haul for Surrey.

Burns and Stoneman play really well, and Surrey go to stumps 88-0 and have put themselves in pole position to win the game tomorrow. They have been challenged and their response has been emphatic.

Interview Morkel after play and head back to the campervan for a well–earned Peroni in the sunshine.

We head into Scarborough and dine at its finest Chinese restaurant. The meal is magnificent and after dinner we head to a pub across the road for a quick drink. It is then decided there is appetite to continue and Barran is dispatched to the bar to ask the locals for suggestions of where might be good to go next.

He returns with a suggestion and we head to another bar where live music is being played and a young man comes onto the stage dressed like Bruce Springsteen. He then produces the most wonderful set of songs that has us singing along with him until 2am!

As he comes off stage, Barran produces his business card and we're soon tottering back to the campervan with a CD of his hits in our back pocket. Has Barran discovered the next big thing? Only time will tell.

A slightly shambolic climb into my bunk leaves me reflecting on a brilliant day of cricket and humming some of the greatest hits of the 90s.

THURSDAY 28 JUNE

Awake at 7am to discover Barran watching his performance on the live stream yesterday. Ever the perfectionist.

Shower and then walk to the ground with Jon. We discuss the impromptu sing-a-long the night before and my voice is regretting getting quite so worked up during the rendition of 'Sweet Caroline' at 1am.

A final breakfast with Kevin Howells in the café, which very kindly provided us with one breakfast too many, which is split between those of us who have only had five hours' sleep.

Back at the ground, there is much excitement that Mike Atherton has written very favourably about the live stream in *The Times*. The only problem is that I'm not sure Barran will be able fit a copy in his car after the 200 copies of the *Guardian* he bought a couple of days ago.

Before play, we record a piece with Barran about our trip to Scarborough for the lunch break on the live stream. I definitely have a face for radio.

Surrey start the day needing another 140 runs for victory. They lose Mark Stoneman early, but Rory Burns plays beautifully to further enhance his England credentials. He looks destined for a 100, but on 97 he picks out the one fielder on the boundary and has to drag himself off.

Scott Borthwick takes Surrey to lunch with Ryan Patel and after the break, he moves past 50. In the end Theunis de Bruyn, in his second and final game for Surrey, hits the winning runs.

A seven–wicket victory and the first time that Surrey have won four consecutive games in Division One since 2000. Another stat that makes good reading for Surrey is that for the past five seasons, the side that have won at Scarborough have gone on to win the Championship.

Rory Burns is understandably delighted at the end, but his players have no time to celebrate as they dash off to get an earlier than planned train back to London.

We slowly pack up the commentary box and I am genuinely feeling sad that the game has come to an end. It has been a wonderful spectacle, and, despite one idiot, Scarborough CC have been lovely hosts. This has been county cricket at its finest.

Say goodbye to everyone and then head back to the campsite. Take a run along the beach with young Jack and then we head back, with Jon and Barran, to the pub to watch England play Belgium. Well, it actually turns out to be England Second XI playing Belgium Second XI, but England's 1-0 defeat is not too disappointing after we discover the pub has an all-you-can-eat carvery.

I discover that baked beans go well with roast beef before we head into Scarborough for a final time, having one last drink in our favourite bar before a return to the campervan to convert the dining room table into a bed for Jack, who has been turfed out of the players' apartments now they've returned to London. This time, we do watch the instructional video beforehand.

What a week. Surrey have been tested and responded brilliantly. I have loved the campervan experience but I am looking forward to not having to walk ten minutes across a field to have a wee!

✻

FRIDAY 29 JUNE

Up early for a final run along the beach before packing up the van, breakfasting at the pub and getting on the road for our drive back to London.

We pull away, leaving Barran doing another 'high intensity workout' in his Lycra.

The drive back to London is pretty steady and I very much enjoy giving my fellow campervan drivers a knowing nod or wave as we pass them on the motorway.

Whilst we're filling up with petrol, Surrey announce that Dean Elgar will be returning for the end of the Championship run in – which is great news.

Five hours after leaving the campsite we leave the security of the motorway and I spend a terrifying hour driving the campervan through central London on a Friday. In rush hour.

Somehow, we make it back to The Oval in one piece and I am really quite sad when I lock Cally the campervan for the last time, pack up Tysoe and say goodbye.

I also say goodbye to Theunis de Bruyn, who is waiting for his taxi to the airport as he heads back to South Africa.

Leave The Oval at 6pm and drive to Mum's. It's been a fantastic couple of weeks on the road.

Surrey are heading into the T20 this season sitting on top of the County Championship. If they keep playing like this I have no doubt they will win the title – and with that thought I embark on a week's worth of washing!

SATURDAY 30 JUNE 30

Back on the road again as I drive to Cardiff to see my girls.

Traffic is awful but eventually get home and it is wonderful to see Isabelle again. She is full of news and by 6pm I'm in the garden, running through the sprinkler with her. Always good to get home.

There is a slight panic when I realise I left most of my clothes hanging in the campervan wardrobe but thankfully it is parked up at The Oval until Monday, so my stuff can be taken off before Cally embarks on its next adventure.

Clockwise from top: On the roof at Guildford; Kevin Howells overseeing things at Woodbridge Road; liberating Virat Kohli and packing him in the campervan for the trip north; getting to know him; with Mum at Guildford.

Clockwise from top: Outside Cally the campervan up at Scarborough; joking around with Jade Dernbach; in the commentary box with Kevin Hand.

HAMPSHIRE V SURREY

Venue: The Ageas Bowl, Southampton
Date: 9th, 10th, 11th June 2018
Toss: Surrey
Result: Surrey won by an innings and 58 runs

Points: Hampshire 3; Surrey 23
Umpires: NA Mallender, BV Taylor
Scorers: KR Baker, PJ Makepeace, JN Green

SURREY	1ST INNINGS	R	b	2ND INNINGS	R	b
*RJ Burns	b Taylor	151	204			
MD Stoneman	c Adams b Edwards	0	2			
SG Borthwick	run out (Taylor)	0	2			
RS Patel	lbw b Taylor	34	74			
+BT Foakes	lbw b Edwards	90	148			
OJD Pope	c McManus b Edwards	41	66			
SM Curran	c Adams b Steyn	13	43			
R Clarke	c Rossouw b Edwards	14	21			
JW Dernbach	lbw b Steyn	6	9			
M Morkel	not out	4	9			
GS Virdi	b Edwards	0	6			
Extras	(10 lb, 4 nb, 1 w)	15				
Total	(all out, 97 overs)	368				

Fall of wickets: 1-1 (Stoneman, 0.3 ov), 2-1 (Borthwick, 0.5 ov), 3-83 (Patel, 22.4 ov), 4-282 (Burns, 70.4 ov), 5-282 (Foakes, 71.5 ov), 6-312 (Curran, 83.5 ov), 7-345 (Clarke, 90.5 ov), 8-364 (Dernbach, 93.3 ov), 9-364 (Pope, 94.6 ov), 10-368 (Virdi, 97 ov)

HAMPSHIRE	O	M	R	W	Wd	Nb		O	M	R	W	Wd	Nb
Edwards	26	5	93	5	-	-							
Steyn	26	2	91	2	-	-							
Berg	12	2	39	0	-	-							
Abbott	17	2	85	0	1	2							
Taylor	16	4	50	2	-	-							

HAMPSHIRE	1ST INNINGS	R	b	2ND INNINGS (F/O)	R	b
JJ Weatherley	c Clarke b Dernbach	9	24	run out (Dernbach)	50	126
JHK Adams	lbw b Clarke	13	69	lbw b Curran	2	20
*JM Vince	c Borthwick b Clarke	14	37	st Foakes b Virdi	28	46
SM Ervine	c Foakes b Morkel	8	17	c Clarke b Virdi	10	28
RR Rossouw	c Pope b Morkel	46	60	not out	39	72
+LD McManus	b Curran	6	21	b Morkel	1	7
GK Berg	lbw b Clarke	8	24	lbw b Clarke	6	10
BJ Taylor	c Borthwick b Clarke	5	19	lbw b Clarke	16	21
KJ Abbott	b Curran	3	14	lbw b Virdi	15	16
DW Steyn	not out	8	10	c Pope b Morkel	0	4
FH Edwards	c Foakes b Clarke	1	3	c Pope b Morkel	0	3
Extras	(10 lb, 4 nb)	14		(1 l, 5 lb, 2 nb)	8	
Total	(all out, 49.2 overs)	135		(all out, 58.4 overs)	175	

Fall of wickets: 1-12 (Weatherley, 8.1 ov), 2-41 (Vince, 19.4 ov), 3-54 (Adams, 23.4 ov), 4-60 (Ervine, 24.5 ov), 5-83 (McManus, 31.6 ov), 6-117 (Rossouw, 40.6 ov), 7-121 (Berg, 41.6 ov), 8-124 (Taylor, 45.4 ov), 9-134 (Abbott, 48.5 ov), 10-135 (Edwards, 49.2 ov)
Fall of wickets: 1-8 (Adams, 7.2 ov), 2-50 (Vince, 21.6 ov), 3-76 (Ervine, 31.5 ov), 4-106 (Weatherley, 39.3 ov), 5-107 (McManus, 40.4 ov), 6-117 (Berg, 44.1 ov), 7-151 (Taylor, 52.1 ov), 8-170 (Abbott, 55.6 ov), 9-175 (Steyn, 58.1 ov), 10-175 (Edwards, 58.4 ov)

SURREY	O	M	R	W	Wd	Nb		O	M	R	W	Wd	Nb
Dernbach	11	2	30	1	-	1	Dernbach	10	3	29	0	-	1
Curran	13	5	31	2	-	-	Curran	15	6	26	1	-	-
Morkel	13	2	33	2	-	1	Morkel	11.4	2	37	3	-	-
Virdi	1	0	2	0	-	-	Clarke	13	0	54	2	-	-
Clarke	11.2	3	29	5	-	-	Virdi	9	2	23	3	-	-

SURREY V SOMERSET

Venue: Woodbridge Road, Guildford
Date: 20th, 21st, 22nd June 2018
Toss: No toss made
Result: Surrey won by an innings and 69 runs

Points: Surrey 24; Somerset 2
Umpires: ID Blackwell, NGB Cook
Scorers: PJ Makepeace, GA Stickley, JH Savill

SURREY	1ST INNINGS	R	b	2ND INNINGS	R	b
*RJ Burns	lbw b Gregory	66	142			
A Harinath	lbw b Abell	48	83			
SG Borthwick	b Groenewald	83	106			
RS Patel	c Davies b Abell	48	102			
TB de Bruyn	c Hildreth b Bess	0	3			
+OJD Pope	lbw b Groenewald	117	134			
WG Jacks	c Gregory b Davey	15	59			
R Clarke	lbw b Gregory	42	62			
M Morkel	b Groenewald	20	22			
JW Dernbach	c Leach b Groenewald	0	5			
GS Virdi	not out	0	5			
Extras	(4 b, 11 lb, 4 nb, 1 w)	20				
Total	(all out, 120.1 overs)	459				

Fall of wickets: 1-83 (Harinath, 26.6 ov), 2-158 (Burns, 43.5 ov), 3-246 (Borthwick, 66.6 ov), 4-247 (de Bruyn, 67.5 ov), 5-299 (Patel, 78.5 ov), 6-351 (Jacks, 96.2 ov), 7-411 (Pope, 109.3 ov), 8-447 (Morkel, 117.1 ov), 9-447 (Dernbach, 117.6 ov), 10-459 (Clarke, 120.1 ov)

SOMERSET	O	M	R	W	Wd	Nb		O	M	R	W	Wd	Nb
Gregory	25.1	0	86	2	1	1							
Davey	27	3	105	1	-	-							
Groenewald	26	6	85	4	-	-							
Abell	22	4	99	2	-	-							
Bess	16	2	50	1	-	-							
Leach	4	0	19	0	-	1							

SOMERSET	1ST INNINGS	R	b	2ND INNINGS (F/O)	R	b
MT Renshaw	c de Bruyn b Clarke	39	69	lbw b Morkel	2	25
EJ Byrom	lbw b Patel	52	144	c Jacks b Morkel	19	32
GA Bartlett	lbw b Clarke	0	5	c Pope b Dernbach	7	16
JC Hildreth	c Harinath b Clarke	2	9	not out	89	127
*TB Abell	c Pope b Clarke	26	47	lbw b Dernbach	5	16
+SM Davies	lbw b Patel	33	53	c Borthwick b Clarke	9	14
L Gregory	c Borthwick b Patel	4	5	c Clarke b Morkel	32	68
DM Bess	not out	6	14	b Clarke	6	25
JH Davey	c Clarke b Patel	0	3	c Pope b Dernbach	21	43
TD Groenewald	lbw b Patel	0	1	b Dernbach	0	2
MJ Leach[1]	lbw b Patel	0	14	c Pope b Morkel	0	3
Extras	(4 b, 3 lb, 10 nb, 1 w)	18		(9 b, 5 lb, 6 nb)	20	
Total	(all out, 59.5 overs)	180		(all out, 61.2 overs)	210	

Fall of wickets: 1-53 (Renshaw, 18.4 ov), 2-57 (Bartlett, 20.3 ov), 3-63 (Hildreth, 22.6 ov), 4-117 (Abell, 40.2 ov), 5-169 (Byrom, 53.1 ov), 6-173 (Gregory, 53.6 ov), 7-174 (Davies, 55.1 ov), 8-174 (Davey, 55.4 ov), 9-174 (Groenewald, 55.5 ov), 10-180 (Leach, 59.5 ov)
Fall of wickets: 1-18 (Renshaw, 8.1 ov), 2-33 (Bartlett, 11.6 ov), 3-33 (Byrom, 12.1 ov), 4-40 (Abell, 15.5 ov), 5-69 (Davies, 20.1 ov), 6-121 (Gregory, 38.4 ov), 7-145 (Bess, 46.4 ov), 8-209 (Davey, 60.1 ov), 9-209 (Groenewald, 60.3 ov), 10-210 (Waller, 61.2 ov)

SURREY	O	M	R	W	Wd	Nb		O	M	R	W	Wd	Nb
Morkel	12	4	39	0	-	2	Morkel	15.2	6	36	4	-	2
Dernbach	15	4	35	0	-	1	Dernbach	15	4	49	4	-	-
Clarke	13	3	32	4	-	-	Clarke	13	1	50	2	-	-
Virdi	16	1	62	0	1	2	Patel	4	1	7	0	-	-
Patel	3.5	2	5	6	-	-	Virdi	12	0	44	0	-	1
							Borthwick	2	0	10	0	-	-

[1] MTC Waller replaced MJ Leach in Somerset 2nd innings, 39.0

YORKSHIRE V SURREY

Venue: North Marine Road, Scarborough
Date: 25th, 26th, 27th, 28th June 2018
Toss: Yorkshire
Result: Surrey won by 7 wickets

Points: Yorkshire 6; Surrey 21
Umpires: PJ Hartley, PR Pollard
Scorers: JT Potter, PJ Makepeace, AJ McCarrick

YORKSHIRE	1ST INNINGS	R	b	2ND INNINGS	R	b
A Lyth	c de Bruyn b Morkel	42	67	c Pope b Morkel	7	20
AZ Lees	c and b Dernbach	0	6	c Dernbach b Morkel	1	6
CA Pujara	c Jacks b Virdi	23	111	b Dernbach	17	43
GS Ballance	b Clarke	54	68	c Jacks b Morkel	15	22
HC Brook	lbw b Virdi	0	2	c Pope b Clarke	6	25
JA Leaning	c Jacks b Dernbach	21	64	c Pope b Morkel	15	44
+JA Tattersall	c Borthwick b Morkel	70	156	lbw b Morkel	23	86
TT Bresnan	b Clarke	48	83	c Pope b Patel	18	51
*SA Patterson	b Dernbach	21	39	not out	25	57
JA Brooks	c Burns b Dernbach	27	28	c Clarke b Dernbach	13	26
BO Coad	not out	0	0	b Dernbach	4	2
Extras	(11 b, 6 lb, 14 nb, 5 pen)	36		(8 lb)	8	
Total	(all out, 102.5 overs)	342		(all out, 63.4 overs)	152	

Fall of wickets: 1-6 (Lees, 1.6 ov), 2-51 (Lyth, 19.4 ov), 3-107 (Pujara, 36.2 ov), 4-107 (Brook, 36.4 ov), 5-139 (Ballance, 47.1 ov), 6-166 (Leaning, 59.5 ov), 7-266 (Bresnan, 90.6 ov), 8-276 (Tattersall, 93.4 ov), 9-337 (Dernbach, 102.3 ov), 10-337 (Patterson, 102.5 ov)
Fall of wickets: 1-3 (Lees, 2.6 ov), 2-8 (Lyth, 4.2 ov), 3-24 (Ballance, 10.1 ov), 4-42 (Brook, 16.3 ov), 5-48 (Pujara, 21.4 ov), 6-70 (Leaning, 30.3 ov), 7-103 (Bresnan, 45.5 ov), 8-115 (Tattersall, 52.4 ov), 9-148 (Brooks, 63.2 ov), 10-152 (Coad, 63.4 ov)

SURREY	O	M	R	W	Wd	Nb		O	M	R	W	Wd	Nb
Morkel	26	7	63	2	-	6	Morkel	16	4	39	5	-	-
Dernbach	24.5	3	104	4	-	1	Dernbach	13.4	5	34	3	-	-
Clarke	20	6	52	2	-	-	Clarke	12	3	25	1	-	-
Patel	11	3	28	0	-	-	Virdi	18	6	32	0	-	-
Virdi	20	1	69	2	-	-	Patel	4	1	14	1	-	-
Borthwick	1	0	4	0	-	-							

SURREY	1ST INNINGS	R	b	2ND INNINGS	R	b
*RJ Burns	c Tattersall b Coad	59	89	c Lees b Bresnan	97	146
MD Stoneman	c Tattersall b Coad	9	6	lbw b Coad	32	77
SG Borthwick	c Tattersall b Bresnan	20	31	b Leaning	62	112
RS Patel	c Brook b Bresnan	32	85	not out	24	56
TB de Bruyn	c Tattersall b Patterson	38	80	not out	8	7
+OJD Pope	not out	69	118	did not bat		
WG Jacks	lbw b Patterson	7	34	did not bat		
R Clarke	c and b Bresnan	0	16	did not bat		
M Morkel	c Lyth b Coad	29	40	did not bat		
JW Dernbach	c Leaning b Coad	0	1	did not bat		
GS Virdi	b Coad	0	2	did not bat		
Extras	(4 nb)	4		(4 lb, 2 nb)	6	
Total	(all out, 83.2 overs)	267		(3 wickets, 66.1 overs)	229	

Fall of wickets: 1-9 (Stoneman, 2.1 ov), 2-71 (Borthwick, 12.5 ov), 3-105 (Burns, 29.2 ov), 4-140 (Patel, 41.6 ov), 5-172 (de Bruyn, 52.6 ov), 6-192 (Jacks, 62.5 ov), 7-197 (Clarke, 67.6 ov), 8-253 (Morkel, 81.5 ov), 9-253 (Dernbach, 81.6 ov), 10-267 (Virdi, 83.2 ov)
Fall of wickets: 1-99 (Stoneman, 28.1 ov), 2-146 (Burns, 42.6 ov), 3-220 (Borthwick, 63.5 ov)

YORKSHIRE	O	M	R	W	Wd	Nb		O	M	R	W	Wd	Nb
Coad	20.2	5	53	5	-	-	Coad	17	6	47	1	-	-
Brooks	15	1	73	0	-	1	Brooks	14	2	53	0	-	-
Patterson	26	7	61	2	-	-	Patterson	14	4	39	0	-	-
Bresnan	21	2	77	3	-	-	Bresnan	9	0	51	1	-	1
Lyth	1	0	3	0	-	1	Lyth	3	1	10	0	-	-
							Leaning	8	3	16	1	-	-
							Brook	1.1	0	9	0	-	-

JULY

"I arrive at The Oval to see Scott Borthwick sporting his shirt from the 1982 World Cup. Sheer class from Badger"

SUNDAY 1 JULY

It's July already. Where is this season going? A morning of gym, paperwork and washing is followed by afternoon in the swimming pool with Isabelle.

We then watch two classic penalty shoot-outs at the World Cup, as Russia and Croatia reach the last 16.

Gary Neville gives me something to think about when he says the size of a goalkeeper's personality is crucial in a shoot-out. Surely the size of his hands is just as important, Gary?

MONDAY 2 JULY

Take Isabelle to school. It's another hot day and she is very excited to show everybody her new watch, which tells her the number of steps she does every day. She will be doing the run instead of me at this rate!

Constructive morning spent writing in the garden and all of a sudden, it's 3pm and time to pick Isabelle up again.

Head home and have an hour running through the sprinkler in the garden – this is now a proper heatwave and it's lovely.

Catch the end of the Brazil v Mexico game and head to the gym. I text Jon Surtees to remind him to fetch my favourite tank top out of the wardrobe in the campervan and then watch Belgium score a brilliant last–minute goal to beat Japan.

This is a great World Cup and England play Colombia tomorrow. There's not much interest in Wales but Colombia seem to be getting better every time I put the telly on. It's great English psychology – make the opposition look really good in case it all goes wrong.

Early night, I'm still shaking off the air conditioning cold from the campervan. Oh yes, Wimbledon started today – no Sir Andy Murray due to injury. What is the country going to do? But a good omen is that he didn't play in 1966 and we won the World Cup that year!

TUESDAY 3 JULY

Whatever 'it' is, it seems to be coming home.

I'm recovering at 10pm writing this after England have beaten Colombia in a penalty shoot-out at the World Cup.

Now I don't watch that much football, but this is the World Cup and after a day doing my tax receipts and a long session in the gym, I decided to quietly sit down at home and watch the game. It would be rude not to.

Having been through Italia 90 and Euro 96, the one thing I was dreading was a penalty shoot-out. Surely not again. However, after Colombia equalised in the last minute, it had that numbing inevitability about it.

My shouting at the American referee had woken Isabelle up, so she came to watch the drama unfold. She also decided this would be a good time to show me her new dance, but I must admit that I wasn't really concentrating on her.

I had already laughed at Mrs Church when she had mentioned something about turning over to watch *Love Island*.

I was tense, Jordan Henderson missed but then – redemption. Pickford saved and Eric Dier stepped up, as cool as a cucumber left overnight in a fridge freezer, and slotted his kick home.

There was a massive hug for Issy and England are in the quarter-finals. Italia 90 and Euro 96 washed away in a second.

Celebrate with peanut butter on toast and then see England have lost to India in the opening T20 – that passed me by!

WEDNESDAY 4 JULY

Wake up to Piers Morgan shouting 'Ingerland' on the TV. And so, it begins.

Take Isabelle to school. Not too much celebrating in Wales it seems.

Head straight to the gym for a very long run and am very touched to see the great Tim Murtagh, of Surrey, Middlesex and Ireland, has donated to my JustGiving page.

After the gym I clamber into Tysoe and head down the M4 back to Mum's. Whilst driving I try to come up with my Surrey XI for the opening T20 game against Middlesex at Lord's tomorrow. There are a few missing – Sam Curran and Jason Roy are away with England, Tom Curran is injured and Nic Maddinson and Aaron Finch do not arrive until next week.

It's the 15th year of T20 and it seems to get bigger every year. I distinctly remember commentating on Surrey's first ever game in 2003. Nobody knew what to expect but I knew it would be popular when over 10,000 people rocked up and the beer sold out after an hour..

I feel the ECB were very lazy with the concept in the early years and, of course, there was the Stanford debacle. By the time they realised what they had, it was too late – the IPL was up and running and everybody else was doing it bigger and better.

Having said that, Surrey will pretty much sell out all their home games again this year and I'm told Lord's is expecting 27,000 tomorrow night.

One question: why the hell are England playing T20s against India in the opening week of our domestic competition? Talk about devaluing it.

I enjoy T20 but there is now so much of it. You do have a competition in place that works though – and surely common sense says you should get this on free-to-air TV and don't make a whole new competition for the sake of it? But that may well be too sensible.

Anyway, by the time I've thought about the team and how proud I am that Jade Dernbach is captaining Surrey (Jade is a lovely bloke and a brilliant bowler who enjoys the big stage – the most rock 'n' roll skipper on the circuit), I am back at Mum's.

Have a quiet afternoon and then watch a bit of the opening T20 game between Warwickshire and Nottinghamshire. The sun is shining, and Trent Bridge looks amazing. Mark Butcher and Rob Key are wearing very bright white plimsolls and even Grant Elliott is telling everyone "it's coming home".

Notts don't score enough and some lad called Ian Bell strokes Warwickshire to victory. He looks a very promising player and, because I'm an expert in these things, I predict he'll score lots of runs during his career.

Enjoy an amazing chicken risotto for dinner and then watch a very interesting documentary about Buckingham Palace. I am all about the culture.

Tomorrow I will be wearing my fabulous new shirt that has very kindly been sent to me by Worboys Shirts. It arrived this week and is rather lovely – I have never been an ambassador before but will wear my shirt for all the big summit meetings I'll be attending.

Head to bed and fall asleep dreaming of Jade Dernbach taking a penalty at Lord's whilst wearing a Worboys shirt.

THURSDAY 5 JULY

An early wake up as Stuart Barnes comes over for a coffee, a catch–up and a look at Dad's 'Motocaddy'.

Barnesy loves a gadget and, after we charge the battery, watch the tutorial video and finally plug all the bits in, the thing works. He reckons it will really help with his golf game. It will certainly save his legs, although the way it shot off down the driveway in fifth gear worries me slightly.

Get packed for the trip to Lord's. I have taken the gamble that the trains are working and head to Borough Green station. I make it to Victoria, where it seems every other line but mine has gone into meltdown due to signalling problems at Streatham. Probably the wrong type of sun.

Have decided to walk to Lord's, again doing the route I'm planning for the run. With the sun shining, I set off and, much to my relief, it seems to be fine. I will get to know Hyde Park very well and my sidestep is going to have to be pretty good on the pavements.

Get to Lord's and make my way to the Media Centre. Kevin Hand arrives, and we have a lovely catch-up. The game is being televised on Sky, so there are lots of people with us in the Media Centre.

Surrey bat first and hand a debut to 17-year-old Academy player Jamie Smith. Not a bad place to make your debut – Lord's, with a full house, live on TV. One thing does strike me – Jamie was two years old during the first year of the competition in 2003. And he will be playing with Rikki Clarke, who won that first tournament with Surrey. Where does time go?

Rory Burns gets Surrey off to a quick start and Rikki Clarke makes a very good 50, but Surrey post a below par total..

During the Surrey innings, Daniel Norcross arrives in the box. For some reason when I say: "I once bruised my knees riding a horse", he chokes on his sandwich and has to make a hasty exit. The atmosphere is tremendous with over 27,000 inside the ground. T20 works,.

Surrey bowl well, but Paul Stirling plays very nicely for Middlesex and they are seemingly in control of the chase. Then Gareth Batty takes two in two, including Stirling, and Middlesex lose four wickets in seven balls. Surrey are back in the game and we are treated to the surreal sound of 27,000 people at Lord's singing 'football's coming home'.

Middlesex get their chase back on track and Hilton Cartwright sends them to victory by three wickets. They deserve the win and it was great to see Dawid Malan and Sam Curran allowed to play, having been temporarily released from England T20 duty. At last, some common sense.

After the game I pack up the equipment and head home. Thousands of people line the streets of St. John's Wood, so I decide to walk to Baker Street. There is a continental feel to proceedings in London, with people out on the pavements enjoying the summer heat.

I get to Victoria and – hallelujah – there's a train. Slowly it rattles to Borough Green and I finally get through the front door at half midnight. It was a long day but there is still time for peanut butter on toast and a coffee. I get to bed at 1.30am and will do it all again in ten hours' time for the opening T20 game at the Kia Oval. The roller coaster has started again.

✻

FRIDAY 6 JULY

Wake up at 5am and struggle to get back to sleep so head off for a run and then help Mum take delivery of some new garden furniture. Very nice it is too, and I enjoy the chance to test it out with a coffee.

Jump back into Tysoe and head back to Borough Green station. Enter the ticket office to purchase a Travelcard and find a poor lad who has booked his ticket to London and has all the details on his phone. However, the charming man behind the ticket desk refuses to give him his ticket. Feeling sorry for the lad I buy his ticket for him, only to get a grumpy acknowledgement from the ticket seller that the transaction has worked.

I inform the ticket man that he needs to work on his customer service, but as usual it has no effect. In fact, he shuts the ticket office and disappears. Good old Network Rail, they try to make you feel so welcome.

The journey to Victoria is uneventful and it is nice to arrive back in the commentary box at The Oval. It has been three weeks since we've had a game here and T20 matchdays are always a big event.

As I settle in to prepare, I am told some wonderful news: Rory Burns has been selected for the England Lions for a three-day game against India A. No one deserves it more and I'm also delighted for Ollie Pope, who has also got the call for the first time.

Celebrate by sitting down with Burns and Scott 'Badger' Borthwick to record our first World Cup football podcast. Twenty minutes of radio gold is constructed as it emerges on air that Badger is best mates with Jordan Henderson and has his number on his phone, albeit with the first name spelt incorrectly. Even though I say so myself, it is a tremendous listen and lovely to sit with these two and talk nonsense.

The whole country is getting very excited about the Sweden game tomorrow and I feel good about everything until I ask Burns and Badger Borthwick about Italia '90 and it emerges they weren't even born. God, I feel very old.

Complete the podcast just in time for the arrival of Matt Cole from BBC Kent and I know the commentary will be in very safe hands tonight. We are also joined by Surrey batsman Arun Harinath, who will be able to point out all the things I miss.

As I see people flooding into the ground the thought occurs to me that over 50,000 people will have watched T20 in London over the last two nights. I'm not sure whether any new competition will be able to compete with those numbers.

Kent win the toss and bat. Joe Denly, a batsman I hugely admire and is a joy to watch, strokes a sublime century. He made a hundred at The Oval last year and looks to be in the form of his life.

We are without Barran on commentary because he is working as the 'voice of God' in the stadium and there is great excitement as he gives Denly his hundred when he is actually on 99. Mercifully for Barran, Denly completes the landmark anyway.

Surrey fight back towards the end of the innings as Mat Pillans takes three wickets and helps keep the total down to something chaseable.

The pursuit starts well and Burns and Foakes are seemingly in control. But Burns then goes and Foakes finds himself fighting a lone battle. He plays incredibly well but wickets keep falling at the other end and he is left high and dry on 76*. Sam Billings takes a brilliant catch to end the game and Surrey's T20 campaign has started with two losses.

Head round to the dressing room to interview Pillans, who is understandably gutted with the result but pleased he got his chance. When you are in the commentary box you are isolated from the crowd but walking around the ground you get a sense of the atmosphere. Rowdy but good-natured is how I'd describe it.

Return to the commentary box, send the interview and then retrace my steps onto the Victoria Line and jump on a train to Kent. I fall asleep on the train home but wake up in time for my station and I'm home by 1am. Another long day, but an enjoyable one.

SATURDAY 7 JULY

Up early for a run and then into Tysoe to drive back to Cardiff today. It's a big day – England are playing Sweden in the World Cup quarter-final.

The build-up starts at 11am on the radio, as all manner of people are being interviewed. We are not too far away from a chat with Gareth Southgate's primary school teacher, who didn't actually teach him, but once took his name at register when his actual teacher was ill.

I'm hoping to be home in time for the 3pm kick off but that is slightly scuppered by two hours sitting on the M25. I think lots of people are trying to get home for kick-off too. I'm not too bothered though because I love sport on the radio, especially in a game as big as this.

I get to the Severn Bridge just as the game gets underway and as I pull into the driveway, Harry Kane puts England one up. Being the superstitious man I am, I stay in the car for the remainder of the first half and then dash into the house to watch the second half in the kitchen.

Isabelle comes home from a party and gives me the biggest hug and a kiss as Dele Alli puts England two up.

This is amazing. England are going to play in a World Cup semi–final! Huge cheers in the kitchen when the full–time whistle goes and Isabelle and I decide to go for a celebratory swim. There is not much chat about the game in Wales – and a lack of huge celebrations on the streets.

It's a cracking swim and we head home for a quiet evening watching the football highlights. It is still coming home.

✲

SUNDAY 8 JULY

A quiet day, soundtracked by lots of people talking about the last time England played a World Cup semi–final, in 1990.

I was 15, on a First XI tour to Eastbourne, the first time I was led astray by some of the senior players. I remember having my first cigarette to celebrate Gary Lineker's equaliser and then drinking too much lager and being violently sick in the pub toilets just before the penalty shoot-out. I then consoled the senior pros as they sat on their pavement and cried into their beers after Chris Waddle smashed it over the crossbar.

How times have changed. This year I'll be watching the semi-final with Mum over a cup of tea.

The girls are packing because they're off on holiday to Spain tomorrow. I would have loved to be going with them, but the summer is no time for a Church family holiday. But it's important that Isabelle and Mrs Church get a holiday, and they're very excited.

Take a quick trip to Sports Direct to buy some new goggles for Isabelle and then listen to Jason Roy smashing India in the T20 at Bristol.

An early night because the girls are up early in the morning to head to the airport. That was the plan, but Isabelle is so excited that she doesn't get to sleep until midnight and I make myself some pasta that I feel I may well be seeing again.

✲

MONDAY 9 JULY

Wake up and promptly see the pasta again, as I suspected.

Pack up Tysoe and run the girls to my in-laws, who are also off to Spain, before spending the rest of the day in bed, feeling awful. Food poisoning during a heatwave is not much fun but the good news is the girls arrive safely in Spain and by the evening I have managed to keep down an ice lolly. Hope I feel better by the morning.

Can't feel as bad as Theresa May though – David Davis and Boris Johnson have resigned, making their early exit from Brexit.

❉

TUESDAY 10 JULY

Woken at 8am by Isabelle Facetiming me from Spain. The breakfast at their hotel looks lovely but after yesterday the sight of her omelette does nothing for my constitution!

Recover from that setback and spend the morning finishing off my accounts (never takes long) and paying the taxman.

After the success of the first podcast with Burns and Badger, we agree to meet at 9am tomorrow to record another episode ahead of the World Cup semi–final.

I repack my bag and get into Tysoe to drive back to Mum's. Ed Miliband is on Radio 2 chatting to David Baddiel about *Football's Coming Home* – I would never have predicted that in 1996!

Nice drive back to Mum's and then head off for a run on arrival. Think it will either make me or break me and decide it has made me, before reconsidering after some toast and peanut butter.

Watch France beat Belgium 1-0 in between Usain Bolt sprints to the toilet.

So, England could be playing France in a World Cup final. Très exciting.

Head to bed for an early night.

❉

WEDNESDAY 11 JULY

Up at 5.30am and drive to the station for the train to Victoria as I have a 9am date with Burns and Badger.

Find a photo of myself from Italia '90, aged 15 with an extraordinary haircut. Realise it was actually taken after I had caught Gary Lineker out in a charity cricket match a couple of months after the World Cup. I think I had taken the place of one of the Kemps from Spandau Ballet who hadn't quite made it on time. Out with Bananarama or something I seem to remember.

There are lots of England shirts in London and I arrive at The Oval to see Scott Borthwick sporting his shirt from the 1982 World Cup. Sheer class from Badger. He is reeling after a picture of his school football team, with Jordan Henderson, was published across the north-east this morning. It was a bad day for him to forget his football kit – he's the only one in school uniform in the photo.

Enjoy a tremendous 20 minutes of insight from the two of them – they are both confident of victory if England can find 'that extra 40 per cent'.

Edit the podcast and unleash it on an unsuspecting nation. Stay for a bit to watch Surrey training and it's good to see that Aaron Finch and Nic Maddinson have arrived. Finch is now officially the top ranked T20 batsman in the world and these two will bring a different edge to Surrey tomorrow night against Essex.

Head back to the station and have a mild panic as all the trains seem to be delayed. After using the time wisely to arrange a round of golf on Friday morning, a train appears.

Get back to Mum's and sit in the garden listening to the build-up to the game on Five Live. Before the tournament, I tweeted: "How many voiceovers will Danny Dyer be doing during the World Cup?" I'm therefore delighted to hear a Dyer voiceover as soon as I turn the radio on.

Mum joins me in front of the telly and she sits in Dad's 'lucky seat'. The whole country is apparently watching, which doesn't turn out to be strictly true when the front door bell goes just as the game kicks off. Apologies to whoever it was we flatly ignored.

I am soon off my seat as the 'Bury Beckham', Kieran Trippier, puts England one up with a free kick that 'Golden Balls' would have been proud of.

The first half goes extremely well, and I celebrate by making us a cup of tea. Mum is not able to get out of the chair, believing it would break England's luck.

The second half does not go so well. Mum is like a mystic footballing genius as she says: "I cannot bear to watch", just before Croatia equalise. I desperately need the loo (the cup of tea at half time) but cannot leave the sofa. I dare not jump up in case I have an accident, so spend 25 minutes with my legs firmly crossed. As the final whistle goes, I sprint to the loo, leaving Mum still sat in the lucky chair.

England play well in the first half of extra time. Mum says she will not be able to bear watching penalties, just before Croatia go 2-1 up. Footballing mystic, as I said.

And then the final whistle goes. Mum is upset, Ian Wright is upset and I'm sure Danny Dyer is upset. I head off to make another cup of tea and have a slice of peanut butter on toast.

The way I see it, nobody expected England to do well but it has been a fantastic month that has got everyone excited again. This bunch seem a smashing set of lads and they have made football fun again. The opportunity has been lost but the sun has shone – and we all love a third and fourth place play-off, don't we?

Head to bed and watch the highlights just to make sure the result was 2-1. I fall asleep but am woken up by a ping on the phone. It's a video of Isabelle swimming in Marbella. Her diving is way better than Neymar's.

✳

THURSDAY 12 JULY

The alarm goes off at 5am – out of bed, shower, dress and then remember the game tonight is a T20 and doesn't start until 6.30pm.

Switch the telly on with my cup of coffee and every channel confirms that England really did lose last night.

Set off for London at 9.30am in Tysoe. Stick the radio on and every channel confirms that England really, really did lose last night. The traffic is pretty bad, and, after a couple of hours, I finally see the 20ft Rory Burns pasted onto the front of the pavilion that lets me know I am at The Oval.

I then remember I am actually parking in the local convent car park (a new destination for Tysoe) and take another 45 minutes to find the sanctuary of "Little Sisters of the Poor". It is about 400m from the ground.

Arrive at the commentary box and set up the broadcasting equipment before making a quick dash across London to see my oldest friend, Jeremy Morris, who is now a director at Google. I love going to meet him because I can sit outside Google HQ and watch the world go by. Today, because Wimbledon is on, there is a large screen outside the offices showing a 20ft Sue Barker and lots of people are sat on deckchairs watching.

It's great to see Jeremy but soon enough I need to head back to The Oval to prepare for tonight's game against the Essex Eagles.

A word about the weather. We are the middle of a heatwave and it is quite wonderful. Blue sky and sun every day is how it should be, and it almost feels like you are living abroad. Plus, you know the cricket is not going to be interrupted, which allows you to just concentrate on the game.

Use the time before the game wisely, negotiating podcast recording with Badger and Burns tomorrow, catch up with Steve Howes and watch a little bit of the ODI between England and India.

I also take a look at Nic Maddinson in the nets. Whilst my commentary may sound completely unprepared, I do like to have a quick watch of a new player before the game starts. I learned many years ago to never wish I had done more preparation before a game or an interview. I used to do hours and hours of preparation and notes but these days I always do just enough, so I feel comfortable when I put the headphones on.

Nick Gledhill and David Brett from BBC Essex arrive and before I know where we are, the captains are in the middle for the toss.

There is another full house at The Oval tonight, even on a Thursday, and the atmosphere is once again really good. Surrey v Essex is always a cracking game and tonight is no different.

Seeing Finch march to the middle to open the batting immediately gives Surrey a more menacing look and alongside Rory Burns he gets Surrey off to a flyer. He hits some massive shots and Ben Foakes comes in and plays beautifully after Burns goes for 30-odd.

Finch and Foakes move past fifty but the real damage is done at the back end by Rikki Clarke and Ollie Pope. Clarke continues to show what a brilliant cricketer he is by striking a quickfire 48 – not bad for a man who won the first ever T20 back in 2003.

As Clarke is launching balls into the Peter May Stand, I turn around to be greeted by the wonderful sight of Mark Butcher at the back of the commentary box. One of Surrey and England's finest batsmen, he is a proper legend. It is really lovely to see him and have a quick catch-up. He was a bloody good player and he is now one of the best pundits on the circuit. Plus, he always looks so cool – it's the musician in him. I have been very fortunate to commentate on the Butchers, Thorpes, Bicknells and Tudors and I'm always very grateful that I saw those blokes at their best – because they were very special cricketers and people.

Anyway, Surrey put on a competitive total and then bowl extremely well. Essex are never in the run chase, especially after Surrey's nemesis Ryan ten Doeschate departs cheaply.

Surrey complete a comprehensive victory and have their first win of the competition. Mat Pillans takes another three wickets and afterwards Rikki Clarke says the arrival of Finch and Maddinson has lifted the dressing room.

Pack up the equipment and slowly make my way back to 'Little Sisters of the Poor'. There is a dramatic half hour as the automatic gates refuse to open. Thankfully, Surrey's commercial director Charlie Hodgson, a fine batsman in his own right, spots a big green button with EXIT on it and we are released from captivity.

Tackle the London traffic and get back to Mum's about midnight. Guess what? Eat peanut butter and toast, accompanied by the ODI highlights. A masterclass from Rohit Sharma and Virat Kohli on how to chase a total.

Head to bed at 1am, I'll be doing it all again in Hove this evening!

FRIDAY 13 JULY

Alarm goes off at 6am, in good time for a tee off at 7.30am with Stuart Barnes and Chris Taylor. Head to the shed and find my 'Johnny Miller California' putter. I acquired it one day after it had been left on a skip, and with no one claiming it I thought, 'I'll have that.' I've never been able to putt but I'm hoping the spirit of Johnny Miller will shine through this morning.

Meet Barnes and Taylor at the club and I am excited to see that Dad's Motocaddy is getting its first outing. We tee off and, three hacks later, I'm standing over my first putt with the 'Johnny Miller'. It's 10ft, left to right and has no chance of going in the hole. I swing Johnny back and, as I make contact, I think 'Come on Johnny'. The ball makes a direct and confident roll towards the middle of the hole and unbelievably, drops straight in.

Maybe this is it? Maybe like Billy's Boots in the *Tiger* comic of my youth, the Johnny Miller is going to turn me into a golf professional?

Sadly, those feelings subside at the next tee when I hit three consecutive balls into a lake. Oh well.

I am treated to Chris Taylor shooting a 74, just two over par for his round. It is the best golf I have ever seen 'live' – and at times I feel like I'm part of a Sky Sports masterclass show. We celebrate his round with a lime and soda and I jump into Tysoe and head to Hove for this evening's game.

Arrive at the ground in the middle of the afternoon and head off to meet Badger and Burns for some podcast recording. Sadly, there is a bit of a technical problem when Burns fills his petrol car with diesel and his arrival is delayed. Thankfully he makes it in time for warm-ups but the podcast on the big third/fourth place clash will have to wait.

The atmosphere in the press box is very jovial and Hove is a lovely ground to come to. In fact, I used to come to Eaton Road a lot when I was younger as I played in the Sussex age-group system. That was the days of Imran Khan and Garth le Roux and I still have a soft spot for Sussex.

Adrian Harms from BBC Sussex arrives, and the toss takes place. The pitch looks a belter and with a full house and the sun shining it promises to be a great night.

Sussex stick Surrey in to bat and we are then treated to an extraordinary performance from Aaron Finch. Dropped on one, he proceeds to make a century built on experience, power and skill. He is a remarkable ball striker and he makes 131* to put Surrey in a brilliant position.

Sam Curran, who has been released by England for the game, then bowls two consecutive maidens at the start of the Sussex chase and Jade Dernbach removes the dangerous Luke Wright.

Surrey's bowlers are once again very good and Sussex are never really in the chase. Hove is not an easy place to come to and get a result, but Surrey secure a comprehensive 52 run victory and are well worth it.

I dash from the commentary box to interview Finch. Not only is he a brilliant batsman, he's a charming fella and it comes across how much he is enjoying being back at Surrey.

I say my goodbyes, manoeuvre Tysoe out of a very tight parking space and slowly make my way back to Mum's. A little like Groundhog Day, I arrive back at midnight, have peanut butter on toast and head to bed after another busy but splendid day.

SATURDAY 14 JULY

Dad had always dreamt of having a holiday home. Ten years ago, his dreams came true when, thanks to all his hard work, he bought a gorgeous flat in Aldeburgh on the Suffolk coast.

It is a wonderful place and today Mum and I are going there for a couple of days. I have not been back since Dad died and it will be another thing to tick off the list of things I've been dreading.

Pack Tysoe and we leave at 9.15am for the two-hour drive. At 10.30am we slow down on the M25 because the junction we are coming off at has been closed due to an accident.

Seven hours later we start moving again. The accident was very bad, and it takes that amount of time to clear the road. Mum sleeps and I listen to the second ODI on *Test Match Special* with the windows open and the sun beating down. We finally arrive in Aldeburgh at 7.30pm but our thoughts are with the poor people in the accident.

It is lovely to be back, but it is sad to be here without Dad. I take Mum for a well-earned glass of wine at a local restaurant and head to bed at 10pm, completely exhausted. We are here until Tuesday and now Tysoe is happily parked. I don't intend on moving him until we leave.

SUNDAY 15 JULY

Up at 6am for the most wonderful run along the beach. The sun is shining, it is incredibly warm, and the legs are feeling good.

Return to the flat to be attacked by a couple of seagulls. They bomb me although I'm not quite sure what I have done to offend them. I then discover there is a baby seagull sitting in the road. It becomes a scene from Hitchcock's *The Birds* as hundreds of seagulls come to protect the baby. They also decide to drop what they had for breakfast on top of Tysoe.

Head to the beach and spend a lovely morning in the sun. The peace is shattered by more seagull bombing raids as a baby seagull decides to come and sit next to me. Don't get me wrong, I'm all for nature, but this was not how I envisaged my morning.

Prior to the renewed bombing, the news had come through that Rory Burns will captain the England Lions next week against India A, which is tremendous.

Escape the angry seagulls to watch Novak Djokovic win Wimbledon and France win the World Cup. What a month it has been for sport. Watch the final World Cup montage wondering what will be happening in four years' time.

Take Mum out for dinner and, as we leave the flat, the seagulls bomb me again. They definitely hate me.

Head to bed at 10pm after a lovely relaxing day. Fall asleep dreaming of a massive seagull bowling 90mph bouncers at me in a Test match.

✳

MONDAY 16 JULY

Wake up early with the sun beating down and go for another gorgeous run along the beach, feeling a little like Sylvester Stallone in *Rocky III*…without the tight–fitting shorts, yellow singlet and long socks.

Spend a lazy morning keeping an eye on Surrey v West Indies A and England Lions v India A. The wifi signal is intermittent on the beach and it does seem rather odd not to be at The Oval when Surrey are playing. Having said that, as I tuck into a chicken ciabatta with a lovely pint of lager, I am enjoying the relaxation of beach life.

The afternoon is spent writing a business plan for my deckchair hiring business, 'Church Pews'. Not a cloud in the sky, sun beating down, that lovely feeling of slightly roasting in my flip flops – that dream seems a little closer.

Take Mum for an ice cream (I am allowing myself some naughty stuff for a couple of days) and manage to get a wifi signal. Burns was out for five for the Lions, but Badger has scored a hundred for Surrey. I'm currently in negotiations with them to continue the football podcasts throughout the season. One of them is demanding a supply of crayons for their football colouring-in book, which is proving to be a sticking point in negotiations.

Head out for dinner with Mum and Mark Fairweather (a lovely gentleman who lives in a flat above Mum and Dad's) and get a very pleasant surprise. Heading for the toilet due to an extra Peroni, a man comes up to me and introduces himself and his family. It turns out he listens to the commentaries and his son is a budding leg-spinner. I invite them to the commentary box at The Oval and end dinner with more ice cream.

A lovely day ends with a slow wander back from the restaurant with no sign of the seagulls, which is a relief.

PS – England are back from Russia, so they, if not it, have come home.

TUESDAY 17 JULY

Early run along the beach and then pack up Tysoe for the drive back from Aldeburgh. This time it only takes a couple of hours to get back to Mum's and in the afternoon, I go for another run. I'm doubling up the training from today, which will be interesting.

Morne Morkel is taking wickets at The Oval and Sam Curran is taking wickets for the Lions at New Road and I take the opportunity to have a kip in the garden.

Speak to my girls in Marbella, who are having a lovely time and I'm delighted to learn that Isabelle's diving into the pool is apparently reaching Olympic standards.

Early night to recover from two runs in a day. I wonder how my legs will feel in the morning?

WEDNESDAY 18 JULY

The legs are feeling surprisingly good and I head out for an early run. Peanut butter on toast to recover and then repack Tysoe because I'm heading back to Cardiff today because my girls are returning from Marbella.

Lovely drive up the M4 listening to the Lions v India on BBC Five Live Sports Extra. There are more wickets for Sam Curran and then runs for Rory Burns and Ollie Pope.

Get home and head to the gym for my second run of the day. Huge result when the TV in front of the running machine I'm using shows coverage of practice from Carnoustie ahead of the first round of the Open tomorrow. The course looks like a desert, with patches of green thrown in and the ball seems to be running a long, long way. Experts think it could be a classic – I fancy Tiger to lift the claret jug; what a story that would be.

Head home to be greeted by Isabelle, who looks very healthy after the trip to Spain. Nothing better than getting home and seeing my girls and we have a lovely evening catching up on all the holiday news.

Surrey have drawn their game against West Indies A and the Lions should wrap up victory against India A at New Road tomorrow.

Fall asleep watching *Alvin and the Chipmunks* with Isabelle and that is me done for the day. The last thing I remember is Alvin causing chaos on his new bike as I drift slowly into the land of nod.

※

THURSDAY 19 JULY

Awake early and head to the gym to get my run out of the way early. It's another beautiful day and I go into town with the girls to get their holiday photos developed.

36,000 snaps later we head home, I repack Tysoe and say a sad farewell because, with Surrey in T20 action tomorrow, I'm back down the M4 to Mum's. It's a good drive, soundtracked by the opening round of The Open, in which Tiger makes a solid start.

Head straight out for the second run of the day, wearing my new cap from Spain with a matador on the front. It's genuinely hot again and the knees are starting to creak a little.

The England Lions beat India A, so Rory Burns has an unbeaten record as captain – his sixth four–day victory of the summer.

A quiet evening is spent in front of the telly, watching highlights of The Open. Tiger played nicely, and I try to get Mum interested but fail miserably.

Head to bed and start reading one of Dad's books on golf called *The Swing Factory*. Fall asleep with the page open on 'the grip' and dream of winning The Open with my new grip, using a bat to play my shots around Carnoustie.

✳

FRIDAY 20 JULY

T20 day! Hooray!

Get my run in early and then say goodbye to Mum who is off to a very proud occasion for us.

For a number of years, Mum and Dad have helped with a sponsored swim at Amhurst School in Kent to raise money for the British Heart Foundation. For the first time today, Mum will present the school with a shield called 'The Tony Church BHF Sponsored Swim' and I know Dad would have been extremely proud.

Jump in Tysoe and start the journey to Canterbury for this evening's game and arrive at the St. Lawrence Ground at 2pm for what I think is a 5.30pm. When I get there, I'm informed by the lovely gentleman on the gate that it is, in fact, a 7pm start. I have five hours to kill!

Take a stroll to the Sainsbury's at the ground and buy the *Daily Mail*, before heading back to the commentary box for a read. Three minutes later I have finished the paper and still have four hours to kill.

I fall asleep and am woken by the Kent chief executive, Ben Green, who used to work at Surrey. We have a lovely catch-up and then Johnny Barran arrives, dressed like a man who owns a million-pound yacht. He is in jovial mood having played for the Lord's Taverners at Hove yesterday, dismissing the former England and British Lions fly-half and now Sussex CCC chief executive, Rob Andrew.

By the time Barran has finished the story of the dismissal a couple of hours have drifted by and it is nearly time for the game to start.

On my way to the ground there had been a few spots of rain and the dark clouds now seem to be stuck above Canterbury. It is a full house; a cracking atmosphere and we're keeping fingers crossed that the rain stays away.

Aaron Finch and Rory Burns march to the middle and get Surrey off to an absolute flyer. The ball is seemingly very attracted to the middle of their bats and the early introduction of Denly gives me the ideal opportunity to remind Barran of his amazing announcement of Denly's 100 at The Oval in front of 25,000 people, when he was actually on 99.

Burns and Finch both play incredibly well. In fact, the start they give Surrey is spectacular. The ball keeps ending up in various tents around the ground and Burns moves to his first T20 fifty. Finch yet again proves why he is the best T20 batsman in the world, making 83, but the light drizzle is getting heavier. Surrey keep pressing the button and move past their previous best score in T20 of 224 back in 2006.

Eventually they finish on 250-6 but the rain is getting heavier. The covers come on and it begins to dawn on everyone that Kent's run chase may never start.

It's hugely frustrating for the crowd but the umpires are left with no choice but to abandon the game. A record score for Surrey but they have to settle for a point.

I pack up and head to Tysoe to get a baby seat we had for Isabelle to give to the actual Alex Tysoe. After the seat has been successfully delivered, I jump back into Tysoe (I hope you're keeping up here) and drive back to Mum's.

Arrive at 11.30pm and(surprise, surprise) have peanut butter on toast and watch highlights of Round 2 of The Open. Tiger is in the mix as I head to bed at 1am. I need to get some kip as the drive to Nottinghamshire for Championship cricket starts this afternoon.

*

SATURDAY 21 JULY

A big day. It's the birthday of Jason Roy and the birthday of my Mum. Jason has a few more international and first-class runs but send him a birthday text first thing and then give Mum a big birthday hug.

I have purchased a rather smart garden lamp for her and cleverly bought a cake on visit to Sainsbury's yesterday. It's a tricky day for Mum without Dad but we have a lovely morning before I pack my bag and set off to Nottingham.

Another four-hour drive passes nicely with The Open on BBC Radio Five Live. It's a fascinating listen and as I arrive in Robin Hood Country, Jordan Spieth pulls out the driver on the first and hits his first shot over 400 yards to within ten feet of the pin. He holes the putt to start his round with an eagle.

Park Tysoe in the National Car Park opposite the hotel I'm staying in and carry my bags across the road and check in. Head straight to the gym for a run and then happily find live coverage of the golf on the TV in my room.

Fall off my bed at about 7pm and go to the hotel bar to find some of the Surrey squad watching the end of the Hampshire v Essex T20 game. It all comes down to the last ball and, amongst great drama and expert punditry from the Surrey players, Ravi Bopara is run out off the last ball and the game is tied.

I leave the hotel to locate the temporary place of residence of Daniel Norcross, who is up at the game for Five Live.

Alongside one of the best in the business, David Hopps, Norcross and I record a T20 cricket podcast for ESPN Cricinfo. It's a lovely chat followed by the realisation that we are sat in the very bar where I was once introduced to former *Good Morning TV* presenter Nick Owen.

Head for a post-podcast curry with Norcross and then walk back to my hotel. Nottingham is certainly lively on a Saturday night.

Safely back in my room, I watch The Open highlights (Tiger still in there) and nod off to sleep dreaming of Tiger opening the bowling for Surrey in the morning.

*

SUNDAY 22 JULY

The first day of the County Championship match against Nottinghamshire starts with breakfast with Burns where we agree that Francesco Molinari may be one to watch at The Open.

I drive Messrs Pope, Foakes and Jacks to Trent Bridge and make my way to the commentary box to see one of the greats of the cricket broadcasting community, Dave Bracegirdle. He is one of the most hospitable men on the circuit and before I know where I am, coffee has been served and he has arranged for me to leave the car at the ground all week, which saves taking out a small loan to pay for the NCP.

I love Trent Bridge. It feels like a proper cricket ground and I have had some great times here. I particularly remember the first T20 Finals Day in 2003, where Atomic Kitten were the musical interlude.

Michael Perkins joins us in the commentary box as the 'third voice' for this week, Barran is due to join us tomorrow and then Norcross arrives wearing another hideous safari shirt. He really isn't the height of fashion.

From a distance the wicket looks green and the boundary to one side is very short. It's a cloudy morning and there is no great surprise when there is no toss and Surrey bowl first.

This is a 'first v second' affair and Surrey are coming off four straight wins. In football parlance, this is Super Sunday!

It proves to be exactly that for Surrey. Jade Dernbach sets the tone by having Steven Mullaney caught behind second ball of the morning and Sam Curran, Clarke and Morkel proceed to dismantle the Notts batting as the home side are knocked over for 210 at tea.

Burns and Stoneman come to the middle and take the game by the scruff of the neck. Stoneman looks back to his old self, which is wonderful to see. He plays 'his' way, like he did last season. It is always satisfying to see a bloke who has a rough trot come back into form. He is a bloody good player, as he showed last summer when he got in the England side. Then some rubbish was thrown out there about his technique and not practising like a Test cricketer. How does a Test cricketer practise, I wonder? Anyway, it was utter guff. It's just very nice to see Rocky go back to playing his way and showing what a quality player he is.

He races to 86 and Burns is very happy to play second fiddle. Surrey are motoring along at six an over – and when Stoneman goes, Burns takes over. The captain yet again looks outstanding in all areas of his game and, alongside podcast partner Borthwick, he takes Surrey to stumps on 223-1. Burns finishes the day on 97 and as a blueprint for a perfect day's cricket, this one is pretty good.

Interview Morkel at the end and fire some more hard-hitting questions at him. He makes the point that to be part of such a good four-man attack is a real luxury because he was always part of a three-man attack for South Africa.

Grab an Uber with Norcross back to the hotel and head to the gym for run number two of the day. Then nip across to Tesco Express, come back to the room and watch Open highlights with a fruit platter.

Delighted that Burns and I have been proven right as Molinari becomes the first Italian to win a major. Tiger was leading at the twelfth but then fell away and Molinari took his chance. Always lovely to see the emotion of a player when years of hard graft come to fruition.

You may have realised by now that I'm a bit of a softie and I fall asleep with tears in my eyes from the brilliant montage at the end of the coverage. Nothing like a really good highlights package, set to the right music.

My personal favourite is Michael Johnson's 'Face of the Games' from the London Olympics in 2012, closely followed by 'The Miracle at Medinah', from the Ryder Cup – also from 2012, with the theme from *Dances with Wolves* underneath. You cannot beat it.

MONDAY 23 JULY

6am wake up and straight to the gym, where I watch the sun come up over Nottingham and am joined by coach Di Venuto, who is always in the gym first thing. 'Diva' is a smashing bloke who has always been very good to me. Not only is a he a bloody good coach, he's also a machine on the cross trainer.

Another breakfast with the captain, joined by Alec Stewart, and today I walk to the ground with Joel Pope. It's really nice to be able to walk to the ground, with the sun beating down, and I arrive at Trent Bridge a sweaty mess.

Head to the commentary box to say good morning to Dave Bracegirdle before sitting in the stands for a while to cool down. It is here I witness one of the more extraordinary greetings between two supporters that I've ever seen.

A gentleman is sitting on his own when his friend arrives. "Morning", he says. "How are you?" "I've got diarrhoea." The two rows in front and behind him clear out and he is left on his own.

I meet a lovely Surrey fan who is also a long-distance runner. He gives me some excellent tips for October and I decide I should spend more time in the stands, in between commentary stints.

Notts start the day much better with the ball and the great Luke Fletcher is outstanding. Burns has to stay patient but, after half an hour, he drives Harry Gurney straight back down the ground to bring up his third century of the summer. Talk about leading from the front. Remember what Dale Steyn said at Hampshire: "It's the way he leaves the ball alone."

Decide to act upon this morning's vow, so when I am not on air I venture into the crowd. Meet some lovely Notts supporters and one of them sets me a cracking quiz question: "On Geoff Boycott's England debut at Trent Bridge in 1964, who did he open the batting with?"

As I mull over this question, Surrey lose Ben Foakes, Aaron Finch and Ollie Pope, but Burns passes 150 for the third time this season. He eventually falls for 153 and there is a slight danger that Surrey may not take full advantage of their position.

Get back in the commentary box to find Johnny Barran has arrived. Once again, he looks like he has dropped in having parked his yacht on the River Trent.

When I'm back on the microphone I ask the question about Boycott's opening partner that I had been set in the stands. A few answers come in via Twitter and it gives me the chance to remember the halcyon days of "Johnny Barran's Cricketing Question of the Day". This was a popular feature on BBC London where Barran would set a question every day but would either not know the answer, have the wrong answer, or the answer would be Alec Stewart. It was a very popular part of the day and we may have to bring it back.

Out in the middle, Sam Curran and Rikki Clarke are putting together an excellent seventh-wicket partnership, making sure Surrey do take advantage of their brilliant position.

Sam goes for 70 but Clarke moves to his first Championship century for six years and his first hundred for Surrey since 2006. I commentated on that one, a double against Somerset at Guildford. Feel very privileged to have been here for this one, although it does make me feel a little ancient. Clarke is a hell of a cricketer these days. He gets better as he gets older – by the time he is 80 he will be the best cricketer in the world in all forms of the game. He eventually falls for 111 but he really has put Surrey into a fantastic position.

All that is left is for Jade to make a cameo 27 *. I knew he was going to have a good day with the bat when he played one of the great straight drives in the nets this morning.

Surrey are all out for 561, the highest score in Division 1 this season. Notts have to bat for 20 overs and Morkel caps another great day for Surrey when he traps Jake Libby lbw before the close.

There is lots of talk of a three-day finish, but it is still a good pitch and Surrey's bowlers will have to work hard tomorrow.

I nip across the ground to interview Clarke. One of the great privileges of our job is being allowed to walk across the ground, and as usual I dream I'm walking back to the pavilion after scoring a hundred in a Test match.

Clarke is very satisfied with the day's work and I retire to the pub with Dave Bracegirdle for a pint. With the weather being so lovely we sit outside and are soon joined by Surrey scorer Phil Makepeace. Phil is in the top 200 chess players in the country and we discuss the merits of live streaming chess competitions.

Norcross joins us and has his usual, a large glass of Pinot Grigio in a pint glass, topped up with soda and ice. I believe he even has cards with his drinks order on them, so he can just hand them over if it is a very noisy bar.

Barran has already gone back to his hotel so we all catch an Uber back into the city centre where Norcross and Makepeace get a table in the all-you-can-eat world buffet, and I spend the next 40 minutes standing outside the restaurant directing Barran the 400 metres from his hotel to us. Eventually I give up and join Makepeace and Norcross, who are already on their second helping of world cuisine.

I do like an all-you-can-eat buffet and I always end up with the most eccentric combination on my plate. Tonight, I have a mix of Chinese, Mexican, Indian and pasta salad. It is delicious and Barran finally arrives, still dressed in his yacht club clothing, and orders sushi.

We're having a lovely night, but then greatest moment of the day occurs when I spot a Mr Whippy ice cream dispenser in the corner. I'm under significant time pressure though as the restaurant shuts in ten minutes. So, using the experience of a seasoned buffet practitioner, I have a Mr Whippy at the dispenser with three more to take back to the table. Genius.

Phil Makepeace heads off but, fuelled by vanilla ice cream, I suggest of one more drink because "the night is yet young".

We go to a very noisy bar, surprisingly full of young people on a Monday night out! We proceed to sit at a table for a couple of hours and have an old man's argument about the merits of cricket and terrestrial TV. The discussion descends into shouting as the music gets louder and Norcross and I are treated to Barran having a dance on his own, looking slightly like a demented yacht club owner.

We head back to our various places of stay full of the joys of summer and when I get to bed I realise it is 2am. Blimey, times flies when you are shouting at each other in the back of a noisy bar! I fall into bed and set my alarm for four hours' time.

Oh, and by the way, Geoffrey Boycott's opening partner on his Test debut in 1964 was Fred Titmus!

✳

TUESDAY 24 JULY

Four hours later the alarm goes off and I head to the gym, A five-mile run wakes me up and that is followed by breakfast and a walk to the ground with Joel Pope.

My early arrival at Trent Bridge is greeted by somebody out in the middle dressed as a cowboy holding a bat, being filmed by a TV crew. Figure it must be a sponsor but cannot quite get my head around the concept and do not recognise the gentleman.

Norcross arrives early because he is interviewing Ollie Pope about the T20 and I see the headline in the newspaper he is carrying: 'The 100 to be played by 15-man teams."

With trepidation, I read the article. Can this get any madder? Last week I tweeted about setting up a rival competition called 'BIB'. This would stand for 'Basically, It's Bollocks'. The competition would be similar but with a few key differences. Mine would be a 99-ball competition (hopefully sponsored by Mr Whippy), teams could use as many players as they liked but would have to select two bowlers who would begin their run-ups in the car park. Each team would be allocated a minor celebrity who has never played cricket before and doesn't understand the game. They would be given a week to train them before that person had to open the batting against one of the car park bowlers.

As I sit and read about the new concept from the ECB I start to realise that, for once, I have hit the nail on the head. Basically, what the ECB is coming up with is bollocks. I just want them to be honest with us. This is all about money, being relevant and trying to play catch-up – it's got nothing to do with cricket and it is now becoming laughable. There is even talk of comedian Michael McIntyre presenting the competition. What next, Jos Buttler doing stand-up at The O2? (I would actually watch that.)

Norcross completes his interview with Ollie Pope and I act as his cameraman for an interview with Aaron Finch. It's a slightly wobbly shot because I've never had the steadiest of hands, but I do remember to press record, which is the main thing.

Another tremendous sight before play is Tom Curran emerging from the dressing room and coming over to say hello. It's been a tough few weeks for TC, who has been carrying an injury, but he is back bowling and looks in good form.

I get to the commentary box and spend 20 minutes sending Norcross's interviews to the right people for him. He may be one of the most talented broadcasters around, but he needs to work on his technicals.

So, Surrey need nine more wickets to make it five straight wins. I think it will be hard work today, but Sam Curran gets them off to the perfect start when he traps Mullaney lbw early in the morning.

Dave Bracegirdle and I are on air for the first 45 minutes of play and it proves to be very eventful. Nothing to do with the cricket, but information reaches us that the cowboy in the middle of the pitch this morning was only Charlie Ross, filming for BBC's *Bargain Hunt*!

Now I think *Bargain Hunt* is one of the greatest programmes on TV and I will admit I got rather over–excited. After my commentary stint I run to the other end of the ground to go and find Charlie, who is apparently filming in the library, in the hope of getting a selfie. I am devastated to discover that he and the *Bargain Hunt* team have already left. What an opportunity missed. If only I hadn't been editing Norcross's videos and acting as cameraman, my dreams might have come true.

I come out of the library to see Ben Foakes take a brilliant catch off Morne Morkel to dismiss Will Fraine. This could be over today, and I go back on air just as Morkel has Samit Patel caught behind. Surrey's quicks enjoy another tremendous morning and Notts go to lunch seven down.

Barran, who I have to admit looks a little tired, refuels still dressed in his yacht club clothes and Norcross spends the lunch break trying to work out which game to go to tomorrow now this one looks like finishing early. His travel arrangements sound horrifically complicated, so I leave him to it and open up the afternoon session with Dave Bracegirdle. Twenty minutes later, the game is over. Two quick wickets for Amar Virdi means it is left to Morkel to finish match with his fifth wicket of the innings.

It's a fifth straight win for Surrey, four of those by an innings. This Surrey side are playing some special cricket and it's a joy to watch.

Interview the captain who is very satisfied with the performance and have a little watch of Tom Curran going through his paces out in the middle. And guess who is with him, offering an ear? Morne Morkel. Surrey have got a good one in Morkel.

Head back to the commentary box, pack and say goodbye to Dave Bracegirdle. Load up a very hot Tysoe and drive back to the hotel. The team have headed home but I decide to go for a run through Nottingham. It's graduation day so I have to sidestep lots of proud looking parents with their offspring in gowns.

Back to the hotel and wander for a coffee. This weather is amazing – it is like being abroad and I sit outside with my Americano watching the world go by and reflecting on the Surrey performance.

I meet Barran for supper at Pizza Express because he has got a special voucher that gets us a free starter – it is very good to know such influential people.

In bed by 10pm, excited by the fact I can get a bonus day back in Cardiff tomorrow with the girls, thanks to Rory Burns and his team.

❋

WEDNESDAY 25 JULY

Early trip to the gym and then a very nice breakfast with Ryan Sidebottom, who stayed last night because he is heading to Lincoln to play for the PCA. He was a magnificent cricketer and is proving to be a superb bowling coach. Not often you have breakfast with a World T20 winner!

Leave Nottingham and have a pleasant journey back to Cardiff. Arrive home at 2pm and then remember Mrs Church is at work and Isabelle is at something called 'Film Club' this week.

So, I fall asleep in the garden and then go to the gym for my second run of the day. The sun is shining in Wales and after a quiet coffee, I make my way home. The girls arrive at 6.30pm and it is lovely to have an evening with them. Isabelle is full of Film Club and sings me one of the songs she has to learn. I can't say I'm familiar with it, but it sounds very good to me.

It's always nice to be back in my own bed, but that doesn't last long as Isabelle has a bad dream, poor thing, and wants her Mum. I fall asleep in Isabelle's room, happy to be home again.

✳

THURSDAY 26 JULY

Early start as Rach heads to work and Issy goes with her for Film Club. I use the morning constructively, doing my invoices and paying the gas and electricity bill.

I then go to the gym and sit with a coffee afterwards, reading about Surrey's signing of Liam Plunkett on a three-year deal. This is another tremendous move from Surrey for a hugely talented and experienced cricketer. I try to beat the rush on Twitter and tweet 'typical Surrey'.

Back into Tysoe and, with my bag packed again, start off back down the M4 to Mum's.

The Test squad has been announced for the opening game with India and it's great to hear that Sam Curran is in there. The big headline is Adil Rashid being picked, even though he has chosen not to play Championship cricket for Yorkshire. He is a fantastic bowler but I'm not quite sure what message it sends to county cricket. I doubt England really care though, as long as they win the first Test.

Back in Kent, I head out for a second run of the day. It is very hot and weather warnings are now in place. We are strange in this country – when snow comes there is a grinding halt to proceedings and now the sun has come out, in the summer, there is a grinding a halt to proceedings. It's the summer, the clue is in the title. And it's great to know the cricket will go ahead – I just hope it doesn't get too hot for cricket in this country!

Surrey announce their squad for the T20 against Somerset tomorrow and Jason Roy is back after a finger injury picked up with England. Last year he made one of the best T20 hundreds I've ever seen against Somerset. Tom Curran is back in the squad too – all his hard work has paid off. A lot of credit should go to Alex Tysoe and strength and conditioning coach Darren Veness for getting him back bowling.

An early night, but not before I watch the news headlines. Tomorrow could be the hottest day ever in the history of the world apparently. At least it's not being exaggerated!

✻

FRIDAY 27 JULY

It's hot, but not the hottest day ever in the history of the world.

A day off training today so enjoy a quiet breakfast with Mum and then repack my bags and drive to The Oval for tonight's T20. I'm going straight to Cardiff after the game. One thing you need to be in this game is organised with your pants.

I listen to Five Live whilst sitting on the M25 for two hours – Adil Rashid seems to be the top story. Michael Vaughan thinks his selection is ridiculous and Rashid is upset nobody from Yorkshire has congratulated him. His selection has certainly caused a debate.

One thing I will say is that I admire Ed Smith for going with his gut and sticking to it. Again, I'm not sure what message it sends to county cricketers, but the fact Jamie Porter from Essex is in the squad seems to have been missed. Here is a lad who is hugely talented, has taken wickets in county cricket, won the title with Essex and it's those performances that have got him picked. But that doesn't seem to get a mention.

The drive up to The Oval is otherwise uneventful, but there is a slight concern on my arrival in SE11 that the weather forecast is now predicting thunderstorms. It is so hot and humid that I shall be sporting shorts in the commentary box this evening. I have never done this before but in this weather, I feel like I've made a very sensible health and safety decision.

After arrival at The Oval and a successful commentary box build I get a fantastic surprise. Back in 2005, Surrey's video analyst was a gentleman by the name of Trent Woodhill. Trent left Surrey and has become one of the best coaches in the world, working in the BBL and the IPL. It's 13 years since I've seen him, but here he is. Time has been kinder to Trent than me, because he looks no different and it is smashing to see him.

He's over for a month doing some consultancy for the ECB on 'The 100' competition and I have a mild panic that he has seen my brilliant idea for the 'BIB' competition and will want to steal my concept. But actually, we just sit and chat about old times, family and the weather – because the heavens suddenly open and we are forced to shelter in the players' dugouts.

The weathermen have got it spot on as there is a massive thunderstorm and the spectacular sight of lightning over the ground. After saying goodbye to Woodhill, I make a mad dash in the rain and head up to the top floor of the Bedser Stand to see another of the great men of cricket. Matt Thacker is the managing director of Trinorth and not only is he a publishing genius, he has always been a huge support during my career. If I had his guts and entrepreneurial skills, I would definitely be sitting on my private beach somewhere in the Maldives.

Matt has very kindly helped sort out 2,000 flyers about the run for me and the poor fella has had to store them in his office for a week. They look amazing and I am very proud that they will be left in the pavilion this evening for people to look at.

Make my way back to the commentary box and await the arrival of Phil Walker, the editor-in-chief of *Wisden Cricket Monthly*. Phil is also somebody I've known for a very long time. He is a fabulous cricket writer and also a very good man. He also looks like a rock star and there is not enough of that in cricket journalism.

Phil is with me on commentary tonight and I am really looking forward to working with him. His enthusiasm for the game is infectious and we have had some fun conversations on air.

Unfortunately, the rain has started again, which means a delayed start. I fill my time wisely, eating the lovely food prepared by the Curran brothers (it's their pictures on the menu, so I presume they must have made it) and catching up with the James Bond of Sky Sports News, Dave Fulton.

This week, my colleague Kevin Hand has published his blueprint for the structure of English cricket. It is an excellent piece of work and one his main points is the introduction of a T10 competition.

He would be delighted tonight, because thanks to the hard work of the ground staff, the game will start at 8.15 and be a ten-over game.

Jade Dernbach wins the toss and decide to bowl and Surrey are outstanding with the ball. Tom Curran picks up two wickets in his first over back and Somerset are indebted to Lewis Gregory's 50*, which gets them up to 99.

Walker calls it at half–time: "Surrey will get these inside seven overs". He is always correct, as Aaron Finch and the returning Jason Roy treat the crowd to a display of pyrotechnic range hitting.

The 50 comes up in the third over and I am quite pleased with myself as I shout down the microphone: "Jason, go into the corner and behave yourself!" as he plays the most amazing shot over long off for six. The crowd are loving it and as long as you've got Finch and Roy at the top of your order, this T10 lark might work.

Surrey stroll to victory inside Phil Walker's predicted seven overs. Top class punditry from him but the overriding feeling is that the game has been cut off in its prime. I guess they do say in entertainment, "Always leave the crowd wanting more."

Make my way round to the dressing rooms and interview Jason Roy. Very good to see him and he sums the evening up when he says: "That was great fun." Whatever the format, that was pretty ruthless from Surrey and leaves them third in the South group.

By the time I get to Tysoe and set off for Cardiff, it's 10.30pm. It takes an hour to get out of London, but I really enjoy listening to Five Live talking about Geraint Thomas, who is about to win his first Tour de France. They'll be dancing on the Severn Bridge tonight.

Finally walk through the front door at 2am. It's been a long day and I fall asleep straightaway, dreaming of yellow jerseys and ten-over cricket.

*

SATURDAY 28 JULY

Really lovely to wake up in my own house. Straight to the swimming pool with Isabelle and then a run in the gym whilst Issy does her 'junior circuits'. She is much better at this running lark than me.

Lovely tuna sandwich for lunch with Mrs Church and then an afternoon of prep for my commentary tomorrow on the Surrey Stars against the Yorkshire Diamonds in the Kia Super League. Really looking forward to it. The women's game is going from strength to strength, but my only fear is, because it's going so well, someone somewhere will try to change it. In fact, that is the talk for 2020 and it would seem plain daft to change a competition just as it is starting to work. But then again, nothing surprises me these days.

One thing I am very much looking forward to is watching the Stars' new recruit Sarah Taylor, because she is without doubt one of the best wicket-keepers in the world.

After prep I fall asleep on the sofa. A long day yesterday caught up with me and Isabelle woke me up because my snoring was ruining her enjoyment of *Alvin and the Chipmunks*.

An early night is enlivened by watching a tremendous programme on Channel 5 called *Worst Gameshow Moments* or some such nonsense and I fall asleep again just as the late, great Richard Whiteley manoeuvres his way around a rude word coming up in the letters game on *Countdown*. Classic.

SUNDAY 29 JULY

Alarm goes off at 6am and after coffee, toast and kissing my girls goodbye, I'm back heading down the M4. I listen to Five Live, who are again focusing on Geraint Thomas and his crowning in Paris this afternoon as the winner of the Tour de France. He sounds like a smashing bloke.

After stopping for petrol and noticing I've just passed 16,000 miles for the season I arrive at Woodbridge Road. It has been raining ever since I left Cardiff and more wet weather is waiting in Guildford. In fact, it is miserable.

Have a cup of coffee and then have the great joy of catching up with Jonathan Batty. JB is a Surrey legend, having captained the side and spent most of his career successfully opening the batting and keeping wicket. He is now teaching geography at Caterham School and coaching cricket. He is back at Surrey as the Assistant Head Coach of the Surrey Stars and it is really lovely to see him.

I also meet a really nice lady called Nicky. It turns out she does sports massage and after telling her about my charity run she gives me some invaluable advice about rehab. It makes me realise how much I still have to do in preparation for October.

The Stars squad appear but the rain is getting heavier. The Yorkshire Diamonds arrive but everyone is getting the feeling that we might not get any cricket today. This fact is reinforced when Jon Surtees arrives in waterproof trousers and wellies.

At 3pm the game is abandoned but I pre-record an interview with BBC Radio London for the afternoon show. All manner of cricketing issues are discussed including Adil Rashid's call-up and Surrey's form in the Championship this season.

Sometimes when you are on air you find yourself on a bit of a roll. For once, I think I am making sense and decide to strike whilst the iron is hot. I'm asked who will replace Ben Stokes for the second Test at Lord's. Stokes will be in court for the well-documented 'incident' outside a Bristol nightclub last summer.

Due to this, he will need to be replaced and because I'm firing on all cylinders, I throw Rikki Clarke's name into the hat. Why not? He is scoring runs, bowling beautifully and catching everything that comes his way. I'd love to see him out there and I know ESPN Cricinfo's chief cricket correspondent, George Dobell, will be pleased with me, because he is actually in love with Clarke.

After concluding my Clarke advocacy, I pick up Tysoe and drive back to Mum's. Despite the rain, I take the opportunity to go out for a run and then the evening is spent discussing the removal of tarpaulins from Mum's new garden furniture. I decide it can be left until the morning and head to bed with the knowledge that the rain will not ruin Mum's new, fully weather-proof garden furniture, due to the £50 plastic sheet that is covering it.

The fact that all the cushions are indoors, and the rain has stopped is just a side issue.

✼

MONDAY 30 JULY

The start of another week and I begin with a run followed by a coffee, paperwork followed by a coffee, a trip to the bank followed by a coffee, and another run followed by a coffee.

I watch a re-run of the 2007 T20 World Cup game between England and India (forgot that Vikram Solanki kept wicket), followed by a coffee.

Prep for tomorrow's double-header at The Oval (Surrey Stars v Lancashire Thunder and Surrey v Glamorgan), followed by a coffee.

I read the excellent news that Gareth Batty will be coaching as well as playing for the rest of the season, followed by a coffee. Head out for another run, followed by supper and another coffee.

Speak to Isabelle who tells me she wants to have a gymnastics party for her birthday and then watch a re-run of England v India in the 2011 World Cup (match tied, Strauss 100), followed by bed.

It's an early night as it's an early start tomorrow for the double header I have christened 'Tremendous Tuesday' as a tribute to the 'Super, Spectacular, Stunning, Smashing, Seminal Sunday' you always see football advertised as on Sky TV.

*

TUESDAY 31 JULY

Alarm call at 5am and into Tysoe to drive up to The Oval. It's a quiet drive and I park up in the local convent where I am the first car in and have a good choice of spaces. I take ten minutes to decide which one to take before heading to the commentary box.

I then enjoy a coffee stroll along the Thames – it feels like a long time since Surrey last played at home. In fact, it was only last Friday but T20 does this to you. It is like the Bermuda Triangle and you get lost in the competition and can't remember what day of the week it is.

Sky are in the building, televising both games. The 'pod' is at the Pavilion End and there will be wall-to-wall coverage today.

An uneventful late morning is brightened by the arrival of BBC Manchester's Scott Read. We will be commentating together on the Stars against the

Thunder. We catch up over lunch and the main topic of conversation is my excitement about a new film coming out about a giant shark called *The Meg*. Lancashire are at The Oval for the day/night Championship game at the end of this month and I offer to take Scott to see it one evening. He doesn't look that excited by my offer.

Out in the middle, Surrey Stars are batting. There is already a good crowd in, but the Stars get off to a bad start. Captain Natalie Sciver holds the innings together with a brilliant 95* but it feels like they may be under par.

Nicole Bolton, the Thunder's Aussie opener, is very classy and the visitors look in control of the run chase. But Sciver bowls the nineteenth over and gets rid of Bolton for 87 and the Stars still have a chance to win. A brilliant game is ended, however, by India's T20 captain, Harmanpreet Kaur, who hits an enormous six off the first ball of the final over.

Read shoots off to do an interview and I immediately do a preview of the men's game against Glamorgan for BBC London. It is a quick turnaround and there is just enough time to grab a coffee and say hello to Nick Webb from BBC Wales. It's always good to see him but before we know it, the toss is taking place in the middle.

Johnny Barran arrives with a special guest, his son 'Little John'. Little John is a very good cricketer and it looks like he has already had a good day having his photo taken with the Surrey players.

Just as the game is due to start, word reaches us that Sam Curran will play tomorrow in the first Test against India at Edgbaston. This is brilliant news, and the series has become even more fascinating before a ball is bowled.

Surrey win the toss and bat. Jason Roy and Aaron Finch fly out of the blocks, playing some wonderful shots but Glamorgan bowl well and get rid of them in quick succession.

Nic Maddinson then plays his best innings for Surrey so far, making an accomplished 70, full of deft touches and timing.

We are treated in our commentary box to the sight of *Test Match Special*'s Charles Dagnall wearing 'the future of shoes', a pair of white plastic sandals. It's lovely to see Daggers but if that's the future of shoes, I think I'll stay in the past.

Surrey post 194-4 and then have Glamorgan on the back foot with a couple of early wickets. It looks like Glammy are going for it and that proves to be the case as Wagg and Carlson drag the game back towards Glamorgan with some powerful shots. Surrey's 194 is now not looking enough but the atmosphere inside The Oval is tremendous again.

Wagg plays a gem of an innings, not for the first time against Surrey, and Glamorgan win with an over to spare, continuing their remarkable record of never losing a T20 game at The Oval.

Say goodbye to Johnny, Little John, Nick and Daggers and head through the crowds back to the convent and Tysoe. It's 10pm and I will be following Glamorgan up the motorway, because I'm back to Cardiff tonight.

It has been another long old day, but I finally get home at 1am. I must be tired because it's straight to bed with no peanut butter and no toast.

Clockwise from top: George Dobell asks Rikki Clarke the questions; the football World Cup podcast boys – Scott 'Badger' Borthwick, Churchie and Rory Burns.

Clockwise from top: *Wisden Cricket Monthly*'s editor-in-chief Phil Walker joins the commentary team; Barran in Man from del Monte model pose; interviewing Morne Morkel at Trent Bridge; Dave Bracegirdle and Daniel Norcross in the commentary box.

NOTTINGHAMSHIRE V SURREY

Venue: Trent Bridge, Nottingham
Date: 22nd, 23rd, 24th July 2018
Toss: No toss made
Result: Surrey won by an innings and 183 runs

Points: Nottinghamshire 3; Surrey 24
Umpires: DJ Millns, RJ Warren
Scorers: PJ Makepeace, R Marshall

NOTTINGHAMSHIRE	1ST INNINGS	R	b	2ND INNINGS	R	b
*SJ Mullaney	c Foakes b Dernbach	0	2	lbw b Curran	23	51
JD Libby	c sub (RS Patel) b Morkel	28	58	lbw b Morkel	18	24
WAR Fraine	c Pope b Morkel	19	61	c Foakes b Clarke	30	77
SR Patel	lbw b Curran	5	10	c Borthwick b Morkel	55	49
WT Root	c Pope b Clarke	15	25	c Burns b Morkel	22	47
MH Wessels	c Clarke b Dernbach	23	29	c Borthwick b Dernbach	5	6
+TJ Moores	lbw b Clarke	27	55	c Pope b Virdi	10	12
SCJ Broad	c Curran b Morkel	3	13	lbw b Morkel	1	2
LJ Fletcher	b Morkel	21	29	b Virdi	8	13
JT Ball	b Curran	16	24	c Curran b Morkel	13	10
HF Gurney	not out	29	22	not out	0	2
Extras	(1 b, 12 lb, 8 nb, 3 w)	24		(2 lb, 12 nb)	14	
Total	(all out, 54 overs)	210		(all out, 47.5 overs)	199	

Fall of wickets: 1-0 (Mullaney, 0.2 ov), 2-59 (Fraine, 19.2 ov), 3-60 (Libby, 19.4 ov), 4-74 (Patel, 23.2 ov), 5-90 (Root, 26.5 ov), 6-121 (Wessels, 32.6 ov), 7-129 (Broad, 37.1 ov), 8-165 (Moores, 46.1 ov), 9-165 (Fletcher, 47.1 ov), 10-210 (Ball, 54 ov)
Fall of wickets: 1-37 (Libby, 8.2 ov), 2-61 (Mullaney, 19.2 ov), 3-108 (Fraine, 29.2 ov), 4-153 (Patel, 39.2 ov), 5-160 (Wessels, 40.4 ov), 6-166 (Root, 41.6 ov), 7-172 (Broad, 43.3 ov), 8-176 (Moores, 44.6 ov), 9-189 (Fletcher, 46.4 ov), 10-199 (Ball, 47.5 ov)

SURREY	O	M	R	W	Wd	Nb		O	M	R	W	Wd	Nb
Dernbach	12	2	38	2	-	-	Dernbach	10	3	47	1	-	-
Curran	13	2	47	2	-	1	Curran	11	0	34	1	-	1
Morkel	14	4	60	4	2	3	Morkel	13.5	2	60	5	-	2
Clarke	15	4	52	2	-	-	Clarke	7	3	21	1	-	-
							Virdi	6	0	35	2	-	3

SURREY	1ST INNINGS	R	b	2ND INNINGS	R	b
*RJ Burns	c Mullaney b Patel	153	248			
MD Stoneman	c Moores b Ball	86	83			
SG Borthwick	c Moores b Fletcher	24	55			
AJ Finch	c Ball b Broad	2	8			
+BT Foakes	c Wessels b Broad	0	3			
OJD Pope	c Moores b Gurney	30	32			
SM Curran	lbw b Patel	70	101			
R Clarke	c Moores b Root	111	134			
M Morkel	lbw b Root	28	37			
JW Dernbach	not out	27	19			
GS Virdi	c Broad b Root	9	12			
Extras	(7 b, 13 lb, 30 nb, 2 w)	52				
Total	(all out, 119.3 overs)	592				

Fall of wickets: 1-147 (Stoneman, 26.3 ov), 2-235 (Borthwick, 46.6 ov), 3-246 (Finch, 49.5 ov), 4-250 (Foakes, 51.2 ov), 5-297 (Pope, 61.6 ov), 6-347 (Burns, 74.6 ov), 7-472 (Curran, 100.6 ov), 8-549 (Clarke, 113.2 ov), 9-564 (Morkel, 115.5 ov), 10-592 (Virdi, 119.3 ov)

NOTTINGHAMSHIRE	O	M	R	W	Wd	Nb		O	M	R	W	Wd	Nb
Ball	23	2	128	1	1	1							
Broad	19	4	80	2	-	5							
Gurney	16	0	119	1	-	2							
Fletcher	20	3	63	1	-	6							
Mullaney	10	1	44	0	-	-							
Patel	27	3	101	2	1	1							
Root	4.3	0	37	3	-	-							

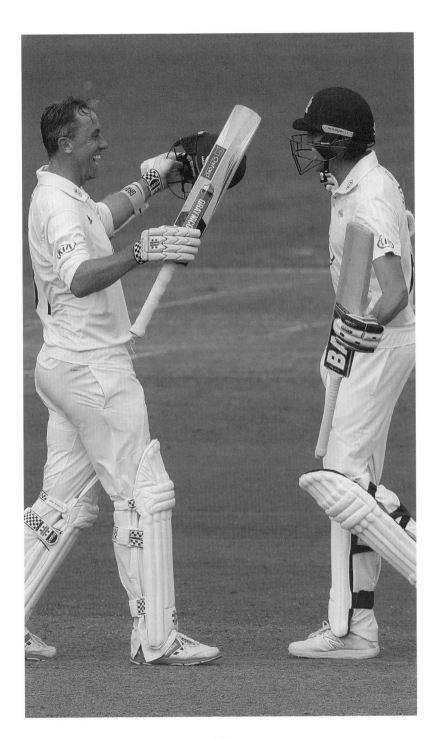

AUGUST

"Not sure if floodlit Championship cricket is good for your health"

WEDNESDAY 1 AUGUST

Where did July go? I am woken by Isabelle at 7am and finally get some peanut butter on toast as we watch some TV programme about a dance group.

The morning is spent at an indoor trampolining centre. I am happy with this decision because it has free wifi, enabling me to listen to *Test Match Special* as Isabelle bounces up and down.

England enjoy a good morning at Edgbaston and Issy and I make our way to the swimming pool. An afternoon of diving and underwater dancing ensues, but I make sure I have a line of sight to a TV with the Test match on it. England are going well until Joe Root is run out for 80, just as I complete a rather good handstand in the pool. A brilliant bit of work from Kohli, who reminds Root that his bat drop at the end of the ODI series may not have been a great idea.

Coffee and hot chocolate watching Sam Curran making 24* and guiding England to stumps nine wickets down. All that focus on Rashid's inclusion but it's still the batting that's the problem.

Take Isabelle home and then head to the gym for a long run in front of Sussex v Gloucestershire in the T20. It's always enjoyable to see the great Bob Hunt of BBC Bristol sitting in the sun commentating, and here he is, live on national TV, resplendent behind a trestle table.

Benny Howell's knuckle balls get me through my run and I head home to put Isabelle to bed. It has been a constructive day and I reckon, if I put the work in, synchronised swimming at the Tokyo Olympics could be an option.

✳

THURSDAY 2 AUGUST

Ten years ago today, I had the huge honour of commentating on Mark Ramprakash's 100th first-class hundred, against Yorkshire. It was a nerve-wracking experience but wonderful to be there for a piece of cricketing history. Where does the time go? A quick quiz question for you: who bowled the ball which he cut for four to bring up that century?*

Spend a nice quiet morning with Isabelle but all of a sudden, my phone starts pinging. My immediate reaction is one of panic, wondering what I've typed on Twitter that has annoyed people. Did I pay the gas bill? Am I being offered PPI compensation again?

However, when I look at my phone, all over Twitter there is just one name, Sam Curran. Sam has just taken three Indian wickets in eight deliveries and his name just seems to be everywhere. I quickly switch on *Test Match Special*, who confirm Sam has just done something pretty spectacular at Edgbaston. Tell Isabelle the good news and she celebrates with a packet of salt and vinegar Hula Hoops.

Virat Kohli is still there, holding everything together for India. I wonder if he is Surrey's greatest overseas player not to have actually played for Surrey? He is definitely the greatest cardboard cut-out I have sat in a campervan with.

Spend the afternoon tackling the M4 and M25 as Kohli does battle with the England bowlers. Sam picks up another wicket but Kohli goes to a quite brilliant century, which, as always, has been beautifully described on *Test Match Special*. Driving never seems as bad when there is cricket on the wireless.

Arrive at Mum's just as Ravi Ashwin bowls Alastair Cook with an absolute beauty for the second time this Test.

Nice quiet evening spent with Mum, watching the highlights of an absorbing day. Mum sums up Sam's day when she says: "Ahhhh, doesn't he look lovely?" Once a mum, always a mum.

Head to bed ready for the big one tomorrow. The London derby in the T20 Blast and an evening in the commentary box with Kevin Hand. What man could ask for more?

*It was David Wainwright, in case you were wondering.

❋

FRIDAY 3 AUGUST

Bad night's sleep. Had a dream that I was on my run and to hurry me up, Jason Roy and Aaron Finch were launching cricket balls in my direction and shouting: "Get a move on! There's a game tonight!"

I clear the cobwebs with a run and then get ready for this evening. Pack up Tysoe and set off to The Oval. *Test Match Special* is on the wireless but by the time I've reached Streatham, England have had an almighty collapse before lunch.

Arrival at The Oval, park in the convent and set up the commentary box. Greeted by the sight of Charles Dagnall dangling the effects microphone out of the *TMS* window. Dagnall, a man with his finger on the pulse, has the Test match playing on his iPad. I spend a happy hour watching with him as Sam marches to the middle at Edgbaston with England in all sorts of bother.

He proceeds to play a quite magical innings, taking on India's bowlers and going to a maiden Test fifty with a cover driven six. We all knew the boy could bat but now the whole world knows.

Daggers nips off to record his new gameshow, *Slogbusters* (don't ask) and I nip to watch the rest of Sam's innings on the TV in the Kia Oval reception area. Sam eventually goes for 63, but he has got the England lead up to 190 and has given them a sniff of victory. His innings looks even better as Stuart Broad takes two early wickets. This is bubbling up to be a classic Test match at just the right time.

Wander back towards the commentary box and bump into Kevin Hand. Lovely to see him as always and we have a proper catch-up in the press room over a glass of The Oval's finest water before shooting up to the commentary box to do a 5.30pm preview for BBC London. It is the perfect day for T20 cricket – hot, sunny and it's another sell out.

The coin goes up and Surrey stick Middlesex into bat. Meanwhile, at the Test match, Sam has taken a wicket and India have closed five down needing another 81 runs for victory. What a morning it will be tomorrow at Edgbaston. Could it be as tense as 2005?

I get a lovely surprise when my oldest friend, Jeremy Morris, and my godson Jake let me know they are in the ground. I remember being so proud of Jeremy when he burgled an international rugby cap for Mexico during his gap year. He is a fully fledged rugby international, something that might surprise you should you ever meet him. Hasty plans are made to meet up at the end of the match.

Out in the middle, Paul Stirling is dropped off the first ball of the game. He makes the most of it as he plays brilliantly and moves to a maiden T20 century. Middlesex bat well and post 221, which looks above par.

The consensus in the press box and on telly is that Surrey will have to bat pretty well to reach that target.

What transpires in the next couple of hours is frankly ridiculous. Aaron Finch sets the tone by pulling his first ball for six and the carnage starts. The way Roy and Finch bat should come with a health warning. They both play the most wonderful shots and the crowd are treated to an incredible spectacle. Middlesex are not sure where to bowl as balls keep disappearing into the stands and the club's sponsor, Kia, must have been panicking that they were going to be bankrupt by the end of game, as each catch in the crowd cost them £1,000.

It is incredible strokeplay from Roy and Finch and when Roy goes for 84, Surrey have 194 in the fourteenth over and are just 26 runs away from victory. Finch then moves to a quite brilliant century and Surrey get to 222 with four overs to spare with Finch 117*.

It was absolute carnage and a wonderful spectacle. The crowd have loved it and it's a wonderful advertisement for T20. Elsewhere this evening Johann Myburgh has smashed a century for Somerset – who'd be a bowler?!

Interview Finch after the game. He is quickly becoming a Surrey legend and watching him and Jason do their stuff has been a real privilege tonight.

Poor Kevin Hand has slightly longer to wait outside the Middlesex dressing room for an interview. I think Middlesex have been on the back end of Surrey's response to the Glamorgan loss this evening. There's not much more the bowlers could have done with the way Roy and Finch have played – they were inspired.

I shoot back to the commentary box and dispatch the interviews to the BBC before saying goodbye to the great and the good in the press box, including Norcross, who appears to be giving a tour of the press box dressed as a safari tour guide.

Meet Jeremy and Jake, who are going to come back to Mum's with me tonight, so we can have a proper catch-up in the morning. It's really interesting listening to Jake, who is 13, talking about his night at the cricket. He loved it and has had a great time. He is wearing his Surrey hat and has Jade, Jason and TC facemasks. He is asleep by the time we get on the Purley Way, enabling me and Jeremy to talk seriously about the game!

That takes about two minutes and we then move onto the important stuff like when we put 100 on together in a school match aged 15. The way we describe our batting, it is just like watching Finch and Roy this evening.

Arrive at Mum's, Jake goes straight to bed and Jeremy and I have peanut butter on toast and then call it a night. I need to be fully awake for the morning to come at Edgbaston.

❋

SATURDAY 4 AUGUST

Up early for a run and back for breakfast. Mum is delighted to see Jeremy and Jake and it is amazing seeing her make breakfast for Jake. It only seems like yesterday she was doing that for Jeremy and I after a night out!

We then sit around the TV and watch a brilliant 90 minutes of Test match cricket. Jimmy Anderson takes the early wicket of Dinesh Kartik but a certain Virat Kohli is still there. It is all very tense and a wonderful spectacle. The Ben Stokes traps Kohli lbw and there is a collective sigh of relief around the TV in the Church house.

India get it down to 31 needed when Stokes take the final wicket. What a Test match. It was reminiscent of the tension in 2005 and it's quite appropriate that my godson is in the house because the day he was christened, Steve Harmison was having Kasprowicz caught behind by Geraint Jones.

Jake and Jeremy depart, and I set out on my second run of the day. While plodding around the lanes of Kent I am secretly delighted that Test match cricket is top of the agenda for all the right reasons. Get home to news that Sam Curran was man of the match. The young man has had quite a week.

Quiet afternoon and evening. Re-watch highlights of the Test and get prepared for a trip to Chelmsford tomorrow. Will leave early because getting through the Dartford Tunnel is always a gamble.

❋

SUNDAY 5 AUGUST

Up early for a run, breakfast and then pack up Tysoe.

I mentioned the Dartford Tunnel last night, and give myself a couple of extra hours, just in case. Of course, there is no traffic and I arrive at Chelmsford far too early.

Park Tysoe and wander into Chelmsford. It is another very hot day and I'm immediately greeted by two bearded men, dressed as fairies doing a fun run. They are followed by Alice in Wonderland, the Incredible Hulk and a wheelie bin. If they didn't have their running numbers on, I would have thought they were all jogging back from a particularly good night out.

Head back to the ground with a coffee but when I get there I find the BBC box is still locked so I sit in the stands and sunbathe. An hour later I wake up and have absolutely no idea where I am.

When I come around the commentary box is open, so I set up and check my phone. I am greeted with the most wonderful news: Ollie Pope named in England squad for the second Test.

There you have it. Less than 12 months after making his Championship debut, Ollie Pope is going to bat four for England at Lord's. I'm so pleased for him and give him a quick buzz to say, "Well done mate". I get a couple of calls to canvass my thoughts on the selection (the experts must still be in church or away for the weekend).

For a lad of 20, Ollie has got everything. He's an incredibly talented cricketer but also a quick learner with a fabulous cricket brain. He is a really lovely lad and, as Chelmsford applauds his selection, after a nice touch from Essex by announcing it over the PA system, I wonder how he must be feeling. Christmas has come early.

After all the excitement, I return to the commentary box to discover Paul Newton and David Brett from BBC Essex in situ.

Paul has been broadcasting for many years and has an encyclopaedic knowledge of Essex cricket. David is a lovely chap who also shares my love of shark films, so today will be a good commentary.

Jade Dernbach wins the toss and bowls. Surrey are very good with the ball and restrict Essex to just 157-5, which looks way below par at Chelmsford.

All the talk is of Jason Roy and Aaron Finch finishing this one early, but Jason goes first ball and then Finch is out for 16. Ben Foakes comes to the middle and plays some lovely shots but, at the other end, Nic Maddinson holds the chase together. Maddinson is a very good player and we are beginning to see the best of him at just the right time.

Foakes goes for 26, allowing England's latest recruit to come to the middle and play some shots that show the Chelmsford crowd why England have selected him. He goes for 24 but Maddinson and Rikki Clarke race Surrey to victory with three and a half overs to spare. A very professional team performance once again.

Say farewells to the press box, including Norcross, who is delighted he decided to do an in-depth interview with Pope at Trent Bridge a couple of weeks ago. You cannot teach that sort of insight and thank goodness I was there to edit and send it out to whoever needed it. Cannot wait to get my 10 per cent.

Drive back to Cardiff and discover, unbelievably, that today was the Community Shield and the Football League season started yesterday. Another seven months of wall-to-wall punditry on the radio has begun! How many more 'experts' can they find for a football debate?!

Head across the Severn Bridge for the third time this week (another £15) and get home to find out that Isabelle has one of her best friends over for a sleepover.

The girls stay up to 11pm but I must admit I'm in bed after something to eat and drink. It has been a long day.

MONDAY 6 AUGUST

A morning of paperwork and then head for a swim with the girls. Mrs Church is at home today, which is lovely and, after swimming, we go for a family lunch.

I do an interview with City AM about Ollie's England selection and then spend the afternoon tweeting someone called "@DanTDM" for Isabelle, who wants to send him her tattoo design for a competition. This is the young man the ECB need to talk to because he has 20 million subscribers on YouTube and films himself playing computer games. Genius, and he certainly appeals to my daughter's generation.

Head to the gym for a long run and then get some fantastic news. Brewin Dolphin have kindly agreed to sponsor my kit for the run. I cannot thank David Quintrell enough and I now have to decide what to wear. It certainly won't be a fairy costume like I saw in Chelmsford yesterday.

Read a lovely article by Vithushan Ehantharajah on Cricbuzz about Ollie's selection. The only other cricket news today is Ben Stokes' court case has started in Bristol – rather depressing to see the news coverage of this, but understandable.

Spend a quiet evening watching TV and trying to find swimming trunks for a trip to the lido tomorrow in Pontypridd. Think I have left them in a locker at the gym, so it could be Surrey shorts circa 2006 tomorrow, which will be a thrill for everyone.

TUESDAY 7 AUGUST

What a smashing day. A trip to trampolining this morning, followed by a slap-up lunch at TGI Fridays. Then an afternoon at the lido with the sun shining. And don't worry, Isabelle was with me and, in the end, I didn't have to revert to my Surrey shorts circa 2006.

Run at the gym this evening and watch Ollie's first England press conference. He looks very composed and gives a great answer to the question, "When did you start dreaming about playing for England?" Ollie's answer? "About two weeks ago." Well batted, lad.

Home and pack bags because I'm on the road for a few days now. Oval to Taunton to Lord's to Bristol.

There is good news as well from Old Trafford. The Surrey Stars have beaten Lancashire Thunder. There are a few big games to come for the Surrey sides and I've also got myself a ticket for Lord's on Saturday. Fingers crossed the weather gods continue to smile on us and I might just get to watch Ollie Pope make his way to the middle to have a bat.

✳

WEDNESDAY 8 AUGUST

A day in Tysoe. Isabelle heads off to the dentist for her annual check-up (she managed to extract a tooth herself a couple of weeks – said she wanted more cash from the tooth fairy!).

Start off down the M4 and drive through the rain in Wales but the further east I go, the better the weather becomes. I arrive in Limpsfield and meet Ronnie

Wilkinson, who is kindly helping to organise a charity Christmas dinner in December to mark the end of my run. She is an expert at this kind of thing and I'm delighted to discover all I need to do is finish the run.

Over coffee we agree that a Q&A with Barran and I would sell about one ticket, so we are aiming a bit higher. I need to get on the phone and see what I can organise.

Arrive at Mum's and fall asleep under blue skies in the back garden. Wake up to see Joe Root confirming that Ollie Pope will bat at four and make his debut tomorrow. Exciting times.

Surrey announce their squad for tomorrow's T20 match against the Sussex Sharks at The Oval and, sadly, there is no Aaron Finch, who has had to go back to Australia due to a family bereavement. Thoughts are with him.

Text Burns and Borthwick to try and arrange a time to organise our first football podcast of the season and then head out for a run.

Return to no answer from Badger and Burns. I wonder if they've had a bigger offer from local hospital radio for their footballing thoughts? That would be disappointing.

Decide not to worry (my offer of free crayons for the football colouring-in books will surely be the clincher on the contract) and head to bed for an early night. Lie in bed reading the 1986 Sussex yearbook, as you do. Colin Wells had a good season!

✳

THURSDAY 9 AUGUST

I wake up really excited for Pope and Curran. As a 44-year-old man, I should not be this excited and should know better!

Up early to run before Tysoe takes me to The Oval. I make sure *TMS* is on for 11am but sadly it's raining at Lord's and the forecast for the rest of the day in London isn't very good. Fingers crossed it disappears before Surrey's game tonight.

Get very wet walking from the convent to the ground, dry off whilst setting up the equipment and then get wet again as I walk to Pret for a coffee and a banana. I am privately cursing all those who have said, "We could do with some rain" during the recent heatwave. They were definitely not cricketers.

There has still been no answer from Burns and Badger on podcast recording and I'm genuinely nervous that hospital radio has gazumped my offer on the crayons for their colouring-in books. If they've offered a supply of Panini stickers, then I'm stuffed. Loyalty goes out of the window when you get to this level of showbiz.

Adrian Harms from BBC Sussex arrives and we agree that we'll be lucky to see any cricket tonight. Play has been abandoned for the day at Lord's, so Pope's debut will have to wait until tomorrow.

But hang on. What's this? The rain has stopped in south London and, thanks to the brilliance of the ground staff, it suddenly becomes apparent that a game of cricket might break out.

It's a funny thing when it's raining and you're sat in a commentary box. You get nothing constructive done, drink lots of coffee and then have a mad rush when cricket threatens to start.

The game does indeed start, with Sussex winning the toss and having a bat. The game is 15 overs a side and we are on BBC Sussex, BBC Surrey and BBC London. Sussex get off to a flyer thanks to Luke Wright and Laurie Evans, but stormclouds are gathering again over the ground and it feels like Armageddon is heading our way.

The atmosphere in the ground is electric, but unfortunately so is the atmosphere in the sky and suddenly thunder and lightning arrive.

The umpires have no choice but to take the players off after 13 overs and it looks highly unlikely we will get back out there. I spend half an hour trying to get a photo of the lightning on my phone but fail miserably.

Unsurprisingly, the game is abandoned, which is a real shame. I pack up, head back to Tysoe and start the journey to Cardiff. It takes four hours and rains the whole way back. I get through the door at 1am and go to sleep thinking that it's been a very long day for 13 overs and one point!

✳

FRIDAY 10 AUGUST

Isabelle in cracking form – she's off to a summer camp today so we grab a quick breakfast together before she heads off.

I repack Tysoe and head back down the M4 for this afternoon's game against Somerset. I listen to *TMS*, where Alec Stewart presents Ollie Pope with his England cap… what a moment. Stewie delivers a rousing speech and there is a photo doing the social media rounds of him presenting Ollie with the Surrey under 9s Player of the Year award. Eleven years later he is presenting him with his England cap. Amazing.

On a cloudy morning at Lord's, Jimmy Anderson is like a kid in a sweetshop, swinging it around corners and taking two early wickets. As I swing into the Taunton car park, Ollie gets into the Test match when Kohli stuffs Pujara on a quick single and Ollie runs Pujara out.

Set up the commentary box and take a moment to enjoy the view, which is truly incredible. You can see the Quantock Hills away in the distance and today the sun is shining in the south west, so the ground looks picture perfect.

Somerset's new media centre opened a couple of years ago and is very nice. You used to have to climb a ladder, go through a trap door and broadcast from a shed on the roof. I gave myself concussion on a number of occasions by whacking my head on the trapdoor. I was also – quite famously in the county cricket world – sick on the roof whilst suffering food poisoning during a game. I remembered to turn off my microphone but sadly left the effects microphone on, so everyone heard the remnants of my hummus and pitta bread being deposited on the roof whilst Kevin Pietersen ran a single to third man.

These days, we are in a very comfy commentary box with easy access to the kettle and coffee making facilities, so I'm in clover.

Preview the game with Charlie Taylor on the BBC Somerset drivetime show. He also very kindly asks about the run and I'm really grateful for the opportunity to chat about it on air. Being the sad man I am though, whenever I'm on a drivetime show I want to end by saying: "Well, that's the cricket. Now Bachman Turner Overdrive with *Let's Rock!*" But I never do. One day, one day.

Anthony Gibson arrives, and we reminisce about out wonderful week in the Guildford sun earlier this year. We are joined by former Somerset bowler Mark Davies as the atmosphere builds ahead of the 4.30pm start (no floodlights in Taunton).

Jade Dernbach wins the toss and decides to have a bat and Rory Burns is run out at the non-striker's end from the first ball of the match. It's a long way to go not to face a ball.

Surrey wobble further but Will Jacks comes in and shows everybody what a massive talent he is, playing some wonderful shots and moving to his first T20 fifty by driving Jamie Overton over extra cover for six.

At the other end, Rikki Clarke eases a couple into the car park but Overton and Max Waller bowl really well and Somerset restrict Surrey to a below par 176-9.

My interval is spent watching the greatest unveiling of a sportsman I've ever seen. Former Arsenal midfielder Santi Cazorla announces his arrival back at Villarreal by emerging from a smoking giant Liebig condenser, aided by a magician. We need to introduce that into our transfer window. Gareth Bale emerging from a steaming kettle aided by Bobby Davro would do for me.

Back in Taunton, Surrey pick up early Somerset wickets and Rikki Clarke takes a stunning catch at extra cover. Earlier in the game, Jerome Taylor had taken a 'worldy' of a catch but this from Clarke is just as good.

Surrey are right in the game but Peter Trego takes it away from them with a brilliant innings. Trego is a marvellous cricketer and quite rightly a cult hero at Taunton.

At the other end, Corey Anderson launches some big shots and, despite a brilliant catch by Jacks on the boundary, Somerset are always in control of the chase. They hit the winning runs off the first ball of the final over and secure a deserved four-wicket victory.

Nip across to do some post-match interviews by the dugouts and chat to Will Jacks, who agrees that Surrey were below par with the bat. They now probably have to win their final three games to make the quarter-finals.

Back in Tysoe, I head from Taunton back to Kent. India were all out for 107 at Lord's so I will get to see Pope bat tomorrow, which will be quite special.

My mood darkens slightly at 10pm as I'm diverted through some villages near Stonehenge. Not ideal and means I don't get to Mum's until 2am. One last task before I go to bed: check my regulation chinos and blazer are ready for Lord's in nine hours' time. Satisfied with their condition, I head to bed to get some sleep.

*

SATURDAY 11 AUGUST

The alarm call after four hours' kip is not welcome until the realisation enters my fuddled brain that I am off to Lord's for a day of Test cricket.

I jump out of bed, dress in the regulation clothes I had checked the previous night and make my way to the station. It is a glorious day and I board the 6.45am from Borough Green to Victoria full of the joys of summer. Before the next stop, I'm fast asleep and wake up at Victoria with no idea where I am.

Stumble to the underground and am just about awake by the time we reach Marylebone. I take the walk up Lisson Grove and find a bench outside the ground where I sit and watch the world go by.

The last time I came to Lord's but not for work to watch a day of cricket was some 25 years ago, with Dad. In fact, it was the 1993 Ashes on the Saturday when Mike Gatting ran Mike Atherton out on 99. Dad and I had a smashing day in the grandstand – brings back some great memories.

The buzz of a Saturday at the Test match is always special and at 10.15am I meet my best mate Jeremy Morris at the Grace Gates. We have always wanted to do a day of Test cricket together at Lord's and, thanks to Jeremy's generosity, today is the day. We are meeting another old friend, Simon Pennington, and it is wonderful to see them both.

We find our seats in the Tavern Stand and take a wander around Lord's, soaking up the atmosphere before the start of play. I must admit that the daydream of playing for England in a Test match starts up again. Very sad at 44.

However, as I settle into my seat with a lukewarm coffee and the sun shining, life is very good.

As the England openers settle in the middle, conversation turns to children, home extensions and swimming techniques. All that stops when Cook and Jennings are both dismissed, meaning Ollie Pope is making his way to the middle on his Test debut.

Now, I could sit and write all that romantic rubbish about "the crowd going quiet", "being on the edge of my seat" and "an overwhelming sense of pride coming over me as Ollie emerged from the pavilion" – but there was none of that for two very distinct reasons. I knew Ollie would be fine and I desperately needed a wee.

The biggest compliment I can give him is that his first walk to the middle in a Test match is about the only thing that would have kept me in my seat; legs firmly crossed.

Even walking to the middle, he looked relaxed and right at home. When he whipped his second ball from Ishant Sharma to the square leg boundary, you could feel the whole ground relax, apart from me because I feared it would cause an embarrassing accident.

Ollie played a very assured innings and watching him on his Test debut was very special – albeit agonising when a couple of times I wasn't sure I'd make it out unscathed. When he went lbw for 28 I have never moved so quickly! I literally leapt from my seat, sprinted in my chinos to the nearest toilet and the relief – well, words can't describe it. Wetting myself during Ollie's Test debut had not been part of the script, and I will never tell him this but there was a little part of me that was delighted when he was out because I knew I wasn't going to have an accident. God only knows what would have happened if he had got a hundred. My regulation chinos may never have recovered.

The rest of the day was spent in the best company watching Chris Woakes score his maiden Test century. He played brilliantly, and it was lovely to watch him bat with Jonny Bairstow while eating sausage rolls, drinking warm lager and listening to a gentleman on my right providing technical advice to the batsmen all afternoon.

The icing on the cake was seeing Sam Curran have a bat before bad light brought an early end to proceedings.

What a day. At Lord's, with friends, watching two Surrey youngsters do their stuff with the sun shining. Not sure it gets better than that.

Walk back to Marylebone and make an uneventful return to Kent, where Mum very kindly picks me up from the station. Spend the evening watching the highlights. It always looks very different on the telly.

Head to bed to get some much-needed sleep before an early start tomorrow for a must-win T20 game against Gloucestershire. Well batted Ollie.

✳

SUNDAY 12 AUGUST

Up early. Run, coffee, Tysoe, Bristol.

TMS soundtracks me all the way to Bath before Surrey Academy director Gareth Townsend (GT) comes on the wireless being interviewed during a rain break. GT is brilliant fellow who has done an amazing job at the Academy. It might be Ollie and Sam making all the headlines at the moment, but GT has also seen the likes of Roy, Virdi, Patel, Jacks, Ansari, Spriegel and Sciver come through the Academy and he deserves a huge amount of credit.

The interview is very good, and I send him a text saying I can't believe he got on *TMS* before me! GT has done quite a few games with me as an expert summariser and not only is he a brilliant Academy director, he can, at times and if the wind is in the right direction, be a very funny man.

In the commentary box I am lifted by the arrival of Bob Hunt from BBC Bristol, the gentleman who was an extra in *Casualty*. Sadly, the weather is not great, persistent drizzle being the order of the day, and we are keeping everything crossed it disappears, so we can get on with the game.

Decide to pass the time by sitting in reception watching a bit of the Liverpool v West Ham game on TV. I am wearing my glasses and, as has been said before, I apparently look a bit like Liverpool manager Jûrgen Klopp. This is proven once again when a group of men walk past and say: "Shouldn't you be at the game, Jûrgen?!"

After that I decide to leave the football and look outside. I am greeted with dry weather and the covers coming off! The groundstaff work tirelessly to get everything dry and, miraculously, we are going to get away on time.

The hosts bat first but Surrey bowl very well and Gloucestershire are dependent on an excellent 50 from one of my favourite cricketers, Kieran Noema-Barnett (so laid back he is almost horizontal) to get them up to 174-6.

During the Gloucestershire innings I have to keep nipping down two flights of steps to do updates for BBC London from a corporate box. This is where the ISDN unit is housed, and I feel slightly guilty sat on my own at a big table with very comfy seats doing my updates. There is a TV with the Test match on and Stuart Broad is having one of his purple patches with the ball; it looks like the Test could be done and dusted today.

Surrey lose Jason Roy and Rory Burns early in their chase, but Will Jacks deposits a delivery straight into the windscreen of a BMW in the car park. This causes Bob Hunt to have palpitations because his car is next to the BMW! Quite tricky to move your car during a radio commentary.

Anyway, Surrey seem very much in control of the chase when Rikki Clarke and Ben Foakes get together, and it seems inevitable that they are going to secure a vital two points.

But Clarke is dismissed for 33 and Foakes goes in the next over for 59. Surrey's chase falls away and Gloucestershire strangle the innings. As the sun finally comes out, Ryan Higgins bowls a very good final over and Surrey cannot find the boundary as the hosts run out winners by five runs.

Bob Hunt is quite rightly delighted because this means Gloucestershire have secured their quarter-final place. For Surrey, the maths is suddenly against them and they now have to win their final two games and hope other results go their way.

Interview a disappointed Ben Foakes, who says that was a game Surrey should have won – and then an amazing thing happens. A gentleman I have never met introduces himself as a long-lost relative of mine. Who would have thought that sort of meeting would occur at the boundary rope in Bristol?

Back into Tysoe and off to Cardiff, where I listen to *TMS* dissecting England's win over India, which was achieved this afternoon after the visitors were rolled over at Lord's.

Arrive home and it is lovely to see my girls. Isabelle is very excited because she has mastered 'the floss' a dance move that has been seen at T20 matches this season.

Head to bed and fall asleep very quickly. Done a few miles in the last three days and there are a few more to come next week.

MONDAY 13 AUGUST

The new week starts with paperwork and a trip to the gym. Mrs Church then has to head out for an emergency dentist's appointment, but when she returns – complete with new filling – we head to the shops to buy Isabelle some new trainers.

I never realised there was such a selection for eight-year-olds and, two hours later, a decision is thankfully made.

Back at home I fall asleep in the garden and then head back to the gym with Isabelle, where we go for a swim.

After a busy few days it is nice to get a proper day at home and the evening is spent watching Isabelle model her new trainers.

*

TUESDAY 14 AUGUST

Today has been spent in the car.

There is an early departure to deliver Isabelle down to Sussex to stay with her best friend for a few days and we divert the journey to stop off at Mum's for a few hours, so she can spend some time with Isabelle.

We then drive on to Sussex where I drop Isabelle off with her friend, say an emotional goodbye, although Issy doesn't notice because she is too busy running around like a lunatic with her friend.

I drive back to Mum's and, on the way, hear the news that Ben Stokes has been found not guilty of affray after the incident outside a Bristol nightclub last September. It's not for me to get into but, in retrospect, a couple of quiet beers and a good book might have been a more sensible way to spend the evening after an ODI?

Back at Mum's I do some preparation for tomorrow's latest 'must win game', this time against Hampshire. Finch is back, which is good news for Surrey, because he puts the fear of God into the opposition.

My phone also tells me that Surrey have signed Jordan Clark from Lancashire. Another very shrewd acquisition – he is a terrific all-round cricketer and another one for the long-term.

End the day with the classic combination of a long run and an early night. The old legs are beginning to feel a little older. There are seven weeks to until I set off on my challenge. Nervous now.

*

WEDNESDAY 15 AUGUST

Early start and immediate relief as I head out for a run – the sun is shining, and my legs are still working!

Head to the station to get the train up to London. Fall asleep somewhere near Otford and seem to be dribbling down my shirt when I wake up at Victoria. Not ideal.

Rebuild the commentary box at The Oval before heading off for a meeting with Maggie Blanks, the CEO of the Pancreatic Cancer Research Fund, about the run. Embarrassingly, I have left all my trousers in Cardiff so have to turn up to a very nice hotel in shorts, feeling very under-dressed.

However, despite my attire it's a great meeting and everything is going in the right direction with the run. Zoom back to The Oval to meet Kevan James for tonight's game against Hampshire and get a very nice surprise when I see Jordan Clarke having his coffee in the press box.

Not Jordan Clark of Lancashire and soon-to-be Surrey, but BBC Solent's Jordan Clarke, who I think is one of the most talented young broadcasters around. We also have Emily Windsor with us tonight in the commentary box. Emily has just signed her first professional contract with the Southern Vipers in the Kia Super League and it is great to have her expertise with us.

Nip over to the pavilion for a catch-up with Roy and Burns. Both are in good form and very kindly agree to host a table at my 'End of Run' dinner. Also getting one of Jason's England ODI shirts for the auction, so it was a very worthwhile trip to the other side of the ground.

The three men and a lady radio team head to the commentary box as Hampshire win the toss and decide to bowl first. I immediately cause chaos on air by talking about this Thursday night game. People are quick to point that it is, in fact, Wednesday, and a gentleman tweets me to say that he has just had a massive panic because he was meant to be in Cornwall on Thursday and thought he had missed his trip. Sorry.

Hampshire have had a terrible T20 campaign and it shows with their batting. Surrey bowl well but, on a slow pitch, the visitors never get going and post just 133-7.

Mad dash down to the press room for a coffee in the interval and straight back on air as Surrey's chase starts badly with Jason Roy bowled first ball (more on that later). They are in a spot of bother at 25-2 but Aaron Finch shows why Surrey missed him when he was away. An aspect of his game he doesn't receive enough credit for is that he is a very intelligent batsman and he reacts very quickly to the situation in front of him.

He works hard for his runs and, alongside Nic Maddinson, steers Surrey's chase through some choppy waters and plays a T20 knock for the purist. He still manages to make 67* off just 57 balls and it's an innings that takes Surrey over the line in the 15th over and continues his remarkable T20 run-scoring this summer.

A must-win game for Surrey has been won and Jade Dernbach seems satisfied with the performance in his post-match interview.

I begin my journey back to Kent by making few friends on the London Underground with four big bags of broadcasting equipment (a particular hold-up is created on the escalator down to the Victoria Line at Vauxhall; thanks to everyone for their constructive advice) and it something of a relief to get the 11.18 from Victoria back to Kent.

Back to Mum's by 12.30 and celebrate completing the journey unscathed with a brand-new pot of peanut butter and Sky Sports News.

Tomorrow, all roads lead to Cardiff because that's where I live – and coincidentally Surrey are playing Glamorgan there on Friday night, in a must-win game.

✳

THURSDAY 16 AUGUST

Guess what? I get up early for a run and then catch up with Mum on a few bits and pieces. She is off to Suffolk for a few days.

Pack up Tysoe and head to Cardiff. It's a pretty good journey and I arrive back in the capital of Wales by mid-afternoon.

Wait for Mrs Church to get home and then head to The Vale where Surrey are staying tonight ahead of the Glamorgan game.

Spend a very nice evening watching Kent v Somerset on the telly with some of the squad and learn some bad news for poor Scott Borthwick, who has broken his wrist batting in the nets ahead of the game last night. His season is over, and I really feel for him. He's a brilliant cricketer and a terrific bloke. I think he would have scored a huge amount of runs in the last six Championship games of the season.

Very excited because tomorrow morning I am taking on the national course at The Vale, alongside Mark Stoneman and Joel Pope. Most of the squad will be out there with their clubs in the morning and I head home having organised to be back for breakfast at 7.30am.

Head home, check my clubs and make sure I have got plenty of balls in the bottom of my bag. Fall asleep dreaming of shooting the course record thanks to my 'Johnny Miller classic', which last time proved to have magical golfing properties.

FRIDAY 17 AUGUST

Back to The Vale at 7.30am and have a nice catch up with Tom Curran over breakfast. Messrs. Dernbach, Clarke, Finch, Jacks, van den Bergh and Stoneman all arrive for breakfast looking like they've just stepped off the pages of *Golf Monthly* and I feel slightly under-dressed in my chinos, polo shirt and tank top.

Head to the pro shop with Stoneman and Pope and am presented with a key. I thought it was for a locker, but Rikki Clarke informs me it is for the golf buggy. The course is so long that we need transport to get around it!

Slightly concerned that my trusty three iron might not be enough club to get me round.

Drive to the first tee and a wonderful morning commences. The sun is shining, the company is fantastic and the golf from me is not too bad. I realise that driving a buggy means club selection is key before playing your shot because you leave your bag on the buggy.

As I slowly smash the ball left and right down the fairway, Stoneman kindly weaves the buggy around The Vale, but it still doesn't prevent me from leaving two of my clubs on the course.

Pope and Stoneman play very well, and I basically follow them round, but it is a hugely enjoyable morning.

As we reach the tenth, news is given to me that Jason Roy will miss tonight's game with a facial injury. To cut a short story even shorter, after being out against Hampshire on Wednesday, Jason went back to the dressing room, threw his bat down only for it to bounce straight up and whack him in the face. Not good for Jason or Surrey, and also very unlucky!

Quick coffee after golf and then home for a change of clothes. Take the short trip to Sophia Gardens. As this is a local game for me, I park Tysoe in the bowls club and take a quick stroll into town to pay our gas bill.

I get a shock when I see a dinosaur's head poking out of a tree along the Taff Trail. Either I have discovered the biggest news story in a million years or there is a dinosaur exhibition in Bute Park. The latter proves to be the case. Still, in the modern way I take to Twitter to break the spotting of a dinosaur in a hilarious manner.

Back at Sophia Gardens I make my way up to the media centre, where tonight I am being joined by one of the great cricket journalists and broadcasters, Edward Bevan. He has been covering cricket, Glamorgan in particular, for over 40 years. When I first started this job,he was always generous with his time and it will be lovely to be back on air with him.

The view from the commentary boxes at Sophia Gardens is fantastic. Slap-bang behind the arm at the Cathedral Road End, there is really isn't any excuse for getting things wrong! That doesn't stop me though and now as most games are live streamed for people to watch, it certainly improves your commentary.

Nick Webb from BBC Wales arrives but there is a problem. It is raining for this must-win game. Nick and I discuss what would happen if the rain continues. Both sides want to play, and we conclude this could be a five-over thrash.

Edward Bevan is giving a weather update in Welsh (no idea what he is saying) but then the rain stops. Hallelujah! There is nothing worse for everybody than sitting around hoping to get a game in. The groundstaff work their magic and we hear it is a 7pm start with no overs lost.

Glamorgan win the toss and, surprisingly, decide to bat with bad weather about. Edward and I settle into the commentary and I pull out all the clichés in the first five minutes.

"Must-win game", "destiny not in their own hands", "must concentrate on this game and not worry about what is happening elsewhere," are all on the table early on. The simple equation is that whoever wins this then has to hope Middlesex beat Sussex to get a place in the quarter-finals.

In gloomy and damp conditions, Surrey bowl extremely well and Glamorgan never really get going. Batsmen get in and then get out, but news reaches us from Hove that Sussex are smashing Middlesex to all parts. It looks like whatever happens here might be academic, plus the drizzle returns at the back end of the Glamorgan innings as the hosts post 183-8 off their 20 overs.

The rain is getting heavier and the thought around the press box is that we might not get back out there because Surrey cannot start their chase in these conditions.

Meanwhile at Hove, Sussex have posted 215-5, but Paul Stirling is off to a flyer and things on the south coast are getting interesting. The drizzle has got lighter and the players are heading back to the middle. Duckworth, Lewis and Stern are going to play their part, which is always bad news because I get handed the DLS scoresheet, a piece of paper with loads of numbers on it. I may as well be handed a piece of paper in Spanish for all the good it does me.

What I do know is we have to have five overs of the Surrey chase to officially have a game. Finch and Burns obviously understand what it says on the piece of paper because they go on the attack as the rain gets heavier and heavier. After five overs Surrey are 60-0 and, according to Edward – who understands the sheet – Surrey need to be on 36. At the end of the fifth, the umpires take the players off as the rain gets heavier and Surrey have done their job because we won't get out here again, meaning Surrey have won on DLS.

There is then a bizarre hour of watching the Middlesex scorecard on a laptop to see if they can do Surrey a favour. For a few minutes it looks like they might, but they then have an almighty collapse and Sussex win, meaning they are through to the quarters at Surrey's expense.

It has all been a bit of an anti-climax and I make my way to the pavilion for interviews. Jade Dernbach is very sensible with his thoughts about tonight. Really, it has been losses elsewhere in the group stage that have done for Surrey and that is why they are out of the competition.

I have a nice chat with Nic Maddinson, as his stay with Surrey has come to an end. He says he has really enjoyed his time with the club and he has certainly made an impact. But this is the nature of modern cricket. Nic heads off to his next port of call as the season keeps rolling on, but hopefully Surrey will see him again.

Send interviews back to the BBC, say goodbye to Edward Bevan and Nick Webb and make my way back to the bowls club.

And now for the biggest irony. I am ten minutes from home but tonight it is back to Kent for me! Mum is away, my girls will be in bed and there is a floodlit County Championship game starting at The Oval on Sunday.

So off down the M4 Tysoe and I go again, arriving in Kent at 2am. Too tired even for peanut butter and toast and go straight to bed to get some much-needed kip.

SATURDAY 18 AUGUST

A lovely quiet day. Up for a run and then breakfast and paperwork. Head to the TV to watch the opening session of the Trent Bridge Test.

The big news is that Ben Stokes returns to the side in place of Sam. I feel for Sam. He has done nothing wrong and I am sure he will be really disappointed. He will play huge amounts of international cricket but sometimes life just isn't fair. Lots of chat about the decision and the morning in Nottingham is pretty even as England pick up a couple of wickets but Kohli is not out at lunch, when I head out for another run.

Return for a shower and then fall asleep in front of the afternoon session. Awake to enjoy an hour of Kohli batting until he is undone by Adil Rashid on 97. India are still having a great day, underlined by Rishabh Pant dancing down the track and lofting Rashid for six on his debut. Maverick.

Head out for a third run. This is getting silly, but I reward myself with spaghetti bolognese and *The Last Jedi*, which is a much better film on a second viewing (I walked out of the cinema in protest on my first viewing at the moment Princess Leia flew across space on her own using the Force).

Head to bed and see Surrey have announced the squad for tomorrow's game. Sam Curran is back but the release confirms that Borthwick's wrist injury is indeed season-ending. It's really sad news for Badger, who has played a big part for Surrey up to this point.

Not sure what time to get up in the morning, as it's the first floodlit Championship game at The Oval. Will leave it to the cricketing gods and see what happens.

SUNDAY 19 AUGUST

Wide awake at 6am so go for a run, come back, have breakfast and am off in Tysoe to The Oval at 8am.

Because it's a Sunday I arrive at the ground an hour later. Only the four and a half hours to kill then.

Set up the commentary box and wander off for a coffee. I am considering giving up coffee because I drink far too much, but I'm still looking for a good alternative. I gave up smoking 12 years ago and am trying not to eat cake at the moment, so the alternatives are few and far between.

Anyway, sit and have a large coffee at the Pret on Vauxhall Bridge. It's very peaceful on a Sunday morning and on arrival back at The Oval I am greeted by the wonderful sight of BBC Manchester's Scott Read and BBC Five Live's Kevin Howells in the commentary box.

We are all in slight confusion with the 1.30pm start and decide it is a bit like a foreign holiday with a time difference. It will just take a couple of days to get used to it.

While we are on the subject, my view on floodlit Championship cricket in this country is that it's pointless. I am sure it was introduced to get players ready for floodlit Test cricket. Well, we don't seem to be having any of that in this country now. And the experiment to see whether or not it brings more spectators in after 6pm certainly didn't work last year.

In fact, it will be fascinating to see whether more spectators come after 6pm to watch this game, because everything is on its side. The weather is good. It's easy to get to the ground. Two excellent sides are going head to head. If it doesn't work here over the next four days, then my theory of pointlessness will be proven correct.

The coin goes up at 1pm and Surrey win the toss and bat. I welcome listeners on the wireless by saying, "a very good morning", then realise it's the afternoon and totally lose my train of thought. This could be a long four days and nights – thank goodness Scott Read is here to pick up the pieces.

Rory Burns falls early, which is a surprise with the way he has been playing this season, and after a nice start Mark Stoneman gets a good one from Tom Bailey and Surrey are suddenly two down.

The peace and tranquillity of the press box is disturbed by the arrival of Norcross. He bursts through the door like a rampaging colossus and there is a palpable shock to see him in a quiet shirt and linen suit. He informs us that he is on 'typing duty' this week for Cricinfo and he has a keen eye on the Test match because he is commentating for *TMS* on the final two Tests.

For the first time in a long while, Surrey do not bat well in the morning session. Arun Harinath goes early, and it's left to Ben Foakes and Aaron Finch to steady the ship. But Finch goes just before the break and Surrey find themselves five down and in danger of not scoring enough first innings runs.

The tea break is very confusing. It feels like the lunch break but it's actually 3.30pm and everyone else in the country is actually having tea, but it's lunch here. If that makes no sense it's meant that way, just like playing Championship cricket under floodlights.

Anyway, after a slice of Victoria sponge and a coffee, balance is restored and Scott Read keeps me calm as the afternoon / early evening session starts.

Sam Curran looks every bit the Test batsman, which of course he is, but Surrey regularly lose wickets and they are indebted to Jade Dernbach's 31 and Morne Morkel's 23 to get them up to and over 200.

Surrey are eventually all out for 208 and we then have the late 'snack break'. I am so confused with the timings that I keep talking, thinking it's the change of innings, but 40 minutes later realise I've missed the pies on offer downstairs. The players are now facing a 43-over final session and Lancashire will have to bat under lights. It will be very interesting to see how the pink ball behaves.

Jade Dernbach makes an early breakthrough and Morne Morkel is introduced into the attack and immediately takes a couple of quick wickets. The lights come on and the ground looks spectacular, but I'm not sure any more spectators have come in after 6pm.

The cricket is fascinating, even though it dawns on the commentary box that the *Antiques Roadshow* is currently on and being missed. A partnership develops between Dane Vilas and Shivnarine Chanderpaul but Sam Curran dismisses Vilas and Rikki Clarke then takes two late wickets, as the moon comes out and Lancashire finish six down.

A 9.45pm finish seems a little late and I feel like I've got jetlag. Make my way to the other end of the ground and proceed to ask coach Di Venuto three of the most muddled questions in interview history. To say I'm all over the shop would be an understatement and I realise it is too late for 'hard-hitting' questions.

Send my disastrous interview back to the BBC and leave the ground at 10.15pm. I get back to Mum's at midnight and catch up with the Test match. India were all out for 329 and England lost wickets regularly to be knocked over for 161. Ollie was unlucky to be caught down the legside, but to be rolled over in 38.2 overs is a worry.

Bed at 1am. Not sure if floodlit Championship cricket is good for your health.

MONDAY 20 AUGUST

Up at 6.30am for a run before a quick shower and drive to the station. Have decided to let the train take the strain for the next couple of days and this seems like a very wise decision when I comfortably sit with a coffee and a paper in an empty carriage.

It does not seem such a wise decision two stops later when everyone in Bromley seemingly gets on the train and I am very grateful to have a seat.

Arrive at Victoria and decide to walk to the ground. It's all very leisurely with the 1.30pm start and I walk through the gates of The Oval at 11am.

Have a cup of coffee in the commentary box with Kevin Howells and Scott Read and then settle into the opening session of the second day. Lancashire start the day confidently, in particular Josh Bohannon on his Championship debut. He looked an extremely good player last night and he picks up where he left off during the first session of the day.

Commentary is proving to be a real joy with Howells and Read. Norcross, still in his 'typing clothes', arrives just in time for the back end of lunch. Timing is everything.

Surrey make the breakthrough after an hour of play when Rory Burns runs out Chanderpaul with Lancashire still 24 runs away from 200. Bohannon continues to play extremely well and moves to a 50 on debut. We all agree on commentary that Lancashire have unearthed a good'un in Bohannon.

Discussions on air also move onto England who are having another tough day against India. Amazing the difference a week makes.

Bohannon eventually falls for 52 to Amar Virdi and Lancashire are all out for 247, a lead of 36 runs.

During the first break of the day, I get overexcited when it emerges that Scott Read may need company for Lancashire's T20 quarter final on Thursday. He is just waiting to see if he can do a joint commentary with BBC Kent, but if not, I can come off the bench. Immediately ring Mrs Church to get my pass for Thursday.

Also, a huge thing happens in the break. As I mentioned, I've been trying to give up coffee and I mention this to Steve, the lovely gentleman who looks after us in the press box at The Oval. Steve immediately jumps into his 'box of teas' and produces something called 'black tea chai'. He pops a bag in a cup of hot water, leaves it to brew for three or four minutes and then hands the cup to me. It is a revelation. I cannot get enough of 'black tea chai' and go back on air with a spring in my step. The only problem is that this new drink also goes through my system very quickly and ten minutes later I'm rushing to the loo.

More importantly than my use of the toilet and getting a pass from Mrs Church, Aaron Finch is awarded his First XI cap. He has been brilliant over the last couple of years for Surrey and you can see how much it means to him to get his 'Brown Cap'.

Back out in the middle, Surrey have some work to do under the lights. Rory Burns once again leads from the front as he continues his fantastic form this season. He doesn't often miss out twice and again today, he plays exceptionally well. Surrey get their noses in front until Bohannon's game gets even better when he bowls Burns late in the day (8.25pm to be precise).

Surrey have a lead at stumps, but the game is delicately poised and after an interview with Amar Virdi at the close I head for a chicken supper withKevin Howells, Scott Read and a very talented young journalist called Bradley Adams.

Tucking into my chicken wings, I have an inspirational thought. During the run, I am going to need to eat so why not see if this very famous chicken eatery will provide me with chicken and rice every night? Leave my details for the manager but my excitement is diminished slightly when Scott Read points out they might want me to run in a chicken costume.

The train home involves listening to a young lady give a ball-by-ball account of her date to her friend on the phone. By the time we reach my stop, it is clear she won't be seeing the poor lad again.

Catch up on Test match highlights. India have declared on 352/7, leaving England two days to bat and score the small matter of 520 to win the game. As the experts say, "it will be a hell of a win from here."

✳

TUESDAY 21 AUGUST

Awake feeling refuelled after last night's chicken dinner. Run, shower and then head back to the station.

The train journey to Victoria is entirely devoid of phone calls about first dates, which is a relief.

On my way into the ground I pop into a couple of well-known supermarkets to look for 'black tea chai'. The only response I get is being asked whether that's the tea you don't put milk in? It seems like black tea chai is very hard to get hold of – like liquid gold apparently.

Arrive at the ground to find England are already four down. Ollie Pope goes for 16, but the pundits are doing their usual trick of forensically taking his technique apart. Ollie is a sensible lad and will just listen to the people who matter, not those who have hardly seen him bat until the last fortnight.

Have a coffee and catch-up with Steve Howes and, as always, the world is put to rights quite rapidly. Very kindly his brother, who is a shirt printer, agrees to do my shirts for the run. What a family the Howes are.

I also receive the fantastic news that Miles Jupp can, in principle, attend the dinner at the end of the run. I am a huge fan of Miles and very touched he would consider attending, amongst his incredibly busy schedule. Miles is a massive cricket fan and is one of the funniest people you could ever wish to meet. It would be a huge honour to have him there.

Wandering back to the commentary box, I have a catch-up with Sam Curran. He is obviously disappointed not to be playing in the Test match, but as always, his attitude is spot on. I wish I had his maturity at 20.

When I reach the Brian Johnston Broadcast Centre, Kevin Howells and Scott Read are gearing up for a day of commentary. I still cannot get used to the fact that all the other games have had a session before we have even started. We all agree that the first hour of the first session in the afternoon will be crucial (even though it doesn't really roll off the tongue).

The good news is that the sun is making an appearance after disappearing for a couple of days.

Well, the first hour belongs to Lancashire. Surrey do extend their lead, but they regularly lose wickets and when Jade Dernbach and Morne Morkel come together, the lead is only 218 and there is still a huge amount of time left in the game. But Dernbach and Morkel bat really well, with Jade in particular playing some handsome shots.

They put on a crucial 51 runs and when Amar Virdi is bowled first ball, Dernbach is 31* and Lancashire need 271 to win the game. Those runs from Dernbach could be key.

Back at the Test match, Jos Buttler and Ben Stokes are getting their heads down against a rampant India.

In our commentary box we are beginning to realise we have a pretty special game on our hands as Alex Davies gets Lancashire's run chase off to a flyer. He cover drives Morne Morkel for six and the game takes another twist. This is a huge match for both sides. Surrey are looking to extend their lead at the top of the table and Lancashire are looking to drag themselves off the foot of it.

Surrey lose Dernbach after one over with a groin strain he picked up bowling earlier in the match. Jade has been exceptional with the new ball this summer and Surrey will now have to try and win the game a bowler light.

The Lancashire openers put on 45 for the first wicket but Amar Virdi makes the breakthrough just before the 'late snack' break when he has Davies very well caught by Will Jacks at short leg for 35.

During the break, I am delighted to welcome David Quintrell and Josh McDonald into the commentary box. David was my Dad's financial adviser for a number of years and Josh works with David and is also a Surrey member. They both work for Brewin Dolphin, who have kindly agreed to sponsor my run and it is really nice to have them in the box.

It was an annual ritual that Dad and David would come to a day at the cricket, have lunch and then come up to the commentary box. It is very nice that David and Josh are continuing that tradition.

Back out in the middle, Surrey take a couple of quick wickets after the break and, when Amar Virdi gets rid of Shivnarine Chanderpaul, Lancashire suddenly find themselves 104-4. Rob Jones is playing nicely but he falls to the Virdi/Jacks combination for 48 and Surrey are in a good position. The lights are coming on and there is talk of the game being over tonight.

But Bohannon and Croft bat extremely well in tough conditions and get the visitors to stumps five down, setting up a brilliant final day. Surrey will need five more wickets and Lancashire 94 more runs.

This is a hell of an advertisement for county cricket. It's just a shame that with everything going for it, the crowd hasn't picked up after 6pm, even with Surrey offering free entry. We would have had exactly the same game if we had started at 11am and used a red ball. I think we have just watched the last session of floodlit Championship cricket in this country.

Set off to the station and catch the 9.30 train. A quiet journey back and get home to see Mum, who has just got back from Suffolk.

Take a quick look at the Test match highlights and Jos Buttler bats brilliantly as he goes to his maiden Test match hundred. England close nine wickets down, so tomorrow India will need just one wicket to win. It could be a very quick day at Trent Bridge.

Take to my bed as I've got an early start tomorrow for a meeting with David and Josh. I only left them two hours ago, but important business needs to be discussed (none of which I understand, but I do a 'knowing nod' quite brilliantly).

✳

WEDNESDAY 22 AUGUST

It's an early departure and as I stand on the platform waiting for the train at 7am I realise how little I miss commuting every day to London. Five years of standing, waiting for the train was utterly soul-destroying. I found myself becoming one of the most irritable individuals, constantly put in a bad mood by the sight of fellow commuters. I'm sure they were all lovely people, but they became the enemy who must be defeated on the 6.57 to Victoria.

Today though, my spirits are lifted when I get on the train to be greeted by two spare seats next to a window. I settle myself into my seat and fall fast asleep within a couple of minutes. We pull into Victoria and after recovering my senses I make my way on the tube to Brewin Dolphin; whose offices are near St. Paul's.

There I have a great meeting with David and Josh. We spend five minutes talking 'business' and 30 discussing what might happen today at The Oval.

After that I make my way to the ground to find Scott Read and Kevin Howells already in situ. Scott breaks the news to me that I won't be required in Canterbury tomorrow night because, quite rightly, he is sharing with the legendary Matt Cole from BBC Kent. I console myself with a cup of black tea and then rush to the toilet as once again it goes straight through me.

So, what will happen today? Anything is possible, and it is decided that this could be a pivotal day in the season. With 20 days still remaining, saying this dramatically on air is tricky though! At Taunton, Somerset have picked up regular wickets during the morning session, so it looks as if the team closest to Surrey in the table are going to get a win.

The Test match is already over after 17 balls and the series is poised beautifully at 2-1 with two Tests to go. Norcross, who is still in his typing clothes, is suitably delighted because he is doing the final two games for *TMS*.

1.30 arrives and, with the Test match over, our commentary is also on the network and fingers crossed we have some tension to make it a good listen.

Surrey strive to make an early breakthrough, but overnight batsmen Croft and Bohannon play extremely well. Without any alarms, they get the runs down to 68 required and we have a classic on our hands.

Read and Howells are both extremely calm, unlike Norcross, who is pacing around the commentary box like a floral-shirted novelist, dreaming up his next page-turner.

The breakthrough finally comes when Morne Morkel has Croft caught behind for 43 and then a clever piece of captaincy from Burns sees Bohannon caught in the gully by the captain himself, again off Morkel. Surrey need just two more wickets and Lancashire still need 62 to win.

I then receive a text from Ollie Pope, who is listening on his way back from Trent Bridge. It's lovely to have the young man with us – and you can tell he's nervous just from the tone of his text.

County cricket is the most wonderful of companions and there is another twist waiting for us all. Graham Onions and Tom Bailey get together and play extremely well. They have their moments but get through to tea (lunch, or whatever you want to call it) having added 37 and the players go to the break with Surrey needing two wickets and Lancashire needing 24 runs.

Scott Read and I join Kevin Howells on *Sports Extra* to discuss a number of cricketing issues of the day. I make my feelings about floodlit Championship cricket very clear, but I've been doing that for the past three days. Read, ever the professional, shows all his experience by using the time I'm banging on and moaning to go and fetch some Victoria sponge from the press room. Norcross is still pacing the corridors of the OCS Stand.

After the break, there is a final twist in this drama. Surrey can roll the dice and take the new ball straight after the break. It would seem an obvious thing to do and, with so few runs required, it would be a gamble – but one worth taking.

The players make their way back to the middle and Surrey decide to take the new ball. And then Graham Onions does the thing everyone least expects. He deposits the first delivery from Sam Curran into the OCS Stand for six. Where did that come from?! It is a great shot and means just 18 are required.

But Lancashire have one major hurdle to overcome. Morne Morkel with the new ball. The tension in the commentary box is growing, so much so that I have to make a mad dash to the loo in between overs. Black tea and nerves are not a good combination.

With 15 needed, Morkel bowls Onions for 29 and Norcross virtually collapses in the back of the box, having given up on his typing duties.

When you are in these situations on commentary, you are trying to sound calm but deep down you are absolutely bricking it. "Don't get this wrong, don't get this wrong", the little man on your shoulder is telling you.

Matt Parkinson joins Tom Bailey and they knock off singles before Parkinson edges Sam Curran for four.

This is getting ridiculous. Seven are needed by Lancashire for an incredible win and everyone is gripped by the tension.

Morkel has the ball from the Pavilion End and is bowling to Parkinson. Another boundary now and Lancashire are favourites. Parkinson pushes forward and turns the ball off the face of his bat into the leg side. And in the blink of an eye, Will Jacks takes the most outrageous catch at short leg.

Surrey have won by six runs – the players run off in different directions to celebrate and Norcross rolls around the commentary box floor kicking his legs and punching the air.

I have had the honour of commentating on the last two deliveries and think I managed to satisfy the demands of the little man on my shoulder.

As the players make their way off, Scott Read and I digest what we have just seen. What an advertisement for County Championship cricket and a huge win for Surrey, which makes it six straight now..Morne Morkel was immense, taking 6-57 and when we turn the microphones off we are exhausted. Norcross has stopped rolling around and started typing and Read and I make our way around to the changing rooms to do some interviews.

I really feel for Lancashire, but Surrey have found an answer when they were tested, and the captain is understandably very pleased on interview.

Also have a chat with Aaron Finch, who now heads back to Australia, having kindly signed one of his shirts for me to auction for the run.

The final player I see is Ollie Pope, who got to the ground in time to witness the final two wickets. It's great to see him after his life has changed so much over the last fortnight.

Head back to the commentary box, send the interviews to the BBC and start packing up. Lancashire will now head to Kent for their T20 quarter final in Canterbury and Surrey will have a couple of days off.

Norcross has finished typing and after saying goodbye to Kevin Howells, I head to the pub with Norcross and Scott Read. It has been a smashing few days and after a pint of the finest lager shandy I say my goodbyes and take on the underground.

A quiet journey back to Mum's sees me wander through the door at 9pm. I must admit I'm very tired, but it has been an exhilarating day. Tomorrow I'm driving back to Cardiff for a few days at home, which will be lovely.

Catch up with Mum and then head to bed feeling satisfied that this game has been a job well done.

*

THURSDAY 23 AUGUST

Up early for a run and then pack Tysoe for the drive back to Cardiff. It's an uneventful journey and I arrive home to be greeted by Isabelle and her best friend, who has come to stay for a few days.

After the initial excitement of seeing Daddy has worn off and the girls are back on their iPads, I head to the gym for the second run of the day. My timing is excellent because I just happen to start running as Kent v Lancashire gets underway on the telly. Watch the Kent innings and then head home and listen to the rest of the game on Five Live. Dagnall sounds as if he is stuck in the crowd and that's because he actually is. It's all glamour on the network!

England announce they have included James Vince for the fourth Test at the Ageas Bowl. He was told to go away and score some runs, which is exactly what he's done. He also knows his way to the ground, which is always a bonus.

Lancashire secure their place at T20 Finals Day and after spending a glorious four days with him, I'm pleased for Scott Read, but sad for Matt Cole.

Head to bed, trampolining is on the cards for tomorrow… hooray!

FRIDAY 24 AUGUST

A morning of paperwork followed by a trip to the trampolining centre in Cardiff. The girls bounce around to their hearts content, whilst I have a coffee with Mrs Church.

I have got out of trampolining by coming up with epic story of how it will be bad for my knees, which is not good at this stage of my training (I think I might have overdone it a bit, but it does the trick for now!).

We then spend an exciting hour in Tesco's and I head to the gym. Bang out 15 miles whilst watching Laurie Evans guide Sussex to victory over Durham in the their T20 quarter-final.

Home for pesto pasta bake and then try and put the girls to bed. Fail miserably and we end up watching *The Last Jedi* for the second time this week.

Head to bed wondering if Rey and Kylo Ren might be related and how Chewbacca goes to the toilet in a confined space.

SATURDAY 25 AUGUST

Quiet morning waiting for a man from British Gas to come and look at the boiler. He's a lovely chap who also changes some light fittings for Mrs Church.

Afternoon in the park and then go to the gym and watch Man City draw with Wolves. Man City spent £60m in the last transfer window and Wolves spent £63m, so I suppose City did well to draw 1-1.

Out for a meal with friends in the evening. It's nice to have an evening out and we return to find the girls still up and Granny watching the telly.

Fall asleep watching *Match of the Day*, only to be awaken by Isabelle at 1am, who has an itchy head. Not quite sure how to cure that but after half an hour of scratching we all go back to sleep.

SUNDAY 26 AUGUST

The big news today is that Isabelle has got nits. The poor thing has two hours of her hair being combed with a foul-smelling potion that, if I were a nit, would definitely make me go and find a new home.

Out in the afternoon to buy new school shoes. It's pouring with rain and it seems the whole of Cardiff has descended on the shopping centre. Three hours later, Isabelle has new shoes and I've lost the will to live.

Send Rory Burns a happy birthday text and then go to the gym. A gentle ride on the bike watching Chelsea beat Newcastle and then home for more pesto pasta bake.

A chaotic evening is spent trying to get the girls to bed and end up watching a documentary called *Mind Games* on Sky Sports. It is a brilliant look at the psychology of sport and hearing the thoughts of Mark Ramprakash and Graeme Hick is fascinating. Ramprakash is one of the greatest batsmen I have ever commentated on and it is interesting to hear him say nerves got the better of him in Test match cricket.

Being a sufferer of depression and anxiety myself, it is a fascinating watch and by the time it ends the girls are asleep and I head to bed thinking how too much thinking can cause us not to perform at our best. That's enough to send anyone to sleep!

✳

MONDAY 27 AUGUST

Wake up to the harsh realisation that I start my run five weeks today. Nerves kick in. There is still a huge amount to organise but today is very busy looking after Isabelle and her friend.

Mrs Church decides we need to go to the shops again and I spend a very happy couple of hours in a coffee shop keeping an eye on the Surrey Stars score at the Kia Super League Finals Day in Hove. The Stars win their semi-final just as we leave the shopping centre and head to the park for an afternoon on the swings.

Return home and go straight to the gym. The timing is perfect because I can watch the whole of the Surrey Stars final whilst trundling along on the running machine.

The Stars win, beating Loughborough Lightning to claim the title for the first time. I'm delighted for head coach Richard Bedbrook and as the final wicket falls, I finish my run.

Elsewhere, Somerset beat Nottinghamshire in the last of the quarter-finals. So, the Finals Day line-up is Sussex, Somerset, Lancashire and Worcestershire. Should be a good one in September!

Home for a pasta supper and packing the girls' bags. Isabelle is coming back to Granny's with me tomorrow and is very excited. We seem to be taking enough stuff for a month and I do wonder how much an eight-year-old needs for a week.

Watch a particularly good edition of, *Can't Pay? We'll Take it Away!* on Channel Five and then make my way to bed. It's a day in the car tomorrow.

✳

TUESDAY 28 AUGUST

A successful day in the car. Set off early to take Isabelle's friend back to Sussex and then Isabelle and I make our way to Mum's.

Go for a long run, leaving Isabelle and Granny to have a proper catch-up and I when I get back the Surrey squad for tomorrow's Championship game has been announced. No Borthwick, Roy or Dernbach because of injury and Pope and Sam Curran are both away with England for the fourth Test.

But Dean Elgar has returned for the final five games of the season and that is excellent news. Since his last game for Surrey he has been in Sri Lanka with South Africa for a Test series, England have reached a World Cup semi-final and Ollie Pope has made his England debut.

Watch the first episode of the new series of *Great British Bake Off*. It's all about biscuits tonight and Isabelle feels the standard is excellent. She gets her expertise from me.

Put Isabelle to bed and then have an early night in preparation for the opening day against Nottinghamshire tomorrow. There is a rumour that Barran might be joining us after his month 'resting' in Corfu.

WEDNESDAY 29 AUGUST

5.30am start and drive Tysoe up to The Oval. It's rather nice being back in the old routine. The only thing that is not good is the drop in temperature. Genuinely chilly this morning.

Arrive at the ground and, because it is before 7am, I manoeuvre Tysoe around the inner concourse to park because the gates at the Vauxhall End are locked. It's a real test of my driving skills and I have been known to park with a wheelie bin attached to the back of the car before.

Rebuild the commentary box and then go for a wander. It is raining, and the heatwave feels a long time ago as I huddle in the coffee shop nursing an Americano.

Back to the ground and await the arrival of Dave Bracegirdle of BBC Nottingham. He spent last night at the Amex in Brighton and has now been to all 92 of the current Football League grounds. A tremendous effort.

Today also sees the return of Barran. He has been missed over the last month and the only contact from him has been from a pedalo in the middle of Lake Garda in Italy. Fingers crossed the rest has done him good. It will be lovely to see him.

Surrey name a couple of changes at the toss. Jade Dernbach is not fit so Tom Curran comes in for his first red ball game of the season and with Sam back playing for England, Conor McKerr comes into the side. Conor has worked very hard to get fit and firing and I'm pleased for him that he's back in the side. Will Jacks is also selected. If Sam or Ollie don't make the England team then Conor and Will are the nominated players to drop out when they return to Surrey.

By 11am the rain has stopped but it's still very gloomy when Rory Burns and Samit Patel (Steven Mullaney has a back spasm) make their way to the middle for the toss, which never happens because Notts choose to bowl first.

Settle down in the commentary box and under leaden skies Burns and Stoneman open up for Surrey. We quickly have the first event of the day, as Burns brings up his 1,000th first class run of the summer. It's incredible consistency as this is the fifth consecutive season he has got to that milestone. But he then gets a good one from Luke Fletcher and is dismissed for ten.

Stoneman is playing very well, and Dean Elgar joins him, but conditions are very testing.

Barran comes on air and is straight into his stride with tales of pedalos, ice creams and sandcastles. Elgar departs for ten and is quickly followed by Ryan Patel. Luke Wood is bowling well for Notts but Stoneman is standing firm.

News reaches us that England have picked their XI for the fourth Test. It takes a few minutes to get my head round what I'm seeing. It seems that England are packing their batting with all-rounders and, because of that, Ollie is missing out. It is no reflection on Ollie, but it is a reflection of the muddle that England's batting is in. I just hope they have sat the lad down and told him the right things. Sam is back in the XI (quite rightly) and I'm delighted for him. All this means that Ollie will be back at The Oval tomorrow afternoon and will take over from Will Jacks. I hope England are paying his petrol money.

Back in the middle, Ben Foakes is playing really well and taking the innings by the scruff of the neck. Surrey go to lunch three down and there is great excitement in the press room when an Oriental banquet is served for lunch.

Dave Fulton is back with us this week and, as always, he is looking like Sky Sports' James Bond. Such a smart man.

After lunch, Foakes and Stoneman continue to build their partnership. Stoneman moves to a gutsy 50 but Foakes falls to Wood for 48. Will Jacks comes to the wicket and immediately pulls Wood for six. This lad is a very special talent.

Jacks and Stoneman move Surrey past 200 but Jacks then goes for a stroke laden 48. Rikki Clarke goes for 14 and Surrey are looking like they could be dismissed tonight.

But Stoneman is back to his very best and Tom Curran joins him, looking assured before he takes the most fearful blow to the side of his head from Matt Milnes. Quite rightly, TC is given plenty of time to make sure he's OK to continue but his helmet has seen better days. Tom is fine to carry on but there is a problem. The first replacement helmet brought out doesn't fit. So, Stuart Meaker, twelfth man, is sent back to get another one. Which doesn't fit. So, sensibly, Stuart gathers up as many helmets as he can and brings them all out to the middle. He looks like a hanging basket salesman in a fluorescent tabard, but eventually a suitable helmet is found, and play continues.

Tom shows a huge amount of guts to help Stoneman guide Surrey to stumps. It has been tremendous to see Stoneman bat like this and he ends the day unbeaten on 99. Take Dave Bracegirdle to the Pavilion End for interviews and grab a word with Ben Foakes, who says the dressing room are happy with their efforts.

Start the journey back to Mum's at 7pm and get there at 9pm where I am greeted by Isabelle, who has had a lovely day with Granny. Put Isabelle to bed and by that time it's 10.30 and there's only time for a quick bowl of cereal, a check of the phone and I'm asleep the minute my head hits the pillow.

THURSDAY 30 AUGUST

Alarm goes off at 5.15am and it hurts. I wander around the bedroom like a zombie until finally a shower and a coffee gets me moving.

Tysoe transports me to The Oval, a journey during which I listen to a very interesting discussion about whether video games are dangerous for young people. They certainly were when I was little because I once dropped my ZX Spectrum on my foot and was hobbling for a week.

Upon arrival at the ground I am delighted to report the sun is out and after a brisk walk (difficult to fit runs in this week) it is wonderful to sit outside and watch the world go by with an early brew.

Back to the ground for a quick sleep in the sun on the TV gantry and I'm awoken by the arriving Bracegirdle, who then joins me on the gantry as we both agree it's a very pleasant way to a launch a day.

Johnny Barran arrives, and another day of fascinating cricket is upon us. Down in Southampton, England have won the toss and decided to bat first. Ollie Pope will be on the M3 up to London.

Stoneman makes his way to the middle having been stuck on 99 overnight. You can probably tell by now that I have an awful lot of time for Mark Stoneman and he very much deserves a first century of the summer. During his struggles with the bat, he has never moaned, just got his head down and worked even harder.

It is therefore a lovely moment when, from the third ball of the morning, he lays back to Harry Gurney and cuts him through the off side for four. Every Surrey player is on the balcony and it shows what a hugely popular member of the team he is. It's horrible watching a batsman go through a bad patch – but it is wonderful seeing them come out the other side.

Tom Curran plays very well and together they move Surrey past 300 and into a dominant position. Curran goes for 43 but Stoneman plays magnificently and his hundred is starting to look like it might be doubled up. He goes for 144, but we are then all treated to Amar Virdi reaching his highest first-class score. Together with Conor McKerr, Virdi takes Surrey past 350 and, just before lunch, he goes for 19 as Surrey are all out for 375.

More excitement in the press box as again it is an Oriental banquet for lunch. I pass, not because I don't like sweet and sour chicken, but because Dave Bracegirdle has been suffering some technical problems this morning and some amateur headphone surgery is the order of the day.

The consensus is that Surrey have batted well, and this could be a tough afternoon for Nottinghamshire. That proves to be the case as the Surrey bowlers are magnificent.

Led by Tom Curran, they dismiss Nottinghamshire for 101. Curran takes five wickets and Morkel, McKerr and Clarke are relentless. The visitors have come across Surrey at the top of their game but will be disappointed to have been rolled over so quickly.

Unsurprisingly, the follow on is enforced – and Surrey are bolstered by the arrival of Ollie Pope, who comes out to field after tea in place of Will Jacks.

The bowlers are still fresh but Notts bat better second time around, despite Morkel making the breakthrough, getting rid of Ben Slater.

Down in Southampton, England have collapsed again but Sam is batting brilliantly to salvage the innings. His stock is continuing to rise! I always thought he would take to Test cricket, but this is something else entirely. He is getting England back into the opening day and is looking every inch the quality batsman he is.

Back in London, Rory Burns has introduced spin for the first time as a partnership begins to develop between Libby and Brathwaite. The decision pays off as Virdi traps Libby lbw, bringing Surrey's fantastic day to a close. They are on course for their seventh consecutive Championship win and again it has been a hugely professional performance.

This afternoon's commentary was a joy, not just for the quality of the cricket but due to the fact we were joined by Nottinghamshire's director of cricket, Mick Newell. He's a tremendous man and it's always good to chat to him, especially with Dave Bracegirdle involved. We also welcomed Phil Walker of *Wisden Cricket Monthly*, who is quite rightly extremely excited that his new edition features a world exclusive interview with Virat Kohli. The actual Virat Kohli, not a cardboard cut-out!

A quiet journey back to Mum's and I'm greeted by a very excited Isabelle, who seems to have spent the best part of the day climbing things at the local 'Clip and Climb'.

I get her off to sleep then watch highlights of Sam's innings at Southampton. He is quite brilliant, making 78 quality runs. I then head to bed, wondering if we'll get a full day of cricket tomorrow.

✳

FRIDAY 31 AUGUST

The alarm seems to go off just as I've fallen asleep and after a stumbling attempt in the shower, a quick coffee is just enough to get me into Tysoe and on my way.

Today Five Live are chatting about the extraordinary moment that has happened overnight in the US Open tennis when Nick Kyrgios had seemingly given up in his match, only for the umpire to give him a pep talk. I quite like that and decide that umpires in cricket should be allowed to encourage the players.

"Ump, how is that not out?!"

"Going over the top but you are bowling really well and mustn't give up. Keep bowling like this and I'm sure at some point my finger will go up. Plus, you look really good in that jumper and I love your new haircut!"

"Thanks Ump, I feel much better now."

Arrive at The Oval and you probably know the routine by now. Commentary box, wander, Pret, coffee, world go by, return, TV gantry, sleep, Bracegirdle arrival, Barran arrival, play starts. This is listed chronologically but sometimes the last two items on the list can be swapped around.

Surrey require eight wickets today, but I think they will have to work hard for them. However, those thoughts change as the Surrey quicks are outstanding once again. Morkel takes two early ones and Conor McKerr bowls beautifully.

Barran is in tremendous form today and utters the immortal words: "I sometimes wonder what my career would have been like if I'd worn a helmet". This immediately starts the listeners wondering and some wonderful suggestions are received, using the hashtag #ifidwornahelmet. Not sure he would have won an Oscar, as one listener suggests.

Lunch arrives with Nottinghamshire eight down and Surrey on the brink of another huge victory. Lunch is enjoyed by the assembled press and I engage a wide conversation with the third estate as to whether mushrooms are the most dangerous vegetable. It's that time of the season.

We don't end up broadcasting for long enough to discuss mushrooms on air because Surrey take the two remaining wickets very quickly after lunch and record another innings victory.

It has been another top-class performance and, just as Surrey win, Sam takes the prize wicket of Kohli in Southampton. A high-quality five minutes for Surrey CCC, that.

Interview Tom Curran and Rory Burns, who are really very satisfied. After finishing the interview with Burns I take a quiet walk with him and tell him I hope I don't see him next week because if there is any justice in the world he will be batting for England at The Oval rather than Surrey in Chelmsford.

After sending the interviews back I engage in a thorough clear out and tidy of the commentary box – it will go on loan to BBC World Service during the Test match next week and I have a reputation to maintain. I'm not sure what that reputation is, but at least it's tidy.

Say farewell to Dave Bracegirdle, who will head back to Nottingham a day early, and then spend a wonderfully peaceful couple of hours sat in the Peter May Stand with the sun shining, reading back over some of this diary.

Wander back to Tysoe and bump into Ollie Pope, who is also on his way home. He's obviously disappointed not to be in Southampton but is characteristically sensible about the whole thing. These Surrey 20-year-olds are so mature. I think I can learn a thing or two at 44.

A quiet drive back to Mum's, listening to *TMS*. Norcross is sounding lovely and I actually speak to him, during a break in commentary stints, about Surrey's performance. Arrive at Mum's to an empty house. Half an hour later, Isabelle bursts through the front door having been treated to a McDonald's supper.

Have a quick look at the Test match highlights, where Pujara has struck a brilliant century and India have a slender lead. This could be a classic.

Put Isabelle to bed and then get a text from a friend saying how much they had enjoyed my commentary of Samit Patel's wicket this morning.

Very good, I think and go to check why it was so good. Was it the perfect description? Had I built the scene up consummately? Did I paint the picture like Arlott?

No. When Morkel hit Patel's pad I had shouted: "That's gout!". Oh dear. Not my finest moment and I head to bed with a new career forming in my mind. Medical analysis from the commentary box. Dr. Hilary Jones will be my summariser, although I'm sure Barran could still find a role to play.

✳

Clockwise from top: Floodlit Championship cricket against Lancashire at the Kia Oval; asking Mark Stoneman the tough questions.

Clockwise from top: Mrs Church and Issy; teatime with Norcross.

SURREY V LANCASHIRE

Venue: The Kia Oval, Kennington
Date: 19th, 20th, 21st, 22nd August 2018
Toss: Surrey
Result: Surrey won by 6 runs

Points: Surrey 20; Lancashire 4
Umpires: M Burns, MA Gough
Scorers: PJ Makepeace, C Rimmer, JH Savill

SURREY	1ST INNINGS	R	b	2ND INNINGS	R	b
*RJ Burns	c Croft b Bailey	6	10	b Bohannon	70	139
MD Stoneman	c Jones b Bailey	14	14	c Parkinson b Bailey	16	31
A Harinath	c Vilas b Bailey	1	10	run out (Bailey)	7	33
AJ Finch	c Bailey b Parkinson	43	63	lbw b Onions	32	34
+BT Foakes	c Davies b Mennie	12	25	c Vilas b Mennie	33	115
SM Curran	c Davies b Bailey	40	50	c Vilas b Bailey	31	34
RS Patel	c Croft b Mennie	12	41	b Parkinson	14	60
R Clarke	run out (Hameed)	15	21	lbw b Onions	19	39
M Morkel	c Mennie b Parkinson	23	46	b Onions	29	36
JW Dernbach	c Croft b Bailey	31	39	not out	24	33
GS Virdi	not out	0	1	b Mennie	0	1
Extras	(2 lb, 12 nb)	14		(9 b, 14 lb, 8 nb)	31	
Total	(all out, 52.2 overs)	211		(all out, 91.5 overs)	306	

Fall of wickets: 1-14 (Burns, 2.6 ov), 2-21 (Stoneman, 4.2 ov), 3-28 (Harinath, 8.1 ov), 4-51 (Foakes, 15.3 ov), 5-108 (Finch, 25.1 ov), 6-130 (Curran, 30.5 ov), 7-154 (Clarke, 36.5 ov), 8-155 (Patel, 38.3 ov), 9-211 (Morkel, 51.5 ov), 10-211 (Dernbach, 52.2 ov)
Fall of wickets: 1-35 (Stoneman, 10.5 ov), 2-73 (Harinath, 23.4 ov), 3-114 (Finch, 32.1 ov), 4-162 (Burns, 49.1 ov), 5-204 (Curran, 59.2 ov), 6-226 (Foakes, 70.2 ov), 7-240 (Patel, 77.5 ov), 8-254 (Clarke, 82.2 ov), 9-305 (Morkel, 90.6 ov), 10-306 (Virdi, 91.5 ov)

LANCASHIRE	O	M	R	W	Wd	Nb		O	M	R	W	Wd	Nb
							Bailey	24	5	78	2	-	2
							Onions	24	3	91	3	-	2
							Mennie	15.5	3	39	2	-	-
							Parkinson	23	2	62	1	-	-
							Croft	1	1	0	0	-	-
							Bohannon	4	0	13	1	-	-

LANCASHIRE	1ST INNINGS	R	b	2ND INNINGS	R	b
+AL Davies	c Clarke b Dernbach	0	6	c sub (WG Jacks) b Virdi	35	38
H Hameed	b Morkel	22	41	lbw b Morkel	20	56
RP Jones	c Clarke b Morkel	10	26	c sub (WG Jacks) b Virdi	48	89
*DJ Vilas	c Foakes b Curran	61	88	lbw b Clarke	3	27
S Chanderpaul	run out (Burns)	45	107	c Clarke b Virdi	2	8
SJ Croft	c Finch b Clarke	10	15	c Foakes b Morkel	43	116
MW Parkinson	lbw b Clarke	0	2	(11) c sub (WG Jacks) b Morkel	7	7
JJ Bohannon	lbw b Virdi	52	108	(7) c Burns b Morkel	32	97
JM Mennie	c Foakes b Virdi	26	55	(8) c Foakes b Morkel	1	24
TE Bailey	not out	6	26	(9) not out	20	58
G Onions	c Burns b Patel	4	4	(10) b Morkel	29	46
Extras	(6 b, 1 lb, 4 nb)	11		(4 b, 6 lb, 14 nb)	24	
Total	(all out, 79.2 overs)	247		(all out, 93.1 overs)	264	

Fall of wickets: 1-0 (Davies, 0.6 ov), 2-34 (Jones, 10.4 ov), 3-41 (Hameed, 14.6 ov), 4-114 (Vilas, 32.4 ov), 5-129 (Croft, 37.1 ov), 6-129 (Parkinson, 37.3 ov), 7-176 (Chanderpaul, 55.5 ov), 8-225 (Mennie, 70.2 ov), 9-242 (Bohannon, 78.3 ov), 10-247 (Onions, 79.2 ov)
Fall of wickets: 1-45 (Davies, 11.2 ov), 2-83 (Hameed, 20.1 ov), 3-97 (Vilas, 28.5 ov), 4-104 (Chanderpaul, 31.6 ov), 5-125 (Jones, 39.5 ov), 6-203 (Croft, 70.1 ov), 7-204 (Bohannon, 72.3 ov), 8-209 (Mennie, 76.2 ov), 9-256 (Onions, 91.3 ov), 10-264 (Parkinson, 93.1 ov)

SURREY	O	M	R	W	Wd	Nb		O	M	R	W	Wd	Nb
Dernbach	9.4	2	31	1	-	-	Curran	11	0	49	0	-	1
Curran	17	1	69	1	-	-	Dernbach	1	0	5	0	-	-
Morkel	16	5	42	2	-	1	Morkel	21.1	5	57	6	-	2
Clarke	16.2	7	42	2	-	-	Clarke	21	2	45	1	-	-
Virdi	19	2	54	2	-	1	Virdi	37	8	95	3	-	4
Patel	1.2	0	2	1	-	-	Patel	2	1	3	0	-	-

SURREY V NOTTINGHAMSHIRE

Venue: The Kia Oval, Kennington
Date: 29th, 30th, 31st August 2018
Toss: No toss made
Result: Surrey won by an innings and 125 runs

Points: Surrey 23; Nottinghamshire 3
Umpires: SJ O'Shaughnessy, RT Robinson
Scorers: PJ Makepeace, R Marshall, AJ Rasheed

SURREY	1ST INNINGS	R	b	2ND INNINGS	R	b
*RJ Burns	c Moores b Fletcher	10	29			
MD Stoneman	c Moores b Wood	144	260			
D Elgar	lbw b Gurney	8	24			
RS Patel	c Moores b Wood	0	5			
+BT Foakes	c Patel b Wood	48	74			
WG Jacks[1]	b Milnes	48	87			
R Clarke	lbw b Fletcher	14	26			
TK Curran	c Root b Milnes	43	69			
M Morkel	c Milnes b Gurney	5	7			
C McKerr	not out	19	45			
GS Virdi	b Patel	19	22			
Extras	(5 b, 4 lb, 6 nb, 2 w)	17				
Total	(all out, 107.3 overs)	375				

Fall of wickets: 1-18 (Burns, 8.1 ov), 2-35 (Elgar, 15.2 ov), 3-36 (Patel, 16.2 ov), 4-126 (Foakes, 40.1 ov), 5-204 (Jacks, 63.2 ov), 6-225 (Clarke, 68.4 ov), 7-309 (Curran, 90.2 ov), 8-315 (Morkel, 91.5 ov), 9-340 (Stoneman, 100.6 ov), 10-375 (Virdi, 107.3 ov)

NOTTINGHAMSHIRE	O	M	R	W	Wd	Nb		O	M	R	W	Wd	Nb
Fletcher	23	3	87	2	-	1							
Wood	22	5	66	3	-	1							
Gurney	26	3	101	2	1	1							
Milnes	19	2	76	2	-	-							
Patel	17.3	6	36	1	-	-							

NOTTINGHAMSHIRE	1ST INNINGS	R	b	2ND INNINGS (F/O)	R	b
KC Brathwaite	lbw b Curran	2	15	c Foakes b McKerr	60	149
BT Slater	c Foakes b Curran	9	14	c Clarke b McKerr	21	34
JD Libby	c Patel b Curran	12	24	lbw b Virdi	17	50
*SR Patel	lbw b Morkel	5	5	lbw b Morkel	15	26
WT Root	c Foakes b McKerr	6	13	c Foakes b Morkel	0	1
MH Wessels	c Jacks b McKerr	12	28	c Foakes b McKerr	0	12
+TJ Moores	c Foakes b McKerr	29	59	c Foakes b Curran	20	55
L Wood	c Foakes b Morkel	8	8	c Pope b Morkel	5	14
LJ Fletcher	c Foakes b Curran	9	21	run out (Curran)	1	1
ME Milnes	not out	0	2	not out	3	15
HF Gurney	b Curran	0	2	c Virdi b McKerr	1	10
Extras	(5 b, 1 lb, 2 nb, 1 w)	9		(2 b, 2 lb, 2 nb)	6	
Total	(all out, 31.4 overs)	101		(all out, 61 overs)	149	

Fall of wickets: 1-12 (Slater, 3.6 ov), 2-13 (Brathwaite, 5.2 ov), 3-20 (Patel, 6.3 ov), 4-38 (Libby, 11.3 ov), 5-39 (Root, 12.1 ov), 6-70 (Wessels, 20.5 ov), 7-80 (Wood, 24.3 ov), 8-101 (Moores, 30.4 ov), 9-101 (Fletcher, 31.2 ov), 10-101 (Gurney, 31.4 ov)
Fall of wickets: 1-41 (Slater, 12.5 ov), 2-78 (Libby, 29.3 ov), 3-109 (Patel, 38.2 ov), 4-109 (Root, 38.3 ov), 5-111 (Wessels, 42.3 ov), 6-122 (Brathwaite, 48.4 ov), 7-132 (Wood, 52.6 ov), 8-135 (Fletcher, 54.1 ov), 9-148 (Moores, 59.2 ov), 10-149 (Gurney, 61 ov)

SURREY	O	M	R	W	Wd	Nb		O	M	R	W	Wd	Nb
Morkel	9	2	21	2	-	1	Morkel	17	3	39	3	-	-
Curran	8.4	1	28	5	-	-	Curran	14	4	31	1	-	-
McKerr	7	1	21	3	1	-	McKerr	12	6	26	4	-	-
Clarke	7	2	25	0	-	-	Clarke	12	5	31	0	-	-
							Patel	3	0	9	0	-	1
							Virdi	3	0	9	1	-	-

[1] OJ Pope replaced WG Jacks in Notts 1st innings, 28.0

SEPTEMBER

"Surrey have won their first
Championship title in 16 years"

SATURDAY 1 SEPTEMBER

Even though I don't have to, I wake up at 5.30am. It slowly dawns on me that it's now September. Blimey.

Early breakfast and then do some paperwork waiting for Isabelle to wake up. Today will be spent in the car, taking Issy back to Cardiff. I would like to thank Surrey for winning in three days and making the Church family life a bit easier on this occasion.

Meet Mrs Church at Reading Services, hand Issy over and say goodbye to the girls because Surrey are playing in Chelmsford this week and I'm still staying down at Mum's.

England have lost early wickets in the Test and Moeen Ali came into bat at three, which was a surprise and had a bit of a 'village cricket' feel to it. I can imagine the conversation in the England dressing room now.

"Lads, who fancies batting at three?"

"Nobody? OK Mo, you give it a go."

Not a great look.

Back to Mum's and head off for a 15-mile run. This is a tester after three days off but the old legs don't actually feel too bad.

Get home and watch Sam batting beautifully for England again. Elsewhere, Somerset have beaten Yorkshire to stay on Surrey's coat tails.

Head to bed and fall asleep watching *Match of the Day*. Just as I nod off Wolves score a late winner and the last thing I see before the end of the day is a Portuguese football manager with a magnificent beard going mad in a technical area.

SUNDAY 2 SEPTEMBER

It is the most beautiful day. There is not a cloud in the sky, the sun is shining and it seems like autumn is staying away for the time being.

The morning is spent doing admin, sitting in the sun and listening to *TMS*. I think it was Meatloaf who said two out of three ain't bad.

England start the morning eight down with a lead of 230 odd and everyone is in agreement that this could be a classic day of Test cricket. Stuart Broad is promptly out first ball but Sam plays a gorgeous shot off Ashwin for four and the crowd goes wild (I say wild… more a gentle roar on a Sunday morning in Southampton).

A mix-up with Jimmy Anderson sees Sam run out for 46 but he has got the lead up to 244.

Just as I'm beginning to feel comfortable in the garden, with the combined tones of Mum, Norcross and Agnew providing my soundtrack, a pigeon lands on my lap. Literally. And it will not move. Every time I stand up it wanders off and then immediately comes and lands straight back on my lap.

I eventually leave my new best friend and head off for a run. I'm hoping by the time I get back, the pigeon will have disappeared.

Two hours later I return to find the pigeon still sat on the deck chair and Kohli and Rahane in the middle of a hundred partnership.

Tension is growing, mainly in the garden where the pigeon continues to sit on my lap. Kohli is playing beautifully and the pigeon really seems to be enjoying *TMS*.

Leave the pigeon to go and catch up with an old friend from school, during which time Moeen Ali dismisses Kohli for 58 and India collapse in a heap, Sam Curran takes the final wicket for England as they wrap up the game and clinch the series.

Come back to Mum's to find the pigeon still sitting on the chair – I think I've made a friend for life.

I watch the Test highlights and go to bed for *Match of the Day 2*. I never make it to Burnley v Man Utd because I'm asleep within seconds. Thankfully, the pigeon is not at the end of my bed.

MONDAY 3 SEPTEMBER

This has been quite a day for English cricket.

The day starts in normal fashion with breakfast, correspondence and saying "good morning" to the pigeon, which is still sitting in the chair in the garden.

Then my phone goes. It is Norcross but I miss the call because I'm trying to get the pigeon off the chair.

I ring him back and he gives me some monumental news. Alastair Cook is going to announce his retirement from international cricket at midday. The Oval Test this week will be his last – the end of an era.

Cook is, statistically, England's greatest batsman. To open for your country for 12 years, you have to be pretty special and I've got married and had a daughter during his England career (not that he would necessarily be aware of that).

He has always come across as a smashing bloke and his numbers are incredible: 160 Tests, 152 consecutive (amazing), over 12,000 runs and 32 hundreds.

The Oval is always the final chapter of the sporting summer and there is no more fitting place for Cook to say goodbye. And surely this now means that Rory Burns will get his chance.

The news comes out at midday and the respect for Cook, and his popularity, is shown by the messages to him on social media.

I say goodbye to the pigeon and head out for a 13-mile run. The realisation hit me this morning that in four weeks time I will have set off on my 1,000-mile trek across London. I know it is not like climbing Everest but it is still terrifying.

The weather is glorious again and it looks really good for this week. As I plod around the lanes of Kent I start thinking about this week's game against Essex. Due to the nature of the fixture list, Surrey are yet to play them in the Championship this season, but now have them twice in the final month. Essex have recently come into some decent form and it should be a cracker and another test of Surrey's title credentials.

Return from the run to find the pigeon still sat on the chair and then get a lovely surprise as I receive a text message from Alex Winter of BBC Northampton, who has sent me a picture of himself on a golf course with a ball cleaner. However, it's not just any ball cleaner, it's Wrotham Heath Golf Course and it is the one that is dedicated to my Dad. I know my old man would have been honoured to know that Alex had cleaned his balls there.

Surrey announce a 16-man squad for tomorrow. I am no detective but I'd say they are covering their bases for England call-ups for the Test that starts on Friday.

The pigeon is still in the garden and I have a quiet evening ahead of an early start tomorrow. Kevin Howells is at the game for BBC Five Live, which is tremendous news – and I always look forward to seeing the BBC Essex crew.

Head to bed and I feel this entry must simply end with: "Well batted Mr Cook".

✶

TUESDAY 4 SEPTEMBER

Clamber aboard Tysoe at 5.30am determined to deal with the Dartford Tunnel before rush hour. Sail through it and arrive at Chelmsford at 6.30am. At least it's September now so there's half an hour less to kill this morning with the 10.30am start.

After a wander and a couple of coffees in Chelmsford I return to the ground and sit in the sun until I am awoken by the arrival of Kevin Howells. His presence indicates that, once again, will be broadcasting on BBC Five Live Sports Extra.

Even though he is nowhere in the vicinity, there is something rather nice about being at Chelmsford on the day after Cook's announcement. Kevin and I discuss his career and then the squad for the Oval Test, which will be announced later today. I wonder if Burns might get the call today? If not, he will definitely be on the plane to Sri Lanka. I think the modern phrase is he has 'earned the right'.

Set up the commentary box and greet Dick Davies and Paul Newton from BBC Essex. Two of the nicest men in broadcasting and if you remember (from the game against Worcestershire at The Oval), Davies shares my love of musical theatre, so there is always much to discuss.

At 10am Rory Burns and Essex skipper Ryan ten Doeschate toss the coin with Dave Fulton and his Sky cameraman seemingly very focused on Burns. No doubt Fults will be asked about the England squad next time he pops up on Sky Sports News.

Essex win the toss and, with cloud shrouding the ground, ask Surrey to bat first. With the uncontested toss rule meaning the away side can either choose to bowl first or ask for the coin to go up, it seems everybody is happy with the outcome.

The only change to the Surrey team is Ollie Pope returning for Ryan Patel and investigations tell us that if Pope is named in the Test squad, he will leave after play on Wednesday. His petrol expenses are going through the roof!

Burns and Stoneman make their way to the middle and it immediately becomes clear that batting will not be straightforward. The ball nips around and the Surrey batsmen show considerable skill not to nick off early.

After 45 minutes, Sam Cook gets Stoneman but Burns is once again looking fully in control of proceedings. He is joined by Dean Elgar and moves past 1,000 Championship runs for the summer with a lovely shot down the ground.

On air, I am waxing lyrical about his chances of being in the Test squad and England's muddled thinking on their batting line-up. I finish my first session, put down the microphone, turn around and who should be sitting in the box but England selector James Taylor! Lovely to see him as always and he is in tremendous form. (Thankfully, like most people, he switched off as soon as I started talking.)

Don Topley, the former Essex bowler and now commentator for BBC Essex, is also in the box – it seems the great and good of cricket are all with us today.

I then have the slightly surreal experience of sitting next to an England selector as the Test squad is announced. I'm delighted for Sam and Ollie to be in there but disappointed for Rory, who isn't named. As I said earlier, I didn't actually expect him to be in for this Test but he had better be on that bloody plane to Sri Lanka.

Out in the middle, the man himself is batting beautifully alongside Dean Elgar and they are forming a significant partnership in the conditions. Surrey go to lunch at 100-1 and during the interval Anthony McGrath (the Essex head coach) and Alec Stewart join Kevin Howells for a chat in the commentary box.

Return from a lunchtime wander to find that Barran has arrived. He had warned me last night he may not be here until lunchtime, but I do wonder if he had remembered the 10.30am start... Very good to see him, as always, and we open up proceedings after lunch, as Burns moves to a fine fifty and the partnership with Elgar moves past 100. The ball is still darting about and Simon Harmer is already finding some turn. Elgar moves to fifty, the third Surrey batsman to show huge amounts of skill today.

Talk once again turns to Cook and I notice that Essex's Australian quick Peter Siddle is paying his own tribute to the former England captain by wearing his shirt and jumper – it's a lovely touch (not sure if Cook is aware or not).

Tea arrives with Burns 86* and Elgar 64*. Both men have played exceptionally well and Burns has once again shown what a cool temperament he has. He knows the media are watching, but he just gets on with his batting.

He looks destined for a deserved century but after the break he drags Siddle onto his stumps and goes for 90.

I then receive an amazing call. I have been bugging Nando's in Vauxhall for a number of weeks about whether they might feed me throughout my run. Now, on the end of the line, is Vinnie from Vauxhall Nando's. We have an excellent chat and I think Vinnie is genuinely interested in the idea. It would be amazing to get them on board and chicken, spicy rice and corn on the cob can definitely push me to 1,000 miles.

Back in the middle, Ollie Pope has joined Dean Elgar. He plays nicely and looks happy to actually have a bat in his hand for the first time since the Trent Bridge Test.

He falls for 21 and then Harmer gets one to really turn and bowls Elgar. Talking of turning, wickets are tumbling on the opening day at Taunton in the game between Somerset and Lancashire.

Back in Chelmsford, the ball is still nipping around and we are watching a tremendous day of cricket. Ben Foakes is the latest Surrey batsmen to play extremely well, guiding the visitors to stumps alongside Will Jacks. Surrey batted like a Championship-winning side today and, chatting to him after play, Dean Elgar was pleased with how things went.

Before leaving I have a nice catch-up with Scott Borthwick, whose arm is still in plaster, poor lad. Despite that, he's still in cracking spirits (probably not exactly the right word to use).

Jump into Tysoe and sail over the Dartford Crossing. Arrive back at Mum's just in time for *Bake Off*, thank goodness. It's a tremendous edition, featuring two Hollywood handshakes in the 'Showstopper' round.

Head to bed after completing the day with a motivational phone chat with Isabelle… school starts again tomorrow!

❋

WEDNESDAY 5 SEPTEMBER

Guess what? I arrived in Chelmsford far too early again. I had intended to leave later but still woke up at 5.15am so decided to get on with it. Sail through the Dartford Tunnel again and pull up at the County Ground at 6.15!

I wander off for a coffee and know it will be a good day when the lady in Pret gives me my coffee 'on the house'. The free coffee helps me overcome the toothache I awoke with this morning – it seems I have an abscess, which is not what the doctor, or dentist, ordered.

Back at the ground I take a quick check of my JustGiving page and receive a bit of a shock when the phone provider informs me that it is blocked for 'adult content'. I did post a picture of my legs on there yesterday, maybe that's what tipped it over the edge?

It is a cloudy morning with a little bit of rain and when Kevin Howells arrives, much of our conversation is about the ongoing game at Taunton, where 22 wickets fell yesterday. Understandably, there is plenty of talk about the pitch. There normally is at Taunton because their wickets take spin. I've no problem with that so long as it's a fair contest between bat and ball. I watched the highlights online last night and it's obviously not in this instance. Some of the shots look like batsmen saying "in a minute, one of these will have my name on it so I better get on with it". Let's see what happens today. Somerset look firm favourites but Lancashire pushed Surrey very close a couple of weeks ago and have plenty of talent in their side, plus a South African international spinner, which could be handy.

Before play starts I pop down to the outfield and have a lovely catch-up with Arun Harinath. He is one of my favourite men in cricket and a hell of a good batsman. He informs me that Surrey fast bowler Matthew Dunn became a proud father a couple of weeks ago – a congratulatory text is immediately dispatched.

Surrey start the day with Foakes and Jacks at the crease and the floodlights are on. Batting is tough again, and Jacks and Foakes both fall in the first hour. Foakes receives two balls from Jamie Porter that are a nightmare. One hits him square in the proverbials leading to a box handover with the twelfth man. The next delivery roars back off the seam and knocks out his off stump. Thankfully, as he walks off, it looks like everything is still in the right place.

Rikki Clarke then starts his day with three consecutive boundaries and Tom Curran, at the other end, looks in fantastic touch. He plays some sumptuous shots, especially off Siddle, and Surrey go past 300.

Simon Harmer comes into the attack and snares Curran but Clarke pushes the 'attack' button and plays brilliantly. He races to fifty, which in these conditions is not straightforward, and he is the last man to go for 56 as Surrey are all out for 351.

Essex get through a tricky couple of overs before lunch and the commentary box head to Anne's Pantry with their lunch vouchers. We have been blessed with the company of Andrew Samson, this morning, the greatest living cricket statistician – you may know him as the *TMS* scorer. It is such a privilege to have him with us that I give him my lunch voucher. He will now have a choice of a top-class curry or burger.

After the interval, the Surrey bowlers get to work and are once again exceptional. Essex have no answer to Morkel, McKerr, Curran and Clarke – although Tom Westley reminds everyone what a fine batsman he still is with 49, and wickets fall at regular intervals.

News is reaching us that it has got very dramatic at Taunton. Kevin Howells makes the executive decision to switch commentary on Sports Extra to the game there – and thank goodness he did.

Lancashire scrambled to a lead of 78 and Somerset have collapsed in pursuit of the target. Maharaj, the South Africa left-arm spinner, is causing chaos and Somerset find themselves eight down still needing another 15 runs. Remarkably, Somerset get the scores level and only need one to win when Maharaj takes the final two wickets to tie the game. It's the first tie in the Championship since 2003 and we are lucky to have Andrew Sansom with us, who has all the tie stats you could wish for right there on his laptop.

Surrey are outstanding with the ball and knock Essex over for 126. The final wicket sees Ollie Pope taking a blinding catch in the gully off Conor McKerr. Ollie will leave this evening to join up with England and the catch is a tremendous leaving present from him.

Burns gets his players together in a huddle. The light is fading but Surrey enforce the follow-on. This season, every time they have had the opposition by the throat, they have tightened their grip and today is no exception.

Essex are 'invited' to follow on. This is not an invitation you can turn down so after tea Browne and Chopra start again. The light is fading and soon it starts to rain. The players make their way off, which gives Kevin Howells and I time to do some maths. Well, it gives Kevin the time to do some maths and me to copy what he's doing.

It transpires that with the tie in Taunton, if Surrey beat Essex, they will need to get six more points than Somerset in their next match to win the title.

The rain gets heavier and play is called off for the day. I interview Rikki Clarke, who has had an excellent day, and head back to the commentary box where I find Kevin, who cannot leave a ground until all the games are completed that day, so he can record his 'scoreboard' for Five Live.

At Worcester, Hampshire are pushing for a win and the sun is shining. So we sit in the commentary box at Chelmsford, listening to Charlie Taylor and Kevan James. Kyle Abbott takes a hat trick and, at 6.45, Hampshire claim the extra half hour with Worcestershire eight down.

Howells and I had planned to have dinner together tonight, but this delay is making things precarious. It gets to 7.15 and I feel terrible making my apologies to the great man but I can't leave it any longer to tackle the Dartford Tunnel.

At 7.45pm, safely back in Tysoe and heading home, I hear Howells' 'scoreboard' on Five Live. Guess what? Worcestershire lost no more wickets in that extra half hour.

Get home at 9pm and am greeted by a number of Mum's friends because tonight is their book club. I'm not sure that Mum has read this month's book but the chicken supreme and rice she has made smells lovely.

Grab a bowl of muesli, watch Sky Sports News and then bathe my mouth with salt water. The abscess is starting to throb. Not a good sign.

Fall into bed feeling a bit sorry for myself but am cheered by a phone call from Isabelle, who tells me she has had a brilliant first day back at school. And you know what? That's all that matters.

*

THURSDAY 6 SEPTEMBER

Up early with the sun shining. Hoo-bloody-ray, summer is back! Tysoe takes me to Chelmsford where my 6.30am arrival means another walk for coffee and, again, it is complimentary from the very nice lady in Pret.

Arrive at the ground to see Kevin Howells arriving, carrying the largest cinnamon bun I have ever seen. Slightly concerned he's been here all night.

We are once again joined by Don Topley, who has very generously turned the back of the commentary box into a bakery by bringing in a cake and lots of sausage rolls.

Essex start the day on 13-0 and the weather looks perfect for batting. However, Tom Curran is exceptional with the ball and picks up two wickets within the first half hour of play. Rikki Clarke then gets in on the act with two of his own and Essex are in trouble at 60-4. They are not the only ones in trouble. The combination of the cinnamon bun and a sausage roll is not agreeing with me so I vacate the commentary box and go and have a sit in the sun.

Now I have a confession to make. The fifth wicket falls as Rory Burns takes a stunning catch in the gully off Morne Morkel, but I miss it because I've fallen asleep. Bun, sausage roll, painkiller for abscess and sun are a good combination if you ever need a kip.

Wake up not knowing where I am as Essex go to lunch five wickets down, still needing 140 to make Surrey bat again. I have a chat with Phil Walker from Wisden, who says he might run extracts of this diary in their October issue. I've never been serialised before.

Fully awake after the break as Ravi Bopara and Michael Pepper bat very well. They have put on 63 when Clarke dismisses Pepper. Harmer and Siddle quickly follow and it is looking like Surrey are going to complete a fifth innings victory of the summer. But quality batting from Bopara and late hitting from Porter and Cook sees Essex take a one run lead.

That leaves us with the rather strange situation of the players heading off for tea with Surrey needing just two to win. That's the thing about cricket – when the sandwiches are on the table you just have to have them.

So Burns and Stoneman head out after tea and the captain hits the winning runs off the fourth ball of the innings. It's the eighth consecutive win for Surrey, the ninth of the season and they can mathematically win the title next week at Worcestershire.

Head over to the pavilion and interview Burns, who is once again very satisfied with the team's performance. Do not tell him that I have announced on air that I will lie on the runway at Heathrow Airport if he is not on the plane to Sri Lanka. What a summer he is having.

England have announced an unchanged XI for the final Test at The Oval tomorrow. No huge surprises but, again, I hope they are saying the right things to Ollie Pope.

Pack up the commentary box and check the league table. Surrey now lead Somerset by 43 points with three games to go. They have been mighty impressive in Chelmsford.

Say goodbye to Kevin Howells and Barran. I will be seeing them both next week at Worcestershire so the farewell is not as emotional as it sometimes is.

Head back to Mum's. Tomorrow will be all about trying to see a dentist, which is something to look forward to. And I may just have a little look at the Test match for Cook's last hurrah.

✳

FRIDAY 7 SEPTEMBER

Up early and can't get a dentist appointment, which is a blow. However, the sky is blue and the sun is shining – so nothing for it but *TMS* on the radio and a comfy chair in the garden. No sign of the pigeon today, and I quite miss the company.

At The Oval, England win the toss and bat. Cook gets a wonderful ovation as he walks to the wicket, bringing goosebumps to the garden as I spend a most enjoyable morning with the dulcet tones of Agnew, Tufnell, Mann and Norcross in my ears.

Cook is not out at lunch and I head out for a long run in the afternoon. When I get back, he has gone for 71 and England have had a bit of a collapse.

I'm off to The Oval tomorrow and it is looking like I'll get to watch Kohli bat, which is good news.

A quiet evening is spent over chilli con carne, washed down with a couple of Peronis, which are medicinal for my abscess.

✳

SATURDAY 8 SEPTEMBER

On the 8.15 rattler up to London for a day at the Test. I am meeting David Quintrell from Brewin Dolphin, who are kindly sponsoring the kit for my run.

We have a lovely day. See Jos Buttler bat brilliantly in the morning and England take wickets in the afternoon.

David and I have a couple of beers to remember Dad and it really is a special day. And Sam Curran produces a pearler of a delivery in the afternoon to put the icing on the cake.

Leave before the close and just as I get on the train, Stokes dismisses Kohli to put England in the driving seat.

Quiet evening watching highlights with Mum (very kind of her). A day in the car awaits tomorrow.

SUNDAY 9 SEPTEMBER

I leave early to tackle the M4 and enjoy a very interesting lunchtime chat with Ed Smith on *TMS*. Arrive in Cardiff in the afternoon and spend a lovely couple of hours with Issy and Mrs Church.

Repack bag and head to Worcester. Surrey have announced their squad. Jade Dernbach returns after injury and Ollie Pope is also made available for the game.

Arrive at the Whitehouse Hotel in Worcester. It is one of my favourites on the circuit because you can park your car in the hotel and walk to the ground. It's the little things in life.

Head to the gym for the second run of the day. Embarrassingly, you have to go through the bar to enter and exit the gym and after an hour's running I leave, sweating profusely, and walk into the bar to see the whole Surrey squad. Lots of jokes about 'have you just been for a walk' etc.

Shower and head out with Joel Pope, Ryan Sidebottom, coach Di Venuto and Chris Taylor to see what fine cuisine Worcester has to offer.

Pope is in charge and we end up in the Chinese all-you-can-eat buffet. It does the job, especially the help yourself to ice cream counter.

Back to the hotel and watch highlights of the Test. Cook is 40 odd not out overnight. It's written in the stars, surely.

MONDAY 10 SEPTEMBER

Alarm at 6am. Gym and then breakfast. Slight fiasco. No peanut butter. Recover from the shock and walk to the ground with Joel Pope. Always a joy to come to New Road. Not only is it the most beautiful location, with the cathedral overlooking the ground, but you also always get a lovely warm welcome.

This morning is no exception and I am greeted by the magnificent sight of Kevin Howells in the commentary box and we are then joined by one of the legends of BBC commentary, Dave Bradley. It is three years since Surrey have been to New Road for the Championship and I can honestly say these are four days I have really been looking forward to.

Dave is in tremendous form and, with the arrival of Barran, the commentary team is complete.

Much talk is of points. What needs to happen? Can Surrey win the title this week? Yes they can, but a lot depends on what happens at the Ageas Bowl, where Hampshire are playing Somerset.

Worcestershire win the toss under cloudy skies and decide to bat. Dernbach comes back into the starting XI and gets the early wicket of Daryl Mitchell. At The Oval, Cook has gone past 50.

Surrey bowl extremely well in the morning but Tom Fell and Olly Westbury get their heads down and see Worcestershire to lunch one down.

And then it happens at The Oval. Cook, in his final Test innings, moves to his century. A wonderful moment and lovely that sport does sometimes give the right people the ending they deserve. Emotional scenes there and also in the press box here at New Road as the sandwiches and jacket potatoes arrive for lunch.

After the break Curran takes two wickets in an over and at the Ageas Bowl Somerset are struggling against Hampshire.

Whilst all of this is happening, Barran is relating the story of the family guinea pig getting stuck in the u-bend live on air. Thankfully, the plumber managed to free the pet.

Surrey chip away during the afternoon session but Worcestershire bat well. After tea, Ross Whiteley and Ed Barnard take the final session by the scruff of the neck. Morkel does get Whiteley for 91 but Barnard is still there at stumps 63 not out as the home side close on 288-6.

Two bowling points for Surrey and, at the Ageas Bowl, Somerset end up 106 all out and Hampshire have closed on 142/9, leading by 36 runs. It's all happening.

Interview Ryan Sidebottom, who as always talks great sense. "We bowled well, but the opposition are allowed to bat well too!"

Back to the hotel and have the honour of chatting to Darren Gough and Jon Norman about my run on talkSPORT. I'm extremely grateful to them for finding the time to chat to me on the day Cook made 147 in his final Test innings.

By the way, Joe Root also made a hundred and India closed three down with Jimmy Anderson drawing level on the most wickets for a quick bowler in Test cricket. What a day in south London.

Dinner with Joel Pope, Barran and Jack (remember the Scarborough road trip?) in an Indian restaurant where the owner greets me like a long-lost friend.

In fact, he is so sure he knows me we get complimentary ice cream, orange segments and sweets. What an evening.

The day ends with a quick trip to Tesco's to buy peanut butter for the morning. Always be prepared.

❋

TUESDAY 11 SEPTEMBER

Up and straight to gym. As always, coach Di Venuto is in there on the cross trainer and I bang out a quick six miles.

Down to breakfast armed with my peanut butter. Manage to break the toaster and almost burn the hotel down but despite that the kitchen agree to look after the jar of peanut butter for me. Result.

Lovely walk to the ground with Alex Tysoe. It's good to catch up with the physio. He is one of the best in the business and also one of the funniest men I know, so it's an entertaining walk.

The only problem – it's raining, which is all rather boring. Arrive at the ground and head to the commentary box. Kevin Howells is already in situ and local knowledge tells us the rain will disappear mid-morning.

Thankfully, local knowledge is proved correct, but it gives the press box the chance to watch events on the final day at The Oval. India are making a decent fist of chasing down a mammoth score, but of course it's written in the stars that Cook will take a hat trick to win the Test.

Lunch is taken at New Road (and thankfully for Johnny Barran I have remembered to fill in his lunch order – have to look after the talent).

Myself, Dave Bradley and Barran settle into the commentary box as Worcestershire resume out in the middle.

Morne Morkel makes an early breakthrough, bowling Ed Barnard for 63 with an absolute pearler. Worcestershire go past 300 and frustrate Surrey, but a couple of wickets from Tom Curran see the hosts dismissed for 336 with Curran taking 4-61 off 32 overs.

The consensus amongst the assembled media throng (myself, Barran, Howells and Bradley) is those are good runs and life could be tricky for Surrey in the afternoon.

That proves to be the case when Wayne Parnell bowls Stoneman and then dismisses Elgar first ball to leave Surrey 4-2. But once again, Burns looks in tremendous touch and, as usual, has me purring on air.

The lovely thing about being with Dave Bradley is that conversation is always entertaining and when Charlie Morris comes on as twelfth man for Worcestershire, Barran announces Charlie's dad is the vicar of Tilford. It is these nuggets of information that make him invaluable.

Burns and Pope set about repairing the innings but I'm feeling under a bit of pressure because one of my great cricketing heroes is in the press box. Jack Shantry is chatting away to the assembled press. Shantry produced one of the greatest all-round performances I have ever witnessed in this fixture, three years ago: ten wickets in the game and a century as Worcestershire were promoted. I honestly think there should be a statue of him in the car park.

I finally pluck up the courage to introduce myself. He is a lovely bloke and it's another reason why I love this job so much.

Down at the Ageas Bowl, huge drama. To cut a long story short, nobody can score any runs and it looks as if Hampshire will beat Somerset. By mid-afternoon they knock off the runs to win the game. With Somerset losing it means Surrey need five more points from this game to win the title. Either five batting points, draw the game or win it to take the Championship.

The five batting points will be tricky but with Burns batting, it is not beyond the realms of possibility. Against a very good Worcestershire attack he shows again why he should be playing for England. Pope makes 48 but life is proving very hard for the batsmen. Burns moves past 50 then loses Will Jacks as a partner. Clarke and Burns move Surrey past 200 and pick up a first batting point, but then Clarke goes for 33.

Poor old Ben Foakes is ill so can't bat (the wrong type of runs) and Tom Curran falls early. But Burns continues to dominate and moves to his fourth century of the summer. It's an unbelievable effort and he is unbeaten at stumps, alongside Morne Morkel.

I interview Morkel, who pays huge respect to his captain's efforts and admits Surrey need a big day tomorrow. He also says the team wants to win this game to claim the title and he means it.

The interview is sent to the BBC and I make my way back to the hotel. Meeting the James Bond of Sky Sport Cricket tonight, Dave Fulton, for a bite to eat – after he has hit some golf balls in his suit!

Very nice evening with Fults, Barran and social media ace Jack. I make the schoolboy error of ordering three 'small plates' (posh pub) and when it arrives I realise they were not joking about the small!

Back in the hotel, watch highlights of the final day of the Test. The fairy tale came true. Cook didn't take a hat trick but Jimmy Anderson took the final wicket to overtake Glenn McGrath in the all-time wicket-taking list, as England won the Test.

It seems everybody at The Oval is crying and I must admit I am a bit choked up when they announce Sam as the Man of the Series. What a summer the lad has had.

Big day ahead tomorrow. One thing about Surrey this season is they have always found an answer to every question they have been asked. I don't see any reason why they can't do it again tomorrow.

✳

WEDNESDAY 12 SEPTEMBER

Slept through my alarm. Not done that for a few years. Skip the gym and head to breakfast to find Alec Stewart having his porridge. Think he's quite impressed when my peanut butter is delivered to me.

Manage to burn my toast again and stroll to the ground. Weather is better today and we should get a full day.

See Ben Foakes heading off for a net, which is a good sign. Kevin Howells arrives and we discuss the day to come over a coffee and a biscuit (he has a biscuit, I abstain). Yesterday afternoon we had a delivery of cakes from the Ladies' Pavilion – they were magnificent and the lovely lady who delivered them broke into a Kevin Howells update on Five Live.

Bradders and Barran arrive and, after yesterday's results, everyone agrees this could be 'moving day' (never really understood what that means – is Wednesday a good day for moving?).

Burns and Morkel start the morning but batting again looks hard work. Morkel is bowled by a beauty from Josh Tongue, bringing Foakes out at number nine. He makes 13 but then departs.

Burns is still doing what Burns does, but he goes for a magnificent 122 and Jade Dernbach follows his captain as Surrey are all out for 268.

In the commentary box, I'm blathering on about how his game is almost a carbon copy of Scarborough. Surrey will have to bowl well to get themselves back into it. They are still just about in touching distance.

Worcestershire start their second innings with a precious lead of 65 runs. They are looking well set at 154-2 and Surrey need some inspiration.

They get it from Morne Morkel. He goes up a couple of gears from the Diglis End and bowls a world-class eleven-over spell, taking 5-10.

All of a sudden, Worcestershire are 188-7 and Amar Virdi and Tom Curran finish off the innings as Worcestershire are all out for 203. They have lost their last eight wickets for 49 runs.

We are purring about Morkel in the commentary box and the target has been set for Surrey – 272 runs to win the title.

Stoneman and Burns make their way to the middle with 20 overs left and bat brilliantly. They are both positive and drive Surrey to 70 without loss at stumps. It has definitely 'moved' today.

Interview Di Venuto, who is happy with how the day has gone but knows there is a lot of work to do tomorrow.

Wander back to the hotel and am quietly sitting in reception when the players come back with an amazing story. Whilst they were packing up at the ground, a group of travellers have broken in and set up home in a field behind the ground. Could caravans stop play? Could Surrey be handed the title by a static home? All will be revealed in the morning.

Quiet drink with Mark Stoneman and Scott Borthwick (who joined us on commentary today and was outstanding. He only mentioned Sunderland AFC once. Well, once an over).

Then take Joel Pope and Jack for a curry to thank them for all their help this season. The Surrey communications team are a well-oiled machine and make my life very simple.

Back to hotel for an early night. Get a slight shock when I turn the TV on to be greeted by a programme called *Naked Attraction*. Extraordinary sighting of lots of 'bits and pieces' so I turn over to catch the end of the news.

Fall asleep dreaming of a barman from Stoke and a teacher from London scoring 202 runs to win the title whilst totally starkers. Wonder if the caravans are at mid-wicket yet?

✳

THURSDAY 13 SEPTEMBER

Up early and open the curtains hoping for blue sky and sun. I'm disappointed but then remember I am looking directly at the brick wall on the other side of the hotel, so have no idea what the weather is like.

I stumble into the gym and slowly start waking up as I trudge along on the running machine. Di Venuto is on the cross trainer and even though this could be a pretty big day, everything is very normal.

After a six-miler I go back to the room and pack my bags. Over the years I have left various pants and jumpers in hotels across the British Isles – but now

I have my routine down to a T and after checking the room five times I head to reception, check out and walk to the car park to load up Tysoe.

As I exit the hotel I am greeted by the most lovely sight – blue sky and sun. It's a batting day.

Back for breakfast and finish off the peanut butter. Everyone is very relaxed and I walk to the ground with the Popes. Discussion turns to whether our friends in caravans who arrived last night have decided to park on the outfield. They might just have been massive County Championship fans but I doubt it.

I inform the Popes that if our caravanning friends have invaded the outfield, they will see me transform before their eyes into a hard-hitting journalist, sniffing out the story. I think they are impressed but we arrive at the ground to find no invasion, just New Road looking a picture in the sun.

Find a quiet corner of the press box in the sun and start focusing on the day. This involves me falling straight to sleep and waking up not quite sure where I am.

Come to my senses and have the wonderful surprise of George Dobell and Will 'Grisham' Macpherson arriving in the press box. It is lovely to see them and means that this is a pretty important day.

Dave Bradley and I head out to the middle and I take a look at the pitch. Unfortunately, it's actually the one for next week's game – but it looks a belter.

Barran arrives and Kevin Howells gets us on air and focuses everyone's attention by saying: "202 runs to win the title".

Could this be the day? Stoneman and Burns head out to the middle and any nerves are quickly dispelled by the way they play. They take their partnership past 100 as they both bring up their fifties. The sun is shining and the commentary box is very relaxed. Bradley and Barran are still discussing the Vicar of Tilford and Surrey look to be making serene progress. But at 11.11 Wayne Parnell bowls Stoneman to leave Surrey 111-1. I briefly wonder what the great old David Shepherd would have made of that many ones in a row? He'd have probably looked like a Morris dancer at square leg.

Everything is still pretty calm in the commentary box but then Dillon Pennington bowls Burns for 66. Pennington looks a fantastic prospect and on commentary the words, "could there be a twist here?" are uttered for the first time.

I am beginning to get very hot, due to a poor selection of clothing this morning. On a hot day, a sweatshirt was probably not the best idea and that is proving to be the case. In fact, I am quite looking forward to lunch and some fresh air.

Kevin Howells is busy organising his lunch panel on Five Live. He has a cracking line-up, but I won't be listening because I'll be trying to stop sweating.

Just before lunch, Josh Tongue bowls Dean Elgar with a beauty and Surrey are still 115 runs away from victory and the title.

Ollie Pope and Ben Foakes guide Surrey to lunch and I go and get some fresh air with Barran and Jon Surtees. There is lots of chat amongst the crowd. "Will Surrey get there?", "Can Worcestershire take seven wickets?", "Will our caravanning friends invade from the adjoining field?"

There are lots more Surrey fans here today and there is the feeling that something special could happen today.

Pope and Foakes make their way back to the middle and start very calmly. In fact, neither is showing any nerves. Whilst everything in the middle is going smoothly, the same cannot be said for the commentary box.

It emerges somebody has had Dave Bradley's tuna salad at lunchtime. This is a massive scandal and I start naming suspects on commentary. It even makes the pages of BBC Sport's cricket page. Somebody, via Twitter, sends a picture of a tuna salad with a ransom demand. Bradders is staying very calm.

Back in the middle, Pope and Foakes take Surrey past 200. And now I start getting nervous. Up until this point I had been very calm about 'that moment' when someone hits the winning runs. But now that little voice starts in my head: "don't get it wrong", "make sure it's good", "16 years people have been waiting for this", "you have one chance to get it right".

I try to stay calm but then Foakes departs for 22. Tension is building again. Plus, Bradders still hasn't had his tuna salad returned.

Will Jacks falls and Surrey are having a slight wobble. But Ollie Pope is delivering again under pressure. There are just 32 needed when he gets a ball from Pennington that doesn't bounce and is bowled for 49. Now Worcestershire are starting to believe.

The tension has gone up a notch but Rikki Clarke is using all his experience to calm the situation and with Tom Curran he takes Surrey to within 12 of victory. But Parnell then dismisses Curran and 'Mother Cricket' is presenting us with a classic.

I am now genuinely nervous. Under the commentary table my feet are going like pistons and none of us have any idea which way this is going.

Morne Morkel strides to the middle and Clarke pulls a boundary to get it to eight needed. Morkel and Clarke seem to be the two calmest people in Worcester.

All the Surrey supporters have gathered by the pavilion and James Bond (Dave Fulton) is down there with his camera ready for action. Photographers are in place and I realise why I love my job so much. Not only is it the cricket and the players but also the people I work with. Bradley, Barran and Howells all take a step back and leave me with the microphone. I'll always be grateful to them.

Morkel and Clarke get the runs required down to just two. This is going to happen and I'm going to be the one to call it. Don't get it wrong.

Pennington bowls a ball on Morkel's hip. He whips it behind square and the ball races to the boundary.

"Don't muck it up, Church", says the little man on my shoulder.

"And there it is, Morne Morkel pulls it off his hip and it runs away for four runs. And Rikki Clarke hugs Morne Morkel. The Surrey players are all up on the balcony. Surrey have won their first Championship title in 16 years!"

What a moment, and I hope I don't muck it up. Surrey Chief Executive Richard Gould joins Kevin Howells and we hand the microphone back to him.

I take a deep breath, shake Barran by the hand and grab my recording equipment. I squeeze past Richard Gould and pat him on the shoulder as he is telling listeners how proud he is of the team.

In front of the pavilion, the Surrey supporters have gathered and I stand with Will Macpherson and watch the Surrey players on the balcony. It is all quite surreal but then I see Alex Tysoe coming towards me. We have known each other a long time. I named my car after him. We have a massive hug.

The team come down the steps and photos are taken on the outfield. I interview coach Di Venuto and then stand quietly with him watching the photos being taken.

Jade Dernbach and I have an emotional hug and what he says to me I'll always remember. But that's between us.

I interview Rikki Clarke after a congratulatory hug and watch Rory Burns conducting an impromptu press conference on the outfield. It's lovely to see the players and supporters all together and you can see how much it means to them all.

I feel for the Worcester players, who now have a massive fight on their hands to avoid relegation. In the two games against Surrey they have played really well, but sadly that's sport.

And I then get my chance to interview the captain. He looks exhausted but finishes our interview with one word, "chuffed". And I must admit I'm pretty bloody proud of him.

With the celebrations continuing, I wander to the commentary box, send back all my interviews, say goodbye to Dave Bradley and thank him for a lovely four days in the box.

Pack up my bags and start walking back to the hotel. On the way out of the ground I find the players heading to their coach with an appropriate amount of beers for a proper celebration. Vikram Solanki is packing the kit van and I shake him by the hand.

I then walk back to the hotel with Steve Howes and the Surrey analyst Natalie Greening-Doyle. We see a few Surrey fans singing away in the city centre and I put my bags into Tysoe and head out of Worcester. An amazing day and I feel very privileged to have been there.

Turn on the radio and I get the shock of my life as I hear my commentary on the winning runs played back on Five Live. "Could have done it better but wasn't too bad," is my assessment of my performance at the critical moment.

Get back to Cardiff at 8pm and I am greeted by Isabelle and her trumpet. She plays me a tune and I get a bowl of cereal and check my phone.

The Surrey media team have done an amazing job on Twitter and Facebook. There are photos, behind-the-scenes videos and all sorts – it is really nice to see all the celebrations.

And then on Twitter I see a photo taken by the Surrey fan Martin Searle of me hugging Rikki Clarke. It's a smashing picture and really sums up how I felt about this team winning the Championship.

Head upstairs with Isabelle and put her to bed. She asks me if Surrey won today. I tell her that they did and she asks if they will get a medal.

"I think so, Issy".

"Good, they deserve it".

"Yes, they do".

❋

FRIDAY 14 SEPTEMBER

Back to the really important things in life after the excitement of yesterday. Take Isabelle to school for the first time this term and then come home to do paperwork. Read the reaction to Surrey's win and, quite rightly, they're getting all the plaudits.

Head to the gym for a long run and sauna. Go to buy a coffee afterwards and am greeted by a massive celebratory photo taken in the Surrey dressing room yesterday on the back page of *The Times*.

Spend a quiet afternoon with Mrs Church and then get a lovely surprise. In the lunch break yesterday, I did an interview with Sam Morshead from the *Cricketer* magazine about the run. He has written a super article that has been published this afternoon. Send it to Mum, who is very happy.

Lots of thoughts today about the journey Surrey have been on over the last 16 years. The likes of Gareth Batty, Arun Harinath, Stuart Meaker, Gary Wilson, Steve Davies, Tim Linley, Zafar Ansari and Chris Tremlett have all played a massive part in getting Surrey to this point. Graham Ford and Stuart Barnes were hugely influential and Kumar Sangakkara certainly played his part. This season Michael Di Venuto, Vikram Solanki, Ryan Sidebottom, Geoff Arnold, Chris Taylor, Alex Tysoe and Darren Veness have been brilliant, and a huge amount of work has gone into getting that moment yesterday.

Back in the present, I pick Issy up from the school and the day is concluded by us playing several games of competitive wordsearch before I head to bed with Vic Marks' book *The Ultimate One-Day Cricket Match*, which he has kindly signed for me. It is a classic – a cricket roleplay book from the 80s that was way ahead of its time. Nod off just as I decide to play "a full-blooded cover drive" against Abdul Qadir!

❋

SATURDAY 15 SEPTEMBER

Up and off again to the gym and then a trip to one of the many millions of retail parks in Cardiff. This one is opposite Cardiff City's football ground, but thankfully they're away at Chelsea.

Play the old, 'you take your time' card with Mrs Church and find a nice comfy chair in a coffee shop. It is T20 Finals Day and I keep an eye on the opening semi-final between Worcestershire Rapids and Lancashire Lightning. The Rapids win to book their place in the final.

Mrs Church certainly does take her time and we buy Isabelle a scooter for her upcoming ninth birthday. Reckon the interest in that will last a week.

Pick Issy up from 'Stagecoach' and then head back to the gym for a watch of the second semi-final, between Somerset and Sussex Sharks. Watch Luke Wright smash it to all parts of Birmingham and Sussex win quite comfortably. It is a final for the romantics – Worcestershire v Sussex.

I would love to watch it but I have a date with Mrs Church and a giant shark. We head to the cinema to watch *The Meg*. It is quite possibly the greatest / worst film I have ever seen. I really hope Jason Statham wins an Oscar because his portrayal of a deep-sea rescue diver fighting a prehistoric shark is definitely the best portrayal of a deep-sea rescue diver fighting a prehistoric shark this year.

Get home in time to listen to the end of the T20 Final on *TMS*. Ben Cox guides Worcestershire to victory and it sounds wonderful on the radio.

Off to bed and discuss the intricacies of *The Meg* with Mrs Church before falling asleep in front of *Match of the Day*.

SUNDAY 16 SEPTEMBER

Early start – gym, where I watch *Match of the Day* again whilst on the treadmill. We then spend a fantastic afternoon in the Forest of Dean with Isabelle at her friend's birthday party.

The girls have an amazing time, climbing trees whilst strapped into a harness. I decide to provide touchline support – not great with heights!

Lovely birthday meal in Pizza Express and then home in time to do some prep for the Somerset game and pack my bags. Off to Taunton tomorrow but I'm taking on BBC Somerset's Anthony Gibson at golf first. Decide to clean my balls and buff up my driver.

❄

MONDAY 17 SEPTEMBER

Cracking start to the week. Take Isabelle to school and then see the dentist to try and sort out my abscess, which is still causing a few problems. A course of antibiotics and a good clean later, I arrive home to find they are digging up the road outside our house. Excellent.

Put bags in Tysoe and then sit for ten minutes, two yards from our front door, waiting for the temporary traffic lights to turn green.

Head to Burnham and Berrow Golf Club to meet Anthony Gibson. It is the most beautiful links course and Anthony proceeds to give me a golfing lesson. He plays very well and I play very badly but the sun is shining, the company is wonderful and it is a glorious way to spend the afternoon.

After a post-round drink I drive to Taunton and check into the hotel. A quiet evening is spent having a couple of bar snacks and recovering from my trouncing.

Surrey have announced their squad for tomorrow and it's very good to see Jason Roy in there. With his talent he could still make the Test squad with a couple of good performances at the end of the season.

❄

TUESDAY 18 SEPTEMBER

Up early and straight into the hotel gym for a run. See coach Di Venuto on the cross trainer and then head to breakfast where I'm delighted to find very big and very deep bowls. Enjoy an enormous helping of granola and then drive myself and the Surrey scorer, Phil Makepeace, to the ground.

It is a breezy morning and after parking Tysoe, I go into Taunton to meet Barry Kitcherside to talk about my run. I could not have got it all organised without Barry's help and generosity and I will always be grateful to him.

Back to the ground and Stephen Lamb of BBC Somerset is already in the box. I have worked with Stephen many times over the years and it is always a joy to be with him. Barran arrives, looking resplendent as always, and we also joined by Kit Harris, who is the captain of Iceland.

Surrey win the toss and bat. Jason Roy is in the starting XI and down to bat at three. I know for a fact Surrey want to win the final two games of the summer, despite the title already being secured. And Stoneman and Burns certainly put a marker down during the morning session. Both bat extremely well although Stoneman falls just before lunch for 84.

During lunch I have the great honour of chatting with Vic Marks. If you remember, he very kindly signed a copy of his book *The Ultimate One-Day Cricket Match* for me and it is nice to be able to thank him in person.

After the break, Roy opens his account with an exquisite drive for four and Burns continues to look every inch a Test opener. He goes for 72 but Roy looks in lovely touch and at the other end, Ollie Pope settles quickly.

Surrey continue to pile on the runs during the afternoon and show why they are already County Champions. Pope goes for 44 but Roy moves past 50 and looks very much at home at number three.

Dean Elgar is a good man to have batting at five and despite losing Roy for 67, he guides Surrey past 350 with Ben Foakes. Surrey close the day with four batting points banked and it has been an extremely dominant performance with the bat.

I interview Jason Roy and then drive back to the hotel. Spend a very pleasant evening watching Champions League football with Barran and Jack, who knows his footie. As mentioned previously, Barran is a die-hard Liverpool fan. His team win 3-2 against PSG, but he misses all three goals because he is concentrating so hard on eating his burger.

❊

WEDNESDAY 19 SEPTEMBER

Up early for trip to the gym. There is a queue to get in but thankfully there is a free running machine. Breakfast consists of another massive bowl of granola and I head to the ground in Tysoe.

Have a lovely catch-up with Academy Director Gareth Townsend, who has quite rightly had an awful lot of plaudits this season.

Barran arrives, still basking in the glory of Liverpool's victory and the weather is lovely, if a little windy.

The morning starts with Elgar and Foakes taking Surrey past 400 to achieve maximum points. Foakes departs for 25 but Elgar brings up his first Championship hundred for Surrey – it has been an extremely good knock from an extremely good batsman.

Surrey look to increase the tempo and wickets start to fall, including Elgar for 110 and I find myself watching in the sun, from a terrace below the media box, as Barran and Stephen Lamb commentate on Surrey eventually being dismissed for 485.

Barran and I enjoy a quiet lunch discussing Liverpool's performance as the sun continues to beat down.

Morne Morkel sets the tone with the first ball of the Somerset reply when he has Marcus Trescothick caught by Rikki Clarke at second slip. The hosts are soon three down and the Surrey bowlers do what they have done all season. They are relentless and Somerset limp past 100 and find themselves 122-9 at tea.

Light rain starts falling but I am touched when I discover a lovely cake has been left by a very kind Somerset supporter called Nicky. She has asked the press to donate money for a slice, all of which will go towards my run – it is an amazing gesture.

The rain gets heavier and, at 4.30, play is abandoned for the day. I dodge the wet stuff and interview Dean Elgar. This is his final game for Surrey and he has been a vital part of the success this season.

Back to the hotel and then go into Taunton with Jon Surtees and, eventually, Barran, who delays his departure from the hotel because he decides to join an aqua aerobics class for the older generation in the hotel pool.

We bump into some lovely Surrey supporters and have a chat about the season over a couple of drinks. Dinner is a rather large burger and chips and, naughtily, I have a Cornetto back at the hotel, lying on my bed listening to the rain come down. It's all rock 'n' roll, this county cricket.

✳

THURSDAY 20 SEPTEMBER

Up early for gym and then breakfast using the magnificently deep bowls for granola. Witness Dean Elgar making his way across the dining room with two grilled tomatoes on a spoon… not only is he one of the world's best opening batsmen, I would also back him in an egg and spoon race.

Walk to Tysoe and get soaked. It's raining and the forecast is indicating we may not see too much cricket today. Arrive at the ground, park and sit in the commentary box waiting for the rain to stop. No sign of Barran, who will be using the hotel facilities (sauna, solarium, pool etc.).

The 10.30am start time comes and goes but, hallelujah, the rain stops. The groundstaff do a terrific job of drying everything up and play gets underway at midday. Kit Harris and Stephen Lamb open up proceedings with Surrey needing just one wicket to finish off the Somerset first innings. It duly arrives when Morkel has Davey caught at cover point and Somerset are all out for 146.

Surrey enforce the follow on and Morkel dismisses Trescothick for the second time in the match and Somerset are 4-2 when Tom Curran has Banton caught down the legside.

Amazingly, it stays dry and despite some excellent Surrey bowling the afternoon belongs to James Hildreth and Azhar Ali. They play very well and put on a hundred for the third wicket.

The England ODI and T20s squad for the tour to Sri Lanka are announced and it's good to see two Currans and a Roy in there.

Curran dismisses Hildreth for 60 but bad light and rain brings an end to proceedings with the hosts on 168-3. Surrey will be confident of pushing for victory tomorrow.

The wonderful thing about Barran staying in our hotel is the fact he has a car and can give a lift back to those that are finishing their work. Sadly, it becomes apparent he left before the final ball was bowled to make use of the hotel facilities again. So five bodies cram into Tysoe and back we go.

Straight to the gym for the second run of the day, and halfway through by 12k, Barran strolls in having obviously had a lovely couple of hours in the sauna, solarium and pool. Always look after the talent.

After the run, I take a walk over to the local Harvester with Barran, Surtees, Mumford-Wilson and Makepeace. It's a tremendous meal, but the sad news is that the recent heatwave has caused the Harvester to run out of jacket potatoes.

Head to bed and watch *Rocky II*. Fall asleep ahead of the final day tomorrow. It should be a good one, the weather forecast is much better and England are announcing the Test squad to go to Sri Lanka. Rory Burns better be in there otherwise I'm lying down on the tarmac at Heathrow.

✳

FRIDAY 21 SEPTEMBER

What a strange old day! There was no hint of what was coming when I went to the gym and then packed my bags into Tysoe.

Back for breakfast and the massive bowls and I'm informed that the Test squad is likely to be announced at 3pm this afternoon.

The weather is lovely. Blue sky and sun and everything looks good as we drive to the ground and park up.

I head to the commentary box and then to the toilet. My phone goes, but now is not the right time to speak to Jon Surtees.

Make my way to the press box and apologise to Surtees for not taking the call. He then tells me some extraordinary news. Today's play has been abandoned.

The sun is shining, the covers are off and all looks good. Pardon?

In the night, the wind has blown the covers off an area of the pitch that has subsequently got wet and the umpires have deemed it unplayable.

I make my way to the middle and am amazed to see the offending area with a tyre mark from the cover through the middle of it.

This is not good. Surely in 2018 there are covers which won't get blown off during a strong wind. Nothing else seems to have been blown over but what do I know?

Interview Alec Stewart who is obviously disappointed and surprised and then listen to Andrew Cornish, the Somerset Chief Executive, explaining that the wind was so strong last night that covers were lifted like the wings on a plane!

It's a sad way to end the game and end Surrey's winning streak – my overriding thought is that Somerset would do well to invest in some new covers.

Send interviews back to the BBC and say goodbye to Stephen Lamb and Kit Harris. We haven't seen Barran, who may still be using the hotel facilities or sensibly heading down the M5 already.

Both sets of players have nets with the sun out and it really is a bizarre sight. Surrey cannot head home because their coach is arriving at 5pm this evening and is now on its way back to Taunton to get here earlier.

Go to Somerset's very own coffee shop 'Stragglers' and then decide to hang around until the coach comes, to say goodbye to Dean Elgar, who has been fantastic this season. I take up a position on a sofa at the bottom of the dressing room stairs to wait for the coach.

Joel Pope comes and sits with me and we make the decision that, if the Test squad is announced before the players get on the coach, then at least I'm here to do some interviews should the opportunity present itself.

And then I have a moment I will never forget. I'm sat on the sofa and Rory Burns comes down the stairs chatting on his phone and looking very serious.

He heads out of the pavilion and the doors shut behind him. A couple of moments later, he comes back and knocks on the door. I push the button to let him back in. He is smiling and I just nod before he goes back up the stairs and into the dressing room.

There is a moment's silence and then the most enormous roar. Rory Burns is in the England squad to Sri Lanka.

Joel Pope comes and joins me on the sofa again to confirm the news but then his namesake, Ollie, comes out of the dressing room on his phone. This is like waiting for your exam results!

He goes round the corner and two minutes later goes back into the dressing room. There is a moment's silence and then the most enormous roar. Ollie Pope is in the England squad to Sri Lanka.

Sam is also in the squad and I am very proud of all three. But particularly Rory. As you may have gathered, I am incredibly fond of the lad, having commentated on his first ever game for Surrey and all the way through to this defining moment. He fully deserves his call-up and it is lovely to see him get his rewards.

Say goodbye to the players as they head to the coach, which has finally arrived. Nip up to the dressing room to give Burns and Pope a congratulatory hug and do quick interviews with them both.

Then they are on a coach and on their way. I wander back to Tysoe. It is a glorious afternoon and I sit with the radio on waiting for the squad to be formally announced.

At 3.30pm the world is told that Burns, Denly and Stone will be going to Sri Lanka. What a day for them all.

Drive out of Taunton and start the journey back to Cardiff. By now it's rush hour so it takes a while. It's a real shame that Surrey's winning run has come to an end in such bizarre circumstances but they will be determined to finish on a high next week against Essex at The Oval.

Arrive home for 6.30 and help Isabelle with her maths homework (which is really very difficult). Pop Sky Sports News on to see reaction to the Sri Lanka squad and am delighted to see Burns' name on the yellow ticker tape.

I then look at Twitter and am amazed by what I see. A Surrey supporter (@my_surrey) has put a picture they have taken of Rory Burns and have said that for every like it gets they will donate £1 to my run. I am humbled and very, very touched.

Put Isabelle to bed and then have an early night. It has been a funny old day. A disappointing end to the game at Taunton but my overriding feeling is of being so happy for Rory Burns. As the captain himself would say… "I'm chuffed."

✣

SATURDAY 22 SEPTEMBER

An extraordinary day. All started very normally with a family breakfast followed by a trip to the gym. The afternoon then takes a strange twist.

Isabelle's birthday is in a couple of weeks. She wants guinea pigs. So off we go to the pet shop for a preliminary look. Two hours later, Isabelle is the proud owner of two guinea pigs, a massive cage and enough hay to fill a small barn.

One problem – with everything, including guinea pigs, packed into the car there is no room for me. So I am left at a retail park in Bridgend whilst my girls head home to 'settle in' the guinea pigs!

Three hours and ten McDonalds coffees later, they return. Get home and meet 'Rikki' and 'Clarke'. They don't seem to be doing much so pop the TV on and watch former England off-spinner Graeme Swann make his debut on *Strictly Come Dancing*. He is actually rather good.

Check on Rikki and Clarke who still aren't doing much. Head to bed. Day in car tomorrow heading back for the final game of the season.

SUNDAY 23 SEPTEMBER

Wake up and check on Rikki and Clarke. Still not doing much.

Mrs Church is worried because they are not using the ladder to go up to the top floor of their cage. My suggestion of installing a lift does not go down that well.

Say goodbye to my girls, Rikki and Clarke and jump in Tysoe. It's raining heavily as I head down the M4 to Mum's for the last time in the 2018 cricket season.

Go for a quiet run on arrival and then head out for a bite to eat with Mum before returning and watching a magnificent episode of *Countryfile*. They are showing the national sheep dog trials and the whistling skills on display are extraordinary.

Surrey have announced their squad for the final game of the summer against Essex at The Oval tomorrow. The game is being televised on Sky Sports and the forecast is looking good.

We will be broadcasting on BBC Five Live Sports Extra, BBC London and BBC Essex and I receive the excellent news that Kevin Howells will be joining us.

Not quite sure where the season has gone. Well, I do know but it has all happened very quickly.

Early night, there is a 5am alarm call to look forward to.

MONDAY 24 SEPTEMBER

Before I know it, the alarm has gone off and I'm sat in Tysoe, powered by coffee (me, not Tysoe) for the drive to The Oval. There is frost on the windscreen, which tells me it's a very late finish to the season this year.

Enjoy an incident-free journey to The Oval and arrive at 7am. Set up the commentary box for the final time this summer. It really looks like we are going to be blessed with glorious weather and a good crowd is expected. This is the week Surrey will officially be crowned County Champions and Surrey Chairman Richard Thompson has announced that beer will be £2 a pint today, rolling back the prices to 2002 when Surrey last won the County Championship.

Potter off for a coffee and on my return am delighted to see that Kevin Howells is already in situ. Sit on the balcony in the sun and greet the great Don Topley, here today with BBC Essex. He arrives with a Suffolk pork pie for breakfast, which is extremely kind of him.

Nick Gledhill, another representative of BBC Essex, and Barran make their entrances and for the final time this season, under a clear blue sky, the coin goes up. Rory Burns calls correctly and Surrey decide to bat first.

At lunch, Surrey are 52-7. The ball nips around and Essex bowl extremely well. This is not what anyone expected, and it is a genuinely lively morning.

I then have the great thrill of being on the BBC Radio Five Live Sports Extra lunchtime panel, alongside Surrey Chief Executive Richard Gould, Will (Grisham) Macpherson from the *Evening Standard* and Mark Baldwin from *The Times* and other esteemed publications.

There is a passionate debate about transfer fees, compensation and the structure of county cricket. It is almost like a cricketing *Question Time* and I do my normal trick of nodding and agreeing with everyone.

Also during the lunch break, Ollie Pope, Mark Stoneman, Scott Borthwick and Morne Morkel are awarded their county caps, all richly deserved.

Back in the commentary box, we have a lovely surprise when Daniel Norcross arrives, in tremendous form as normal. It also lovely to see Stuart Barnes, who is at the ground watching his former charges.

The afternoon belongs to Essex too. Surrey are all out for 67 and, despite the early loss of Nick Browne, the visitors bat themselves into a very strong position. Nothing much happens for the bowlers and the second wicket eventually falls when Jade Dernbach has Murali Vijay caught behind for 80. Essex close on 197-2, with Tom Westley on 91*. Unbelievably, we are still going at 6.30pm on September 24th!

Across the country, some of the greats are embarking on their final games before retiring. Paul Collingwood, Jonathan Trott, James Tredwell, Jimmy Adams and James Foster are all hanging up their bats and gloves this season. It's always sad to see the men you have admired for so many years calling it a day, but whatever they do next, I'm sure they will be hugely successful.

Nip around the ground and interview Ollie Pope, who is very honest about Surrey's day. He also describes how proud he is to be awarded his Surrey cap. There cannot be too many who got their England cap before their county cap. Although, thinking about it, Mark Stoneman was exactly the same, so I may not ask that question on air tomorrow.

An exciting end to the day with delivery of lots of protein from Protein World, who have kindly sent me provisions for the run. With the amount of protein I'm going to consume, I shouldn't lack energy!

Drive back to Mum's and on the way I receive news that Rikki and Clarke have got a new cage with no stairs. A bungalow I suppose.

Arrive at Mum's for a quick bowl of granola and then straight to bed. Only three days of the season left sadly. Oh, and by the way. Tiger Woods won his first golfing competition in five years yesterday. And it is the Ryder Cup this weekend. They do say timing is everything.

TUESDAY 25 SEPTEMBER

You could write this now. Alarm – shower – coffee – Tysoe – Oval – commentary box – Pret – coffee.

The normal routine is followed again it is a lovely day in south London. The weather gods are being extremely kind this week.

Today could decide the fate of Lancashire, Yorkshire and even Nottinghamshire. The permutations are discussed with Kevin Howells upon arrival. It has been a fantastic summer but with two relegation spots it means someone has to join Worcestershire for the drop.

Spend the morning trying to be constructive but failing miserably. Open up the broadcast on BBC Five Live Sports Extra and then have a catch-up with Gareth Townsend, Surrey's Academy Director, who is a guest at lunchtime on both Five Live and Sky Sports.

Rikki Clarke takes the early wicket of Dan Lawrence and Tom Westley then moves to a deserved hundred. It is good to see such a talented player coming back to his best form.

Surrey bowl well in the morning but the pitch is playing really well and Essex look determined to bat themselves into an even more commanding position under the September sun.

Westley goes just before lunch for 134 and I proceed to have an extremely exciting lunch break.

Firstly I get an e-mail saying my running kit has been dispatched to the printers – that is a relief because I'm not sure running in my pants would convey the right impression. I then take delivery of another box, this time from Science in Sport, which contains more protein drinks and bars for my run. Their support is much appreciated and will definitely get me through 1,000 miles of running.

The afternoon belongs to Simon Harmer. He bats extremely well and moves to his first century for Essex. The Surrey bowlers stick to the job with Jade Dernbach taking four wickets, but as Harmer reaches his century the declaration comes with Essex on 477-8, leading by the small matter of 410 runs.

During the afternoon it is confirmed that Lancashire have been relegated. It transpires that with Notts collapsing against Somerset, they only needed one more batting point to stay up. On such margins can your season be decided.

After the tea break, Burns and Stoneman head to the middle for the final time this season. They got the season started against Hampshire five months ago and now they are back here together for the final time this summer.

Surrey face a tricky 20 overs but the opening pair bat extremely well. Stoneman plays a couple of drives that will last all winter and they put on 63 for the first wicket until Burns is out for 21. The captain has had an incredible summer with the bat and he quite rightly gets a standing ovation from the pavilion.

Roy joins Stoneman and they guide Surrey to stumps with no further damage. Lots of work for Surrey to do over the next couple of days but I know they are desperate to finish the season unbeaten.

Interview Jade Dernbach after play, and he looks tired. I'm not surprised, it's 25 September after all.

Receive some excellent news from Barran before the end of the day. Tomorrow night is Surrey's end-of-season awards night and I am doing the Q&A with the players. There is a room to stay at Barran's Mum's, so I don't have a late night drive back to Kent facing me. Plus I might be persuaded to have a final beer before the run.

Jump into Tysoe and listen to an excellent Ryder Cup preview on Five Live. Excitement is building in Paris and in me. Love a Ryder Cup.

Arrive back at Mum's at 9.30pm. Find her packing medals for the British Heart Foundation sponsored swim on Friday that she has organised. Very proud of her.

Head to bed but lay out chinos and blazer for the morning. Must look at my smartest for the end-of-season awards. Now, where are my best shoes?

✻

WEDNESDAY 26 SEPTEMBER

A 5am alarm call allows me time to find my best shoes before embarking on the normal routine.

The quality of my early coffee and sit-down is enhanced by the presence of genuinely warm late-summer sun before I join Kevin Howells for a quick preview of today's action. We both think that Surrey can bat their way back into this game, and whilst we are chatting a gentleman sticks his head in the commentary box window. He is here for a conference and tells us that he loves cricket and asks if he would he be allowed to look in the *TMS* box?

He's a lovely chap and, as we show him the room with a couple of desks and lots of plugs you would have thought we'd taken him to Disney World. Again, another reminder of how lucky we are to do this 'job'.

Howells and I start coverage on BBC Radio Five Live and we get a very nice surprise when James Foster pops up to say hello. He is retiring this year and I can honestly say he is the best wicket-keeper I have ever had the privilege of commentating on.

Roy and Stoneman make their way to the middle in perfect batting conditions. They both play extremely well, batting positively and laying down a marker for the rest of the day. If anybody thought Surrey were just happy to go through the motions, then they were very wrong.

Roy proves once again that no matter the colour of the ball, he is quality. He dominates the scoring and the partnership races past 100. Jason has so much talent and when he is in this sort of mood, he is a joy to watch. He can definitely play Test cricket. He races to his first Championship century of the season and eventually falls for 128. The partnership with Stoneman has been worth 181 and Surrey are back in the game.

Stoneman follows for 86 but the rest of the afternoon belongs to Ollie Pope. He caps off a brilliant summer with a magnificent innings. The runs continue to flow and it is starting to dawn on us that something special is happening. In fact, just after telling us that he once sang on stage with Frank Bruno and Roy Castle, Johnny Barran informs the listeners that if Surrey go past the 410 run deficit and win the game, it will be a world record. (Thank goodness Andrew Samson was listening!)

With the end-of-season awards this evening, I pop down to the Jardine Suite for a run-through. The room looks magnificent and it is very nice to see Laura Woods there. Laura is a tremendous presenter and reporter for Sky Sports and talkSPORT and, thankfully for me, she knows what she's doing. Seeing her arriving makes me feel much more relaxed about this evening.

Because of my job, people think I find talking in front of lots of people easy. That is not the case. It terrifies me. When you are on the radio you are in your own world and nobody can see you. But tonight there will be a large audience and all the Surrey players will be in the room and I don't want to make a fool of myself. Fortunately, Laura will be there to guide us through the evening.

As I rush back to the commentary box, I pause to watch Pope go to his fourth Championship hundred of the summer. When he is dismissed for 114, Surrey are 418-5 and lead by eight. Could a world record be in the offing? I wonder if anyone has got Kriss Akabusi on stand-by?

Ryan Patel and Will Jacks guide Surrey to stumps. Another pair of hugely talented batsmen and an outstanding day with the bat is ended with Jacks moving to his first Championship fifty. Surrey close on 477-5 and lead by 67.

Rush to the dressing room and grab a word with Jason Roy. He is very pleased with how the day has gone and tells me that Surrey are desperate to finish the season unbeaten.

Run back to the commentary box, send the interviews to the BBC and then perform a quick change into the chinos and blazer and head off with Barran to the end-of-season awards. I look like a scruffy school teacher, Barran looks immaculate.

The awards are a lovely occasion. Members, supporters and players are all together and sharing the success of the team.

Laura is a brilliant host and all I have to do is ask my usual hard-hitting questions to the players. Quite rightly, Rory Burns is the Players' Player and Members' Player of the Year and it is very nice to look back at the season amongst the Surrey Family.

After the awards finish, I get the lovely surprise of seeing Zafar Ansari. Zafar retired last season but played a huge part in Surrey's journey to winning the Championship and it is smashing to see him.

As I'm staying with Barran tonight, I make my way to The Beehive pub and enjoy a celebratory evening with the supporters. Barran very kindly takes me to a bar that serves late-night 'posh eggs on toast'. What a lovely end to the day. Eggs on toast with a pint amongst friends.

The bar contains some very glamorous individuals but I do not care that I am the only person dressed like a scruffy teacher in ill-fitting chinos. This has been a special summer and it will all end tomorrow. And we might be witnessing a world record!

✳

THURSDAY 27 SEPTEMBER

So, the final day of the season arrives. Awake with a slightly sore head and walk to The Oval still dressed as a scruffy teacher. 7.30am arrival, change of clothes, coffee and good to go.

The weather gods are in a wonderful mood because blue sky and sun seems to have been the order of the day.

Turn on the broadcasting kit for the final time in 2018 and greet Kevin Howells, who brings exciting news. *Test Match Special*'s Henry Moeran is coming today and, due to his technical genius, I will be able to interview the players 'live on air' when Surrey are presented with the Championship trophy at the end of the game.

Howells and I wonder where the season has gone – and agree it has been a tremendous summer.

Paul Newton and Dick Davies from BBC Essex arrive, as does Barran, who seems to be drinking gallons of coconut milk. It is free entry for the final day of the season and as the players make their way to the middle for the final morning of the season, a good crowd is building.

Will Jacks falls for 53 but Rikki Clarke joins Ryan Patel and together they move Surrey' lead past 100. Barran joins me on air and reveals he once sang at Buckingham Palace and was in the *Taming of the Shrew* with the Royal Ballet. Sadly, he tells the listening public his singing career was ended when his voice broke. In cricket, it is always a shame when you see balls dropped, but I think on this occasion it was a blessing for the music industry.

Clarke departs for 39 and is immediately followed by Morne Morkel. Patel continues to play sensibly but goes for 39 and when Jade Dernbach is bowled by Jamie Porter, Surrey are all out for 541. The lead is 131 and the world record is on.

During lunch, I join a panel of distinguished cricket journalists to discuss the season on Five Live Sports Extra. It is an interesting discussion but does mean I miss out on a rather delicious chicken pasta that is being served for lunch. Well, it looks delicious as Barran devours a massive plate of it at the back of the box.

This post-lunch session could well be the final one of the season and all four results are possible. You couldn't ask for any more.

Morne Morkel gives Surrey the perfect start when he bowls Murali Vijay with an unplayable delivery. Amar Virdi then dismisses Nick Browne and Jade Dernbach has Dan Lawrence caught in the slips with his first delivery.

Excitement is growing in the commentary box and when Ravi Bopara goes without scoring, Essex are in trouble at 47-4. That becomes 55-5 and the final day of the season is turning into a classic.

This Surrey team just do not lie down but Ryan ten Doeschate and Adam Wheater put on 42 until Morkel dismisses Wheater and then immediately has Simon Harmer caught behind without scoring.

Dick Davies, Paul Newton and Barran are describing everything perfectly and I sit in the back of the box with Kevin Howells, delighted we have such a brilliant game of cricket on our hands. I also get a very pleasant surprise when one of my favourite broadcasters, Simon Mann, pops into the commentary box to say hello.

Henry Moeran comes to see me and explains what will happen at the end of the game so I can get reaction during the trophy presentation. It all sounds very straightforward but I must admit I am slightly distracted with what is happening in the middle. Morkel has dismissed Jamie Porter and Essex are eight down, still needing 21 to win.

I take a deep breath (there are a few nerves about) and join Dick Davies on commentary. Immediately, Matt Coles is run out for two and Surrey need just one wicket to finish the season unbeaten.

I think it must be nerves but I am busting for a wee. Obviously now is not the time to excuse myself. Essex are eight runs from victory and Ryan ten Doeschate is still there.

Alongside Matt Quinn, the Essex captain gets it down to two runs required. Three of the four results are still possible as Jade Dernbach stands at the top of his mark to bowl to ten Doeschate. This is brilliant theatre and the little man is back on my shoulder warning me not to mess this up.

Dernbach charges in from the Vauxhall End and ten Doeschate nudges the ball off his hip and down to the long leg boundary rope. Essex have won by one wicket and ten Doeschate has played a gem of an innings.

The unbeaten season is not to be for Surrey and as the players make their way off, I hand the microphone to Kevin Howells and dash off to the other end of the ground for the trophy presentation. First though, I need the loo, and in my haste I go through a wrong door and end up in a part of The Oval I do not recognise. This is not the time to get lost. I find a loo, recalibrate my radar and sprint to the other side of the ground.

I leap the fence and dash onto the outfield. Burns is already out there and Henry Moeran is chatting to him on Five Live. At the end of the interview (which was very good), Henry passes me the headphones and microphone and I describe the trophy presentation on Five Live Sports Extra.

It is a wonderful occasion. The sun is beating down, the pavilion is packed with Members and you can see what it means to everyone as Rory Burns finally gets his hands on the Championship trophy.

Because I am down on the pitch, I am able to grab several live interviews with a number of players and it again comes across how much winning the title means to them.

The photographers take hundreds of photos of the celebrations and I hand back to Kevin Howells in the commentary box, leaving the celebrations to walk back and join him. By the time I get there, he has rounded off the season on the BBC and the broadcasting kit can be packed up for another year.

The end of the season is always strange, especially when you have a thrilling ending like today. You can get so caught up in the action, grabbing interviews and trying to make sense to the listener that you completely forget that that it's all over for another six months.

Howells and I pack up all the microphones and gadgets that keep us on air and we say goodbye to Paul Newton and Dick Davies.

I give Barran a hug (please don't tell him but I will miss him over the winter) and then say cheerio to Kevin. I pack all of my bags into Tysoe and then say goodbye to some of the wonderful Surrey supporters I have got to know over the years.

As I leave the pavilion I can hear lots of cheering from the dressing room. Family and friends have arrived and this is the players' time. They have earned their celebrations and it has been an absolute privilege to follow them again this season.

I wander back to Tysoe and then drive back to Mum's. The last day of the season finishes with peanut butter on toast and the preview of the Ryder Cup, which starts tomorrow. I am very tired and decide to head to bed.

As I'm heading upstairs, Mum says: "Well done this season, you must be so proud of them all."

How right she is.

*

FRIDAY 28 SEPTEMBER

Up early to watch the start of the Ryder Cup. Change into t-shirt, shorts and trainers.

I've got 1,000 miles to run.

❋

SPECSAVERS CHAMPIONSHIP DIVISION ONE TABLE

	M	W	L	T	D	N/R	Pts
Surrey	14	10	1	0	3	0	254
Somerset	14	7	2	1	4	0	208
Essex	14	7	4	0	2	1	187
Yorkshire	14	5	5	0	3	1	158
Hampshire	14	4	5	0	5	0	144
Nottinghamshire	14	4	8	0	2	0	133
Lancashire	14	3	7	1	3	0	133
Worcestershire	14	2	10	0	2	0	104

SPECSAVERS CHAMPIONSHIP BATTING AND FIELDING

	Matches	Innings	Not Out	Runs	Avg	H/S	50s	100s	ct	ct/st
SG Borthwick	8	12	1	444	40.36	83	5	0	13	0
RJ Burns	14	22	1	1359	64.71	193	7	4	11	0
R Clarke	13	17	1	500	31.25	111	2	1	19	0
SM Curran	8	10	1	209	23.22	70	1	0	2	0
TK Curran	4	5	0	81	16.20	43	0	0	0	0
TB de Bruyn	2	3	1	46	23.00	38	0	0	2	0
JW Dernbach	10	13	2	129	11.73	31	0	0	2	0
MP Dunn	2	3	1	10	5.00	9*	0	0	2	0
D Elgar	7	10	0	387	38.70	110	2	1	6	0
AJ Finch	2	3	0	77	25.67	43	0	0	1	0
BT Foakes	12	18	1	624	36.71	90	4	0	37	37/1
A Harinath	2	3	0	56	18.67	48	0	0	1	0
WG Jacks	6	8	0	168	21.00	53	1	0	8	0
C McKerr	5	5	2	64	21.33	29	0	0	0	0
SC Meaker	1	1	0	13	13.00	13	0	0	1	0
M Morkel	10	13	2	172	15.64	29	0	0	1	0
RS Patel	9	14	3	276	25.09	48	0	0	5	0
OJD Pope	12	15	2	965	74.23	158*	1	4	20	8
JJ Roy	2	3	0	196	65.33	128	1	1	0	0
MD Stoneman	13	21	1	660	33.00	144	4	1	4	0
GS Virdi	14	16	8	68	8.50	21*	0	0	5	0

SPECSAVERS CHAMPIONSHIP BOWLIING

	Overs	Maidens	Runs	Wickets	Average	BBI	5WI	10WM
SG Borthwick	18	1	67	0		0-4	0	0
R Clarke	363.1	87	1012	47	21.53	5-29	1	0
SM Curran	192.2	37	608	25	24.32	6-54	1	1
TK Curran	120.4	30	312	19	16.42	5-28	1	0
JW Dernbach	285.5	65	929	32	29.03	4-49	0	0
MP Dunn	44.3	10	171	3	57.00	2-41	0	0
C McKerr	67.2	13	246	13	18.92	4-26	0	0
SC Meaker	22	1	93	0		0-93	0	0
M Morkel	315.4	82	845	59	14.32	6-57	4	0
RS Patel	87.1	14	279	8	34.88	6-5	1	0
GS Virdi	360.3	46	1184	39	30.36	6-105	1	0

Clockwise from top: At the Championship-presentation with Jade Dernbach; the commentary box at New Road, Worcester with Kevin Howells and Dave Bradley.

Clockwise from top: commentating on the Championship presentation with Johnny Barran; interviewing skipper Rory Burns; giving Rikki Clarke a big hug after the title-winning performance at Worcester.

ESSEX V SURREY

Venue: The Cloudfm County Ground, Chelmsford
Date: 4th, 5th, 6th September 2018
Toss: Essex
Result: Surrey won by 10 wickets

Points: Essex 2; Surrey 22
Umpires: JH Evans, NJ Llong
Scorers: AE Choat, D Beesley, GJ Lee

SURREY	1ST INNINGS	R	b	2ND INNINGS	R	b
*RJ Burns	b Siddle	90	217	not out	2	4
MD Stoneman	c Westley b Cook	12	29	not out	0	0
D Elgar	b Harmer	75	179	did not bat		
OJD Pope[1]	c Harmer b Siddle	21	57	did not bat		
+BT Foakes	b Porter	30	65	did not bat		
WG Jacks	c Lawrence b Siddle	16	52	did not bat		
R Clarke	c ten Doeschate b Porter	56	69	did not bat		
TK Curran	c Lawrence b Harmer	26	41	did not bat		
M Morkel	b Cook	1	3	did not bat		
C McKerr	c Lawrence b Cook	0	5	did not bat		
GS Virdi	not out	0	1	did not bat		
Extras	(14 b, 6 lb, 4 nb)	24			0	
Total	(all out, 119.2 overs)	351		(no wicket, 3 minutes, 0.4 overs)	2	

Fall of wickets: 1-30 (Stoneman, 9.4 ov), 2-178 (Burns, 64.6 ov), 3-200 (Elgar, 75.3 ov), 4-233 (Pope, 85.6 ov), 5-257 (Jacks, 97.5 ov), 6-279 (Foakes, 102.5 ov), 7-324 (Curran, 115.4 ov), 8-325 (Morkel, 116.1 ov), 9-325 (McKerr, 116.6 ov), 10-351 (Clarke, 119.2 ov)

ESSEX	O	M	R	W	Wd	Nb		O	M	R	W	Wd	Nb
Porter	28.2	3	87	2	-	-	Harmer	0.4	0	2	0	-	-
Cook	25	7	71	3	-	-							
Siddle	29	6	86	3	-	1							
Harmer	29	12	62	2	-	-							
Westley	2	0	8	0	-	-							
Bopara	6	1	17	0	-	1							

ESSEX	1ST INNINGS	R	b	2ND INNINGS (F/O)	R	b
NLJ Browne	c Elgar b Morkel	7	19	c Patel b Clarke	21	89
V Chopra	c Clarke b Curran	3	8	lbw b Curran	5	28
T Westley	c Burns b Clarke	49	66	b Curran	7	24
DW Lawrence	lbw b Curran	3	22	c Burns b Clarke	3	10
RS Bopara	c Foakes b Clarke	6	26	not out	81	122
*RN ten Doeschate	c Foakes b Clarke	2	7	c Burns b Morkel	11	18
+MS Pepper	b Curran	9	30	c Stoneman b Clarke	21	48
SR Harmer	lbw b Clarke	0	1	c Elgar b Morkel	0	3
PM Siddle	not out	21	20	c Stoneman b Clarke	8	25
JA Porter	lbw b McKerr	12	21	c Jacks b Morkel	31	36
SJ Cook	c Pope b McKerr	2	6	b Virdi	12	22
Extras	(4 lb, 4 nb, 4 w)	12		(9 b, 11 lb, 4 nb, 2 w)	26	
Total	(all out, 37.2 overs)	126		(all out, 70.3 overs)	226	

Fall of wickets: 1-10 (Browne, 4.2 ov), 2-10 (Chopra, 5.1 ov), 3-20 (Lawrence, 9.6 ov), 4-47 (Bopara, 19.2 ov), 5-53 (ten Doeschate, 21.3 ov), 6-86 (Pepper, 28.6 ov), 7-86 (Westley, 29.2 ov), 8-87 (Harmer, 29.6 ov), 9-122 (Porter, 35.6 ov), 10-126 (Cook, 37.2 ov)
Fall of wickets: 1-16 (Chopra, 9.5 ov), 2-28 (Westley, 17.6 ov), 3-31 (Lawrence, 20.5 ov), 4-60 (Browne, 28.5 ov), 5-86 (ten Doeschate, 34.1 ov), 6-139 (Pepper, 47.6 ov), 7-140 (Harmer, 48.4 ov), 8-157 (Siddle, 55.5 ov), 9-208 (Porter, 64.3 ov), 10-226 (Cook, 70.3 ov)

SURREY	O	M	R	W	Wd	Nb		O	M	R	W	Wd	Nb
Morkel	9	3	18	1	-	2	Morkel	20	3	68	3	-	1
Curran	13	2	36	3	-	-	Curran	20	8	46	2	-	1
McKerr	6.2	0	40	2	4	-	Clarke	17	3	47	4	-	-
Clarke	9	1	28	4	-	-	Virdi	8.3	1	36	1	-	-
							McKerr	5	1	9	0	2	-

[1] RS Patel replaced OJ Pope in Essex 2nd innings, 7.1 overs

WORCESTERSHIRE V SURREY

Venue: Blackfinch New Road, Worcester
Date: 10th, 11th, 12th, 13th September 2018
Toss: Worcestershire
Result: Surrey won by 3 wickets

Points: Worcestershire 6; Surrey 21
Umpires: M Burns, NA Mallender
Scorers: SM Drinkwater, D Beesley, JC Hathaway

WORCESTERSHIRE	1ST INNINGS	R	b	2ND INNINGS	R	b
*DKH Mitchell	c Burns b Dernbach	13	25	c Burns b Clarke	15	67
TC Fell	lbw b Clarke	69	163	b Morkel	89	134
OE Westbury	b Curran	22	83	lbw b Virdi	15	27
JM Clarke	c Clarke b Curran	0	3	(8) c Jacks b Virdi	0	1
RA Whiteley	c Pope b Morkel	91	142	b Morkel	10	26
+AG Milton	c Foakes b Morkel	7	20	(4) c Pope b Morkel	24	45
EG Barnard	b Morkel	63	108	(6) lbw b Morkel	12	20
WD Parnell	c Clarke b Virdi	42	104	(7) b Morkel	2	22
BJ Twohig	c Foakes b Curran	2	21	not out	7	20
JC Tongue	c Virdi b Curran	5	7	c Elgar b Curran	6	21
DY Pennington	not out	2	27	lbw b Virdi	1	4
Extras	(5 b, 7 lb, 6 nb, 2 w)	20		(2 b, 8 lb, 8 nb, 4 w)	22	
Total	(all out, 116.4 overs)	336		(all out, 63.5 overs)	203	

Fall of wickets: 1-22 (Mitchell, 8.2 ov), 2-88 (Westbury, 38.1 ov), 3-88 (Clarke, 38.4 ov), 4-134 (Fell, 52.6 ov), 5-165 (Milton, 61.5 ov), 6-248 (Whiteley, 83.1 ov), 7-290 (Barnard, 97.5 ov), 8-311 (Twohig, 104.3 ov), 9-323 (Tongue, 106.3 ov), 10-336 (Parnell, 116.4 ov)
Fall of wickets: 1-65 (Mitchell, 19.4 ov), 2-91 (Westbury, 27.3 ov), 3-154 (Milton, 44.3 ov), 4-157 (Fell, 46.5 ov), 5-181 (Whiteley, 50.2 ov), 6-187 (Barnard, 54.6 ov), 7-188 (Clarke, 55.4 ov), 8-188 (Parnell, 56.4 ov), 9-200 (Tongue, 62.4 ov), 10-203 (Pennington, 63.5 ov)

SURREY	O	M	R	W	Wd	Nb		O	M	R	W	Wd	Nb
Dernbach	17	3	70	1	-	-	Curran	10	1	34	1	-	1
Curran	32	11	61	4	-	-	Dernbach	11	3	33	0	-	-
Virdi	19.4	4	65	1	-	1	Morkel	17	8	24	5	-	2
Morkel	26	8	62	3	1	2	Clarke	6	0	29	1	-	-
Clarke	22	6	66	1	1	-	Virdi	19.5	2	73	3	4	1

SURREY	1ST INNINGS	R	b	2ND INNINGS	R	b
*RJ Burns	c Parnell b Barnard	122	206	b Pennington	66	126
MD Stoneman	b Parnell	0	4	b Parnell	59	83
D Elgar	c Barnard b Parnell	0	1	b Tongue	21	45
OJD Pope	c Milton b Parnell	48	68	b Pennington	49	70
WG Jacks	b Twohig	17	33	(6) c Westbury b Barnard	12	13
R Clarke	c Milton b Whiteley	33	39	(7) not out	18	24
TK Curran	c Whiteley b Tongue	0	2	(8) c Whiteley b Pennington	7	17
M Morkel	b Tongue	16	37	(9) not out	9	8
+BT Foakes	c Fell b Pennington	13	33	(5) c Whiteley b Parnell	22	44
JW Dernbach	c Tongue b Pennington	6	3	did not bat		
GS Virdi	not out	0	3	did not bat		
Extras	(3 b, 10 lb)	13		(1 b, 6 lb, 4 nb)	11	
Total	(all out, 71.3 overs)	268		(7 wickets, 71.2 overs)	274	

Fall of wickets: 1-4 (Stoneman, 1.2 ov), 2-4 (Elgar, 1.3 ov), 3-101 (Pope, 24.1 ov), 4-135 (Jacks, 36.3 ov), 5-203 (Clarke, 50.6 ov), 6-204 (Curran, 51.3 ov), 7-232 (Morkel, 59.5 ov), 8-262 (Foakes, 69.6 ov), 9-262 (Burns, 70.3 ov), 10-268 (Dernbach, 71.3 ov)
Fall of wickets: 1-111 (Stoneman, 30.2 ov), 2-135 (Burns, 39.4 ov), 3-157 (Elgar, 44.6 ov), 4-210 (Foakes, 59.1 ov), 5-228 (Jacks, 62.1 ov), 6-240 (Pope, 63.6 ov), 7-260 (Curran, 69.2 ov)

WORCESTERSHIRE	O	M	R	W	Wd	Nb		O	M	R	W	Wd	Nb
Tongue	16	0	63	2	-	-	Tongue	11	2	36	1	-	-
Parnell	18	3	56	3	-	-	Parnell	21	3	101	2	-	2
Barnard	14	2	48	1	-	-	Twohig	11	2	36	0	-	-
Pennington	9.3	3	36	2	-	-	Barnard	16	3	53	1	-	-
Twohig	11	2	44	1	-	-	Pennington	12.2	3	41	3	-	-
Whiteley	1	0	5	1	-	-							
Mitchell	2	0	3	0	-	-							

SOMERSET V SURREY

Venue: The Cooper Associates County Ground, Taunton
Date: 18th, 19th, 20th, 21st September 2018"
Toss: Surrey
Result: Match drawn

Points: Somerset 6; Surrey 13
Umpires: RT Robinson, AG Wharf
Scorers: LM Rhodes, PJ Makepeace, GA Trett

SURREY	1ST INNINGS	R	b	2ND INNINGS	R	b
*RJ Burns	b Groenewald	78	130			
MD Stoneman	c C Overton b J Overton	85	127			
JJ Roy	lbw b J Overton	63	89			
D Elgar	c Davies b Abell	110	185			
OJD Pope	c J Overton b Davey	44	67			
+BT Foakes	b Groenewald	25	77			
R Clarke	st Davies b Leach	18	30			
TK Curran	c Banton b Leach	5	8			
M Morkel	c Davies b Abell	7	13			
C McKerr	lbw b Abell	6	15			
GS Virdi	not out	21	11			
Extras	(9 b, 11 lb, 2 nb, 1 w)	23				
Total	(all out, 125.1 overs)	485				

Fall of wickets: 1-147 (Stoneman, 36.6 ov), 2-206 (Burns, 51.2 ov), 3-263 (Roy, 63.4 ov), 4-345 (Pope, 85.3 ov), 5-414 (Foakes, 108.4 ov), 6-446 (Clarke, 116.6 ov), 7-446 (Elgar, 117.2 ov), 8-458 (Curran, 120.4 ov), 9-458 (Morkel, 121.1 ov), 10-485 (McKerr, 125.1 ov)

SOMERSET	O	M	R	W	Wd	Nb		O	M	R	W	Wd	Nb
C Overton	22	1	83	0	1	1							
Davey	21	3	72	1	-	-							
Leach	24	2	107	2	-	-							
Groenewald	22	4	64	2	-	-							
J Overton	23	4	87	2	-	-							
Abell	13.1	0	52	3	-	-							

SOMERSET	1ST INNINGS	R	b	2ND INNINGS (F/O)	R	b
ME Trescothick	c Clarke b Morkel	0	1	b Morkel	0	6
T Banton	c Foakes b Virdi	30	62	c Foakes b Curran	4	3
Azhar Ali	c and b Morkel	2	9	not out	61	114
JC Hildreth	lbw b Curran	6	22	c Foakes b Curran	60	81
*TB Abell	c Foakes b Clarke	21	26	not out	21	50
+SM Davies	c Burns b McKerr	5	6	did not bat		
C Overton	b McKerr	0	2	did not bat		
J Overton	c Virdi b McKerr	9	11	did not bat		
JH Davey	c Stoneman b Morkel	36	74	did not bat		
TD Groenewald	lbw b Clarke	11	23	did not bat		
MJ Leach	not out	15	30	did not bat		
Extras	(1 b, 9 lb, 1 w)	11		(13 b, 9 lb)	22	
Total	(all out, 44.2 overs)	146		(3 wickets, 42.2 overs)	168	

Fall of wickets: 1-0 (Trescothick, 0.1 ov), 2-2 (Azhar Ali, 2.1 ov), 3-11 (Hildreth, 7.1 ov), 4-37 (Abell, 15.2 ov), 5-42 (Davies, 16.3 ov), 6-42 (C Overton, 16.5 ov), 7-53 (J Overton, 20.3 ov), 8-84 (Banton, 25.3 ov), 9-109 (Groenewald, 32.4 ov), 10-146 (Davey, 44.2 ov)
Fall of wickets: 1-0 (Trescothick, 0.6 ov), 2-4 (Banton, 1.3 ov), 3-107 (Hildreth, 26.3 ov)

SURREY	O	M	R	W	Wd	Nb		O	M	R	W	Wd	Nb
Morkel	8.2	1	19	3	-	-	Morkel	8.2	4	16	1	-	-
Curran	14	2	32	1	-	-	Curran	9	1	44	2	-	-
McKerr	7	1	20	3	1	-	Clarke	7	0	24	0	-	-
Clarke	10	1	32	2	-	-	McKerr	11	3	38	0	-	-
Virdi	5	0	33	1	-	-	Virdi	7	0	24	0	-	-

SURREY V ESSEX

Venue: The Kia Oval, Kennington
Date: 24th, 25th, 26th, 27th September 2018
Toss: Surrey
Result: Essex won by 1 wicket

Points: Surrey 2; Essex 22
Umpires: MJ Saggers, AG Wharf
TV Umpire: BV Taylor
Scorers: AE Choat, PJ Makepeace

SURREY	1ST INNINGS	R	b	2ND INNINGS	R	b
*RJ Burns	c Harmer b Quinn	19	52	c and b Porter	21	37
MD Stoneman	c Wheater b Porter	2	10	b Harmer	86	167
JJ Roy	lbw b Porter	5	6	c sub (ASS Nijjar) b Quinn	128	151
OJD Pope	c Bopara b Cook	26	53	lbw b Coles	114	120
+BT Foakes	lbw b Quinn	0	1	lbw b Quinn	32	75
WG Jacks	b Cook	0	5	c Harmer b Coles	53	87
RS Patel	lbw b Cook	5	19	c sub (MS Pepper) b Coles	38	148
R Clarke	lbw b Porter	0	5	c sub (MS Pepper) b Coles	39	53
M Morkel	c Wheater b Porter	1	7	c Browne b Coles	0	2
JW Dernbach	b Cook	4	3	b Porter	2	14
GS Virdi	not out	1	1	not out	2	3
Extras	(4 lb)	4		(14 b, 5 lb, 6 nb, 1 w)	26	
Total	(all out, 27 overs)	67		(all out, 142.2 overs)	541	

Fall of wickets: 1-13 (Stoneman, 4.1 ov), 2-23 (Roy, 6.4 ov), 3-41 (Burns, 15.3 ov), 4-41 (Foakes, 15.4 ov), 5-48 (Jacks, 18.3 ov), 6-54 (Patel, 22.4 ov), 7-55 (Clarke, 23.4 ov), 8-57 (Morkel, 25.4 ov), 9-62 (Dernbach, 26.3 ov), 10-67 (Pope, 27 ov)
Fall of wickets: 1-63 (Burns, 13.2 ov), 2-244 (Roy, 57.5 ov), 3-249 (Stoneman, 60.3 ov), 4-364 (Foakes, 85.6 ov), 5-418 (Pope, 96.3 ov), 6-479 (Jacks, 118.1 ov), 7-532 (Clarke, 133.6 ov), 8-532 (Morkel, 135.2 ov), 9-539 (Patel, 141.3 ov), 10-541 (Dernbach, 142.2 ov)

ESSEX	O	M	R	W	Wd	Nb		O	M	R	W	Wd	Nb
Porter	10	0	26	4	-	-	Porter	26.2	3	127	2	-	-
Cook	11	5	27	4	-	-	Quinn	28	3	115	2	1	1
Quinn	6	2	10	2	-	-	Harmer	50	10	122	1	-	-
							Coles	32	5	123	5	-	2
							Bopara	1	0	17	0	-	-
							Westley	4	0	13	0	-	-
							Lawrence	1	0	5	0	-	-

ESSEX	1ST INNINGS	R	b	2ND INNINGS	R	b
NLJ Browne	b Morkel	2	14	(2) c Clarke b Virdi	12	22
M Vijay	c Foakes b Dernbach	80	127	(1) b Morkel	2	6
T Westley	c Foakes b Clarke	134	282	c Clarke b Dernbach	20	46
DW Lawrence	lbw b Clarke	17	77	c Clarke b Dernbach	10	11
RS Bopara	b Virdi	8	24	c Jacks b Virdi	0	7
*RN ten Doeschate	c Pope b Dernbach	27	40	not out	53	62
+AJA Wheater	retired hurt	68	105	c Patel b Morkel	11	11
SR Harmer	not out	102	156	c Foakes b Morkel	0	3
JA Porter	lbw b Dernbach	1	13	lbw b Morkel	4	13
SJ Cook[1]	c Foakes b Dernbach	1	4	run out (Jacks)	5	11
MR Quinn	not out	4	6	not out	0	6
Extras	(7 b, 13 lb, 12 nb, 1 w)	33		(4 b, 5 lb, 8 nb)	17	
Total	(8 wickets, dec, 140.2 overs)	477		(9 wickets, 32.2 overs)	134	

Fall of wickets: 1-12 (Browne, 4.2 ov), 2-158 (Vijay, 47.2 ov), 3-205 (Lawrence, 70.5 ov), 4-236 (Bopara, 79.3 ov), 5-276 (ten Doeschate, 91.6 ov), 6-282 (Westley, 94.5 ov), 7-449 (Porter, 134.6 ov), 8-456 (Cook, 136.6 ov)
Fall of wickets: 1-13 (Vijay, 3.2 ov), 2-25 (Browne, 6.4 ov), 3-42 (Lawrence, 11.1 ov), 4-47 (Bopara, 12.5 ov), 5-55 (Westley, 15.6 ov), 6-97 (Wheater, 21.2 ov), 7-97 (Harmer, 21.5 ov), 8-111 (Porter, 25.5 ov), 9-124 (Coles, 29.3 ov)

SURREY	O	M	R	W	Wd	Nb		O	M	R	W	Wd	Nb
Morkel	30	6	84	1	-	2	Virdi	11	0	73	2	-	2
Dernbach	29.2	8	95	4	1	-	Morkel	12	3	28	4	-	1
Clarke	29	9	65	2	-	-	Dernbach	9.2	2	24	2	-	1
Patel	25	3	92	0	-	1							
Virdi	27	1	121	1	-	3							

[1] MT Coles replaced SJ Cook in Surrey 2nd innings, 8.0 overs

ACKNOWLEDGEMENTS

Rach, Isabelle.

Mum, Dad, Pete Stevens, everyone at BBC London Sport, Kevin Howells, Adam Mountford, Charles Dagnall, Henry Moeran, Johnny Barran, Daniel Norcross, Kevan James, Scott Read, Isabelle Duncan, Chris Egerton, Anthony Gibson, Steven Lamb, Dick Davies, Paul Newton, Nick Gledhill, Don Topley, David Brett, Dave Bradley, Dave Bracegirdle, Dave Townsend, Martin Emmerson, Kevin Hand, Dave Callaghan, Charlie Taylor, Edward Bevan, Nick Webb, Jordan Clarke, Emily Windsor, Matt Cole, Will Macpherson, Elizabeth Ammon, Vithushan Ehantharajah, Bruce Talbot, Mark Baldwin, George Dobell, Dave Fulton, Mel Farrell, Adam Collins, Tanya Aldred, Phil Walker, Matt Thacker, Laura Woods, George Foster, Alex Davidson, Peter Miller, Richard Spiller, Marcus Hook, Jeremy Morris, Maggie Blanks, Eric Coleman, Karen Coleman, Christine Fairweather, Barry Kitcherside, Ronnie Wilkinson, James Hickman, Joel Pope, Jon Surtees, Jack Wilson-Mumford, Lee Fortis and all his groundstaff, Emily Clark, Steve Kitcher, Rebecca Lockyer, Steve who runs the press room at The Oval, Daryll Leith, Dave Gangadeen, all the press officers at the other counties, Michael Di Venuto, Steve Howes, Alec Stewart, Vikram Solanki, Darren Veness, Stuart Barnes, Geoff Arnold, Chris Taylor, Alex Tysoe, Daryll Leith, Natalie Greening-Doyle, Callum Doyle, Richard Gould, Richard Thompson.

Every listener and Surrey supporter.

The entire Surrey squad.